Marital
Distress

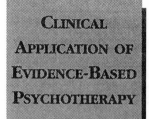

CLINICAL APPLICATION OF EVIDENCE-BASED PSYCHOTHERAPY

A Series of Books Edited By
William C. Sanderson

In response to the demands of the new health care environment, there is a movement in psychology (and in all of health care) toward defining empirically supported treatment approaches (i.e., treatments that have been shown to be effective in controlled research studies). The future demands of psychotherapy are becoming clear. In response to pressures from managed care organizations and various practice guidelines, clinicians will be required to implement evidence-based, symptom-focused treatments.

Fortunately, such treatments exist for a variety of the most commonly encountered disorders. However, it has been extremely difficult to disseminate these treatments from clinical research centers, where the treatments are typically developed, to practitioners. More often than not, the level of detail in treatment protocols used in research studies is insufficient to teach a clinician to implement the treatment.

This series, *Clinical Application of Evidence-Based Psychotherapy*, will address this issue. For each disorder covered, empirically supported psychological procedures will be identified. Then, an intensive, step-by-step, session-by-session treatment application will be provided. A detailed clinical vignette will be woven throughout, including session transcripts.

All books in this series are written by experienced clinicians who have applied the treatments to a wide variety of patients, and have supervised and taught other clinicians how to apply them.

Social Phobia:
Clinical Application of Evidence-Based Psychotherapy
Ronald Rapee and William C. Sanderson

Overcoming Shyness and Social Phobia:
A Step-by-Step Guide
Ronald Rapee

Specific Phobias:
Clinical Applications of Evidence-Based Psychotherapy
Timothy J. Bruce and William C. Sanderson

Cognitive-Behavioral Treatment of Depression
Janet S. Klosko and William C. Sanderson

Marital Distress:
Cognitive Behavioral Interventions for Couples
Jill H. Rathus and William C. Sanderson

Treatment of Obsessive Compulsive Disorder
Lata K. McGinn and William C. Sanderson

Marital Distress

COGNITIVE BEHAVIORAL INTERVENTIONS FOR COUPLES

JILL H. RATHUS, PH.D.
WILLIAM C. SANDERSON, PH.D.

JASON ARONSON INC.
Northvale, New Jersey
London

Library of Congress Cataloging-in-Publication Data

Rathus, Jill H.
    Marital distress : cognitive behavioral interventions for
couples / Jill H. Rathus and William C. Sanderson.
      p. cm.
    Includes bibliographical references and index.
    ISBN 0-7657-0000-X
    1. Marital psychotherapy. 2. Couples—Counseling of. 3. Marriage
counseling. 4. Cognitive therapy. I. Sanderson, William C.
II. Title.
    [DNLM: 1. Marital Therapy—methods. 2. Cognitive Therapy—
methods. 3. Marriage—psychology. 4. Couples Therapy—methods.
WM 430.5.M3 R235m 1998]
RC488.5.R36 1998
616.89'156—dc21
DNLM/DLC
for Library of Congress   98-21980

Printed in the United States of America on acid-free paper. For information and catalog write to Jason Aronson Inc., 230 Livingston Street, Northvale, New Jersey 07647-1726. Or visit our website: http://www.aronson.com.

I dedicate this book to my husband, Lloyd,
whose love, support, and humor enrich my life
immeasurably.

—JHR

This book is dedicated to my parents,
who, among other valuable lessons,
showed me firsthand how to have a wonderful marriage,
as they celebrate their fortieth anniversary.

—WCS

Contents

Acknowledgments

I first must acknowledge K. Daniel O'Leary, my mentor at the State University of New York at Stony Brook, whose influence on both my dedication to couples therapy and research and my professional development in general has been profound. Dina Vivian, my first supervisor in the Marital Therapy Clinic at Stony Brook, also made important contributions over several years to my training and love for working with couples. I would also like to acknowledge the work and influence of the many additional pioneers of behavioral and cognitive-behavioral couples interventions who developed and researched the interventions discussed in this book, including, but not limited to, Donald H. Baucom, Aaron T. Beck, Andrew Christensen, Norman Epstein, Frank Fincham, John M. Gottman, Kurt Hahlweg, Hyman Hops, Neil S. Jacobson, Gayla Margolin, Howard J. Markman, Gerald R. Patterson, Richard B. Stuart, and Robert L. Weiss.

A special word of appreciation goes to my co-author, Bill Sanderson. As a mentor, supervisor, collaborator, and friend, Bill has played a major role in my professional development. I feel privileged to have worked closely with him at Montefiore

Medical Center/Albert Einstein College of Medicine. I also wish to acknowledge my colleagues in the Department of Psychology at Long Island University/C.W. Post Campus for their support and friendship.

Family and friends have provided love and support throughout the book-writing process and throughout my life. I want to particularly thank my parents, Karen Shawn, Spencer Rathus, Keith Breiman, and Lois Fichner-Rathus, and my grandmother, Rose Shawn, and to acknowledge the memories of Bernard Shawn, and Sophie and Gus Rathus. Each of my parents and grandparents has served as an inspiration and as a role model in one way or another, and thus each owns a portion of this book. And I'd like to express my appreciation to my husband, Lloyd, for his comments on the manuscript at various stages as well as his patience during the writing process (he too owns a portion of this book). As I sat around the conference table with him in the Marital Therapy Seminar at Stony Brook in the fall of 1989, I would have been more than pleasantly surprised to know that I would dedicate a book on marital therapy to him as my husband nearly a decade later.

I would also like to acknowledge the editorial and production staff at Jason Aronson for their professionalism and hard work throughout the various stages of publishing this book. Last, I would like to thank the many distressed couples who have shared their most difficult struggles with me and entrusted me with their relationships. They, of course, are the ultimate teachers and supervisors.

—JHR

First, I would like to acknowledge the individuals who have been directly involved and have had a significant influence in my professional development: David H. Barlow, Aaron T. Beck, Susan G. O'Leary, and Jeffrey Young. I would also like to acknowledge T. Byram Karasu, Chairman of the Psychiatry Department at Albert Einstein College of Medicine, who has provided me with the opportunity to be productive in my academic endeavors. Numerous colleagues have served as collaborators, advisors, and friends over the years, including Tim Bruce, Janet Klosko, Lata McGinn, Alec Miller, Ron Rapee, Scott Wetzler, and of course, the co-author of this book, Jill Rathus. I would like to express my gratitude to my wife, Lynn, who has been my greatest support over the past 15 years, and to my children, Kristen and Billy, who have limited my productivity, but provided life's greatest reward. Finally, I would also like to acknowledge the many patients I have treated who have provided the motivation and challenge to evolve as a psychotherapist.

—WCS

1

Rationale for a Cognitive-Behavioral Approach to Relationship Distress

"We're just not happy."

"He really annoys me."

"We don't communicate."

"We can't agree on anything."

"It's not like it used to be."

"She has an awful temper."

"It's never going to get better."

These statements are often among the first a therapist hears when a distressed couple[1] begins treatment. Members of a distressed couple naturally want to convey to a therapist their pain and their perspective on the problems in the relationship, and thus rarely enter treatment singing the relationship's virtues. By the time the partners arrive in the marital therapist's office they are often having feelings of rage or despair, cognitions of blame and hopelessness, and urges to at the very least "fix" the partner, if not leave the relationship altogether.

Unlike individual therapy, in which the therapist must form a therapeutic alliance with one presumably self-referred client, the marital therapist faces the difficult tasks of (1) forming a

---

1. We will refer to couples, relationships, marriage partners, and spouses interchangeably throughout this book. Although the cognitive-behavioral model presented was originally developed and validated as a *marital* treatment, the model applies to nonmarried couples and same-sex partners as well.

working alliance with both partners, who are likely at odds with each other vis-à-vis treatment goals, and (2) fostering a working alliance *between* partners, so that they can participate jointly in working toward improving the relationship. Further, clients who have waned in their commitment to the relationship may arrive with a foot out the door; some clients may regard the marital therapist as the last stop before the divorce lawyer. However, a wealth of outcome studies suggests that a majority of couples can significantly benefit from marital therapy.[2]

In this volume, we aim to familiarize the practitioner with the various components of cognitive-behavioral marital therapy (CBMT), an empirically based treatment model. We hope that what may at first seem to the therapist like an endless array

---

2. At least three forms of couples treatment can claim established efficacy: (1) the cognitive-behavioral relationship therapies, (2) emotion-focused couples therapy (Johnson and Greenberg 1985), and (3) insight-oriented couples therapy (Snyder and Wills 1989, Snyder et al. 1991). Other novel couple treatments have received promising preliminary support, such as Christensen and Jacobson's integrative behavioral couples therapy (Christensen et al. 1995). However, cognitive-behavioral approaches have accrued by far the greatest volume of empirical support, through numerous randomized studies evaluating global intervention packages and "dismantling" studies evaluating separate treatment components. In this volume we thus present a cognitive-behavioral intervention, consisting of empirically supported treatment components in a manualized format. Studies demonstrating efficacy of the various treatment components, alone and in various combinations, are listed in Appendix I.

of problems and complaints will become patterned into a logical and coherent set of tasks. In this chapter, we present a cognitive-behavioral conceptualization of the development and maintenance of marital discord, as well as a discussion of the various problem areas targeted in a brief treatment format. We will also touch on when *not* to conduct couples treatment, as certain presentations call for interventions other than the model presented here. The remainder of this volume will present a detailed, session-by-session intervention procedure for marital distress.

A COGNITIVE-BEHAVIORAL MODEL OF RELATIONSHIP DISTRESS

The cognitive-behavioral model of marital relationship distress is derived from theory and research in a variety of areas including Bandura's (1977) social learning theory, social exchange theory, family systems theory, and cognitive psychology. How then, according to this model, does a relationship that at one point brought joy, love, and commitment go so awry that the very same relationship causes pain and despair? The cognitive-behavioral model focuses on both environmental and individual variables (i.e., behavioral skills, cognitive processes, affective states) as determinants of marital satisfaction. The learning theory side of this perspective holds that by analyzing the interaction between our behavior and our environment, we can understand and modify the difficulties that led to seeking treatment. More specifically, the consequences provided by a partner are seen as controlling the behaviors "emitted" by a spouse; spouses continually act in ways that are reinforcing or punishing to their partners. Each partner's behavior constantly influences and is influenced by the partner through a series of behavior-consequence sequences.[3] This view of the interdependence and circularity of partner behaviors is also consistent with a family systems perspective. The cognitive contribution to the model highlights idiosyncratic perceptual factors as mediators of the person–environment relationship. From these perspectives, problems in the following areas collectively contribute to the development and maintenance of marital distress: low rates of pleasing behavior coupled with high rates of displeasing behavior, reciprocity of negative behaviors, communication and problem-solving skill deficits,

---

3. We wish to point out here that we feel this view may be misleading and even harmful in the case of domestic violence, where this perspective may appear to suggest that the *recipient* of violence emits (i.e., the victim *evokes*) behaviors that influence a partner's use of violence. While at times this model may apply (e.g., a partner's compliance following violence may reinforce its use), research demonstrating the occurrence of violence independent of a victim's behavior suggests dispositional causes as well as *intra*personal reinforcement factors (e.g., violence being negatively reinforced by the reduction of aversive arousal) as important determinants of partner-directed aggression. Most important, and regardless of the determinants, we feel it is critical to hold the violent partner solely responsible for the use of violent behavior. While an interactional model implicates both partners in marital conflict, we generally do not advocate couples-based interventions for marital violence, as explicated at the end of this chapter.

dysfunctional relationship cognitions, and dysfunctional anger expression.

Low Rates of Pleasing Behavior

The CBMT model highlights the frequency with which spouses exchange rewards and punishments as central determinants of marital satisfaction. In 1969, in one of the earliest published models of this approach, Richard Stuart characterized distressed relationships as providing a paucity of positive outcomes for both partners. Researchers including Robert Weiss (1978) and John Gottman (Gottman, Notarius, Markman et al. 1976, Gottman et al. 1977) substantiated this view in the 1970s with findings showing that distressed couples indeed tend to exchange low rates of pleasing behavior and high rates of displeasing behavior compared to nondistressed couples.

When distressed spouses make vague or global statements such as "He doesn't make me happy anymore" or "She doesn't pay attention to me," they are referring to a lack of rewarding or subjectively pleasing behaviors expressed by one spouse toward the other. Although we do not typically think of closeness this way, enjoying time with a partner, sharing pleasant activities, and feeling connected and fulfilled all depend on the occurrence of discrete behaviors—behaviors that we can identify and observe. We can translate the statement "My partner makes me happy" into "My partner *engages in particular positive behaviors* that make me happy." The nature of these behaviors will vary from person to person but may include acts such as "laughs at my jokes," "makes supportive statements about my career," or "takes time to explain things to the children." These seemingly small rewards in fact form an important part of the fabric of intimate relationships.

Reinforcements and punishments have both an immediate and a long-term impact on ongoing behavioral sequences between spouses. For example, the immediate impact of criticizing a partner who reveals bouncing a check may lead to a countercriticism by the partner, resulting in an angry escalation and discouraging such honest revelations in the future. On the other hand, validating the partner's frustration at having bounced the check might lead to a warm interaction and reinforce this type of communication; that is, the check-bouncer might be more likely to communicate such transgressions in the future. These patterns have a cumulative effect over time. If a spouse has been disturbed about a partner's irresponsible handling of money over the past several months, the spouse might be more likely to express anger than support over a bounced check. Thus, one's behaviors toward a spouse may reflect one's happiness with the relationship at a given period of time, but *classes* of reinforcers and punishers accumulate over time and influence the emotional climate of the relationship.

Reinforcement Erosion

In new relationships, mutual reinforcement is at its peak. Positive feelings, novelty, sexual attraction, and idealized expectations of future rewards all contribute to each partner's motivation to donate rewarding behaviors frequently and noncontingently. Further, during courtship, couples typically spend time together that is primarily pleasure-focused and void of "real-life" hardships. At the same time, punishing experiences are rare in newly developing relationships, as individuals reveal their best behavior, downplay differences, and sacrifice needs in order to accommodate a desired partner. Over time, of course, novelty fades and couples face the challenges inherent in sharing life with a partner. Demands increase and change, stressors accumulate, and shared time and activities lose some of their initial reinforcement value. For satisfaction to remain, couples must adjust to changing demands while developing expanded repertoires of mutually reinforcing activities. Difficulties arise when couples are not able to make these needed adjustments.

Through a process known as *reinforcement erosion*, relationship rewards tend to trail off for both partners over time (Jacobson and Margolin 1979). The mechanism underlying this process is twofold: first, behaviors or activities that were at one point highly reinforcing yield diminished reinforcement value because of habituation. In other words, partners get used to each other and the positive intensity of attributes or shared activities simply fades. One of the most common examples of this tendency is the reduced reinforcement value of sexual activity as the relationship ages; countering this typically requires that couples expand their sexual repertoires to maintain their level of interest.

Second, over time, many partners gradually begin to emit fewer rewarding behaviors. In distressed relationships, partners complain that these positive behaviors have markedly decreased. This reduction may occur for a variety of reasons, both malevolent and benign, such as a sense of security leading to a reduction in active efforts to attract the partner, a shift in priorities (e.g., "The relationship is solid now, so I better focus on work"), an assumption that "She *knows* I love her—I don't need to show her," lack of recognition of the value of such gestures to the partner, outside stress, or willful withholding because of anger or resentment. Ironically, even very positive intentions or assumptions, such as increasing the family's living standard by taking on extra work, or assuming one's love is obvious and needs no expression, can lead to the neglect of such behaviors and ultimately the decline of satisfaction in marriage.

High Rates of Displeasing Behavior

In addition to low rates of rewarding behavior, marital distress can develop from an abundance of aversive behaviors exchanged between spouses. When relationships are newly developing, partners tend to display only their best behavior, but with comfort and commitment comes a letting down of one's guard. After a time, many partners become more likely to disagree, criticize, raise their voices, and so on. Qualities that partners might have concealed early in the relationship might emerge, such as messiness, overspending, overinvolvement with family, or other behaviors that a spouse might find displeasing. While all relationships contain some degree of displeasing behavior, the level can grow extreme for a couple who share few common interests (e.g., jogging becomes one

partner's self-involved habit instead of a couple's shared rec-
reation time), differ in needs for affiliation, face outside stress,
have communication and problem-solving difficulties, or have
become so angry about other issues that they make no effort
to inhibit hostile gestures.

In addition to the positive or negative consequences provided within a relationship, factors outside of the relationship
can carry important weight as well. According to social exchange theory (Thibaut and Kelley 1959), relationships are
maintained by one's sense that the rewards within a relationship outweigh the punishments or costs, and that the reward-
to-punishment ratio within the relationship is higher than one
could attain outside of the relationship. Thus, distress arises
not only when a spouse perceives an absence of rewards in
the relationship or a preponderance of costs, but also when
the reward:cost ratio compares unfavorably with other potential relationships or with being out of a relationship altogether.
Thus, spouses will be less tolerant of aversive behaviors and
more demanding of rewarding ones if they perceive the avail-
ability of appealing alternatives to their present relationship.
A relationship might have a favorable balance of rewards and
punishments, but if opportunities develop outside of the relationship that pose a better reward:cost ratio, the relationship
will lose its stability unless its internal rewards increase or its
punishments decrease. Thus, a potential lover, an appealing
relocation offer rejected by a spouse, or other enticing extramarital choices can threaten marital satisfaction even in a relatively stable relationship, especially when the rates of pleasing
and displeasing behaviors change gradually over time.

Reciprocity of Negative Exchanges

We have described the development of marital distress as it emanates from *base rates* of positive and negative behaviors partners direct toward one another in the relationship. However, we can also differentiate distressed from nondistressed couples on the basis of the *contingent exchange* of negative behaviors.

According to family interaction researcher Gerald Patterson (Patterson and Reid 1970), reciprocity refers to the approximately equal rate of exchange of rewarding or punishing behaviors between spouses. Reciprocity can occur both in moment-to-moment interactions and over the long term. *Positive reciprocity* refers to the exchange of rewarding behaviors at approximately equal rates, and occurs in both distressed and nondistressed relationships. That is, regardless of marital satisfaction, pleasing behavior rates between spouses tend to be highly correlated over time, such that spouses who are giving to their spouses will tend to be given to in return. However, *negative reciprocity*, or the relatively balanced exchange of punishing behaviors, is a phenomenon more pronounced in distressed couples. Marital interaction researchers such as Kurt Hahlweg and colleagues (1984) have found that, in distressed dyads, spouses show an increased probability of responding promptly to their partners' aversive behaviors with an aversive behavior of their own, leading to a coercive escalation process. In contrast, happy couples are less likely to reciprocate negative behaviors, usually viewing them as aberrations or making otherwise benign appraisals of their occurrence. Since reciprocity holds for interactions over time, unhappy couples can expect an equitable exchange of punishing behaviors over the long run as well.

The implication of this tendency is that in couples for whom marital satisfaction has waned, the phenomenon of negative reciprocity maintains punishing response sequences. Although reciprocity of positive behavior appears similar in nondistressed and distressed couples, distressed couples exchange lower rates of positive behaviors overall. This combination of fewer positive behaviors and negative reciprocity traps couples in aversive interaction sequences.

The following examples illustrate how these processes work for nondistressed and distressed couples. Because nondistressed couples are less likely to reciprocate negative behaviors and yet reward each other at equal rates, they tend to attain a pleasing momentum and to exchange behaviors based on positive reinforcement (i.e., a behavior that increases the likelihood of a behavior it follows, such as praise or compliance). An example of behaviors exchanged on the basis of this *positive control system* is a husband preparing a nice dinner, which pleases his wife, who then compliments her husband, and voluntarily begins cleaning following dinner. The husband might then begin cleaning at the wife's side, the wife may reciprocate with lively conversation and a kiss, the husband may suggest sharing an after-dinner drink, and so on, and so goes a positive evening. Not only is the interaction pleasant and likely to remain pleasant, but the reinforcement value of each spouse's gestures strengthens the chances that each partner will engage in similar behaviors in the future.

In contrast, distressed couples engage in an *aversive control system* by which they interact, exchanging behaviors on the basis of negative reinforcement and punishment. *Negative reinforcement* refers to an increase in the likelihood of a behavior following the *removal* of an aversive stimulus, while *punishment* refers to the decrease in the likelihood of a behavior following the *presentation* of an aversive stimulus. Aversive control strategies include threats, demands, criticisms, nagging, expressions of anger, ignoring, and negative facial expressions. An example of an aversive control system involves a husband who has made his wife dinner and asks her to do the dishes. She replies that she needs to make some phone calls now and will get to them later. An hour later, when the wife is off the phone, the husband finds the dirty dishes still piled up in the sink. Troubled by the sight of dirty dishes remaining in the sink, the husband escalates his request to an angry demand that she do the dishes now. When she protests that she'll do them when she is ready, he begins yelling at her for her general lack of participation in the household chores. Not wanting to endure a tirade, she reluctantly begins the dishes, which immediately "shuts off" his angry criticisms. Thus, she is negatively reinforced for her compliance (through the cessation of her husband's yelling), while her husband is positively reinforced for using an aversive control strategy to attain the behavior change he desires. Patterson and his colleagues (Patterson and Hops 1972, Patterson and Reid 1970) have labeled this aversive control strategy based on the exchange of negative and positive reinforcement *coercion*. Following such interactions, both partners will be more likely to rely on these coercive processes in the future than to negotiate an alternative solution.

As an example of interactions under the control of punishment, consider the example of a husband who arrives home two hours late on the night of his anniversary. The wife yells at him for arriving late, resulting in a lengthy argument, and their evening is spoiled. Alternatively, the wife might apply a punishing strategy through the withholding of rewards, such as sulking and refusing affection upon the husband's late arrival. If, in the future, he arrives home on time for special occasions, we can assume the wife's yelling or sulking had a punishing effect, in its suppression of her husband's tardy behavior. In either case, aversive behavior has been an effective strategy in securing behavior change, and so the wife is likely to continue coercive control tactics. The problem is that although these tactics may lead to short-term behavioral compliance, they tend to be reciprocated with similarly aversive tactics. These aversive control patterns therefore develop into entrenched patterns of mutual hostility, and contribute to a gradual decay in satisfaction.

In addition to a lower ratio of rewards to punishments and a characteristic pattern of negative reciprocity, Neil Jacobson and colleagues (1982) have found that distressed spouses are particularly *reactive* to rewards and punishments from a partner. That is, unhappily married couples' relationship evaluations are highly contingent on immediate consequences, and as such tend to fluctuate rapidly. We have all observed tense marital interactions that demonstrate this lability, in which one partner says or does "the wrong thing" and the other partner's anger surfaces immediately. In contrast, we can probably think of a more stable couple, for whom a similar mistake by one partner would either be met with little reaction or ignored. Happy couples, who have received a steady enough supply of rewards over time with a relative minimum of irritants, are less dependent on any given interaction for their evaluation of the relationship and thus more resistant to fluctuations in satisfaction. In other words, good marriages are simply more resilient.

Communication Skill Deficits

In addition to the role of behavior exchange in the development and maintenance of marital relationship distress, communication difficulties can contribute to the decay of satisfaction as well. Stable marriages rely not only on mutually rewarding interactions but also on strong communication skills. In fact, marital researcher Howard Markman (1979, 1984) has shown that early communication difficulties predict the development of later marital discord.

The maintenance of intimacy and the thwarting of a downward, destructive interactional cycle requires each partner to be skillful both in expressive (i.e., speaking) and receptive (i.e., listening) communication. As a speaker, a spouse must be able to express feelings, ideas, problems, and requests, while avoiding blaming attacks or contemptuous remarks. As a listener, a spouse must be adept not only at monitoring whether he or she is receiving the message correctly, but also at offering validation and support while avoiding defensiveness or withdrawal. Speaking and listening styles in couples are mutually influential; a partner receiving criticism will naturally tend to respond defensively, and a speaker encountering a defensive response will likely intensify the complaint in an attempt to be heard. In order to handle the changes and challenges that couples inevitably encounter, partners must have the skills to constructively express feelings, assert desires, and listen to and discuss options for negotiation. Through these means couples can develop new repertoires for reinforcement and new rules or scripts to handle novel situations or routines. Good communication skills enhance mutual understanding and diffuse conflict. As such, good communication can also become a source of positive reinforcement in a relationship.

Early in a relationship, communication may be sufficient even in partners who are not expert communicators. Partners may devote extra effort to expressing feelings and listening as part of the larger package of investing rewarding behaviors at a high rate in a desirable new relationship. With an overall halo surrounding the relationship, partners may take extra pains to negotiate or convey empathy. Moreover, since partners put their best foot forward early in a relationship, and critical decisions regarding issues such as finances or child-rearing are not yet facing the couple, there may be fewer challenging issues about which to communicate. While a long-term relationship with poor communication may be characterized by hostile communication or no communication at all, due to factors indicated above, partners in a newly forming relationship are not yet burdened with such issues. Thus, early communication-skill deficits may go unnoticed for some time, masked by the prominence of other rewards.

Faulty communication strategies inevitably lead to the escalation of conflict, the deflection of problem-solving, and ultimately the beginnings of marital distress. Although anger and disagreement are normal and at times adaptive aspects of relationships, deficits in communication skills lead to the painful escalation of conflict and a frustrating lack of resolution. Rather than feeling heard or accepted, members of a distressed dyad typically feel invalidated and attacked after attempts to communicate. Specific communication difficulties include destructive expression of feelings, failure to listen to and validate the partner's point of view, or shutting down completely during conflict.

Difficulties in communication can arise not only from lack of skill, but also from affective and cognitive factors that *inhibit* the use of skillful means to communicate. For example, a husband might become so emotionally flooded during conflict that he withdraws from any interaction; his wife might come to develop the expectation that bringing up problems will prove hopelessly frustrating. Thus, communication difficulties may not only lead to but also result from relationship distress. Some couples remain stuck in a pattern of relentless arguing, while others come to view attempts to communicate as a signal for frustration and simply withdraw.

Marital communication researchers have revealed a variety of factors that differentiate distressed from nondistressed couples. Weiss and colleagues (Birchler et al. 1975, Weiss et

al. 1974) have identified higher overall rates of negative communication behaviors in distressed couples during both con-
flict-resolution discussions and casual conversations. Specifically, they have highlighted deficits in specifying complaints,
expressing empathy, and negotiating disagreements as differ-
entiating the communication of distressed from nondistressed
couples. In some of his early research, Gottman (Gottman et
al. 1977) (a major innovator of couples communication interventions; see Chapters 4 and 5 on Enhancing Communication) found that, compared to nondistressed couples, not
only did distressed couples engage in *higher rates of negative
nonverbal behaviors* (e.g., rolling eyes, expression of disgust),
but they also exhibited *greater reciprocity of negative verbal behaviors*. Thus, as in overall behavior-exchange patterns, distressed spouses are more likely to respond to negative *communication* behavior, such as an insult, with another negative
communication. Because of this reciprocity, distressed couples
become submerged in negative interaction patterns, finding it
harder to disengage from conflict.

Gottman's work (Gottman, Notarius, Markman et al. 1976)
also revealed that while distressed and nondistressed spouses
indicated equivalent levels of positive *intent* behind their verbal messages, distressed partners rated the *impact* of these
messages as significantly worse. For example, a spouse in
either a happy or distressed marriage might intend to show
interest in a partner's day with the question, "Did you go shopping today?" While a maritally satisfied spouse might interpret the question as an expression of interest, a spouse in a
distressed marriage might interpret the question as an accusa-

tion of mishandling money. These frequent negative misperceptions contribute to the downward spiraling of many marital interactions for distressed couples.

In addition to differences in impact of messages, Gottman's research (Gottman et al. 1977) revealed that distressed couples differ from nondistressed couples in their use of validation. For nondistressed couples, spouses engaged in problem-solving discussions typically follow a problem statement by the other spouse with a validation, that is, some show of support or understanding. For distressed relationships, in contrast, spouses typically respond to such expressions by registering a complaint of their own. These cross-complaining patterns lead to sequences of mutual problem statements and attacks, with little opportunity for either partner to feel understood or achieve resolution.

More recently, Gottman (1993a,b, Gottman and Krokoff 1989) has found that while several styles of handling conflict characterized stable marriages, couples with marriages heading toward dissolution tended to share strongly negative interchanges, including communication marked by criticism, contempt, defensiveness, and withdrawal from interaction. Spouses typically intensify their speaking to include critical comments, and, ultimately, displays of contempt, often in the context of repeatedly feeling that they are getting no response to their expressed complaints (which may be the result of the listener being unwilling to listen, or the speaker sending an unclear message in the first place). In response to these hostile, judgmental, and hurtful communications, spouses on the receiving end tend to become increasingly defensive, a pattern

that practically ensures a lack of resolution. As attacks escalate and frustrations mount, many partners will become
flooded with physiological arousal (i.e., increased heart rate,
blood pressure, and high adrenaline production—as in a "fight
or flight" reaction). Finding it nearly impossible to engage
effectively in this state, individuals experiencing this reaction
may suddenly shut down completely, often appearing cold and
nonresponsive, or physically leaving the situation (Gottman
and Levenson 1986). Once relationships reach such a point
of distress, less intense stimuli produce the same high-intensity physiological reactions; cynical, distress-maintaining
thoughts become ingrained; and partners tend to distort positive memories into negative recollections (Buehlman et al.
1992). At this point, it becomes nearly impossible for couples
to steer the relationship back on course on their own.

Finally, observational and physiological research has identified gender-based incompatibilities in communication style
that also contribute to the development of relationship distress in heterosexual couples. Women are more comfortable
expressing their feelings and conflicts, and thus report being
troubled by their spouses' tendencies to avoid expression of
emotions, problem-solve instead of listen, and withdraw from
interaction. In contrast, men prefer to calm down alone, avoid
discussing feelings, and think and behave rationally (as opposed
to emotionally). They thus report being troubled by their
wives' tendencies to criticize and badger them and to harp on
problems. Obviously, these stylistic clashes can set the stage
for discord as couples with conflicting needs develop "demand–withdraw" cycles, each partner vying for a satisfying

mode of interaction. In fact, in congruence with these differences, Gottman (1994, Gottman and Levenson 1986, 1988, 1992) has reported that men are (1) much more likely than women to become flooded with arousal during conflict, and (2) slower to calm down once aroused. These findings suggest a potential physiological basis for the observed gender differences in communication; this physiological pattern can be addressed within CBMT (see Chapter 9 on Addressing Marital Anger).

Problem-Solving Skill Deficits

Unlike difficulties with communication, which are often a presenting complaint of the couple entering treatment, difficulties with problem-solving can go unrecognized. Well-meaning and confused spouses may report that for some reason, each time they try to discuss a problem, things either "go nowhere" or "blow up." They thus develop a sense that they are "walking on eggshells," learn to avoid certain topics, and come to feel hopeless about getting needs met. Of course this pattern becomes self-fulfilling, and continues to generate negative perceptions and expectancies about the relationship.

Communication is a necessary first step in clearly identifying a problem. However, even if communication skills are in place, efforts to communicate may reach a dead end as couples encounter seemingly irreconcilable differences. Thus, partners may feel they have gained insight into a difficulty but are still faced with an unsolved problem. A couple's reaction to this type of problem may pose a greater threat than the actual problem itself. Rather than viewing problems and disagreements as a normal part of an intimate relationship, members of a distressed couple may come to feel overwhelmed and hopeless as differences accumulate with no satisfying resolution. While a lack of problem-solving skills can set this frustrating process in motion, it can be exacerbated by poor communication throughout the process, lowered motivation to negotiate with a partner, outside stress that presents many new problems for a couple, unrealistic relationship standards (e.g., couples should agree on everything), or overwhelming affect that interferes with engagement in the task of problem solving (e.g., one partner storms out in an angry rage each time the other partner brings up the problem). Alone or in combination, these factors can sow seeds of marital dissatisfaction.

As mentioned above, a particular hallmark of distressed relationships is the tendency to engage in aversive control strategies to effect change in a partner. Thus, over time, a pattern of coercion may develop in place of successful problem-solving ability. Despite their immediate effectiveness in bringing about behavior change, coercive interactions occur at great cost to marital satisfaction, becoming strengthened over time and leaving spouses angry and unhappy.

Dysfunctional Relationship-Linked Cognitions

The cognitive aspect of the cognitive-behavioral model of relationship distress refers to the areas of marriage affected not by outward behaviors or capability deficits but by internal, interpretive processes relevant to partner interaction. This area originates from the clinical application of cognitive psychology and from social cognition theories of social psychology. The application of cognitive models to couples therapy stems largely from cognitive models of individual psychopathology championed by such clinician-theorists as Aaron Beck (Beck et al. 1979), Albert Ellis (1962), and Donald Meichenbaum (1977). The cognitive contribution to the CBMT model is based on the empirically supported premise that faulty information processing leads to many of an individual's maladaptive dysfunctional emotional and behavioral responses. The faulty information processing generally takes one of two forms: either invalid appraisals of reality, or valid appraisals based on unrealistic standards. Beck (1988) notes the further complication that people seldom step back to evaluate either the accuracy of their moment-to-moment cognitions or the appropriateness of their standards, but instead regard them as unwavering truths. Naturally, both transient cognitions and long-standing assumptions significantly impact emotional and behavioral reactions within the marital relationship. Thus, relationship malfunction is related not only to *what spouses do* but also *how these actions are appraised* by their partner.

Donald Baucom and Norman Epstein (1990, Baucom et al. 1989) have proposed five categories of cognitive phenomena central to the development and maintenance of marital relationship distress. *Perceptions* involve subjective notions of what events occur, *attributions* involve the causes of these events, *expectancies* involve predictions of what events will occur, *assumptions* involve views of how events relate to one another and of how things are, and *standards* are beliefs about how things should be. Other important cognitive phenomena include cognitive distortions and negative framing.

Perceptions

Perception refers to the process of attending to and categorizing information. Through a process Beck (1988) terms *selective abstraction*, people tend to notice particular aspects of their environments and neglect to notice others. What we perceive is influenced by our past learning, our assumptions and standards, and our mood states. Biases in perceptions occur frequently in marital relationships; research indicates that spouses may have trouble agreeing whether particular behaviors did or did not occur even on the same day about which they are reporting. Such perceptual biases can create and maintain problems when spouses selectively attend to negative aspects of the partner or the relationship, neglecting to focus on positive qualities or efforts to change. Once partners develop negative feelings about the relationship, they tend to attend to marital events that confirm their views and minimize events that disconfirm them.

Attributions

Attributions are the reasons partners assign to the occurrence of events. Attributions that spouses make for partner behavior and relationship conflicts relate to marital quality, such that spouses who make negative attributions for their partners' behaviors experience greater marital distress (Holtzworth-Munroe and Jacobson 1985, Jacobson et al. 1985). Frank

Fincham and Thomas Bradbury (1990) have found that, compared to nondistressed couples, distressed couples make more negative causal and responsibility attributions for marital events. *Causal attributions* made by distressed couples include the beliefs that troublesome spouse behaviors are due to stable, global, and internal factors on the part of the spouse (a process parallel to that found in the *self-directed attributions* of depressed or anxious individuals about negative or threatening events). For example, in a distressed relationship a spouse is likely to view a partner's inconsiderate oversight as part of a pattern of ongoing behavior, likely to occur across many situations, and caused by some intrinsic quality in the partner. (In a happier relationship the same oversight might be viewed as a one-time or rare occurrence, specific to one situation, and due to a particular set of circumstances, such as a rough day.) In contrast, positive events by the partner are more likely to be regarded by distressed spouses as transient, specific, and external. *Negative responsibility attributions* include viewing undesirable partner behaviors as selfishly motivated, intentional, and blameworthy. Like perceptions, attributions are influenced by standards, assumptions, and prior learning experiences. Innacurate attributions can aggravate marital difficulty by exaggerating the apparent representativeness of displeasing partner behaviors, while reducing the reinforcement value of positive ones. As anger or discord develops, partners make increasingly negative attributions for each other's behaviors, viewing negative acts as intentional and positive acts as flukes that are unlikely to recur. Thus, relationship improvement becomes difficult as spouses discount partners' efforts to improve.

Expectancies

Expectancies concern the events we anticipate, including consequences and outcomes of particular events in marriage. They are formed through learning (e.g., instruction, modeling, and direct experience), and are influenced by assumptions and standards. Generalized expectancies involve predictions such as "Anyone I get close to will let me down," while specific expectancies involve predictions pertaining to particular situations, such as "When I express my feelings to my husband he will belittle them." Sometimes expectancies occur in the form of long-held blueprints for a marital relationship, such as "I always envisioned that my wife would stay home with the children." Clearly, expectancies influence both affect and behavior in marriage. For example, a wife holding the expectancy that her husband will belittle her should she express her feelings would likely harbor resentment toward her spouse while keeping her feelings private.

Assumptions

Assumptions are conceptions about characteristics of one's partner, one's relationship, or the world. Maladaptive marital assumptions can develop from one's learning history, inaccurate perceptions of events in one's history, or previous assumptions that bias inferences and become self-perpetuating. *Schemas*, or stable cognitive structures that organize complex relationships among events or characteristics, provide the framework from which individuals move beyond clear evidence and develop assumptions. Ample evidence indicates that schemas self-perpetuate because they bias perceptions, leading individuals to attend to schema-confirming information while disregarding disconfirming information. Epstein and Eidelson (1981) have reported that negative marital assumptions, such as "disagreement is destructive," or "the relationship cannot change," are strong predictors of both marital distress and diminished motivation to cope with marital difficulties.

Standards

Standards are beliefs about how things should be. Standards for one's relationship or partner can prove distressing and lead to maladaptive behavior when one's experiences of relationship events or partner characteristics compare unfavorably to one's beliefs of how they should be. Take, for example, an individual who adheres to the relationship standard that "spouses should anticipate each other's needs without having to be told." If this person's spouse fails to recognize a particular need, the individual may feel angry and hurt, and may choose to angrily confront the partner. If, however, the individual did not espouse this standard and instead believed partners were not mind readers, he or she might experience neutral emotions in response to an unrecognized need and instead make a clear request to the partner. Although many personal standards are valid and serve important self-protective or relationship-protective functions (e.g., "partners should remain faithful; I will not tolerate infidelity, nor will I be unfaithful"), unrealistic or extreme relationship standards can be problematic. Examples of potentially problematic relationship standards include "my partner should want to spend all of his or her free time with me," "we should always see eye-to-eye on important issues," and "sex should be perfect." Additional trouble can arise when partners hold realistic but incompatible standards, such as different views of the roles in-laws should take with regard to the couple's major decisions.

Cognitive Distortions

Although each of these areas of cognitive functioning serves valuable adaptive functions vis-à-vis organizing and interpreting information into manageable and predictable pieces, difficulties for the marital relationship arise from the fact that each of these areas is subject to cognitive distortions, or errors in information-processing, leading to erroneous depictions of reality (Abrahms and Spring 1989). Relationship problems thus develop in part from the formation of inaccurate inferences based on ambiguous or inaccurate information, faulty prior learning, and an absence of proper distinctions between one's beliefs and reality. For example, while one partner might be making loving gestures toward the other, the spouse on the receiving end may not find these behaviors pleasing for a variety of reasons, perhaps minimizing them because of unrealistic standards, inferring malevolent intentions behind the behaviors, or failing to perceive them at all. Similarly, a couple may possess the skills to communicate effectively but may inhibit communication because of the expectancy that open communication would be fruitless, or because they hold the standard that married couples shouldn't have to discuss their needs.

In these ways, faulty cognitions can undermine even the best of marital intentions or behavioral skills.

Negative Framing

A related facet of the cognitive model of relationship distress concerns the tendency for couples in discordant relationships to negatively frame qualities in their mates that they once found appealing. Thus, over time, a partner's confidence and conviction might come to be regarded as stubbornness; a partner's admirable ambitiousness might come to be seen as workaholism. Characteristics once viewed as desirable become liabilities, and couples seem no longer able to recognize the positive sides to these features in their partners.

Dysfunctional Anger Expression

While the ability to identify, label, and constructively express the range of one's emotional experiences to a partner is an important part of intimacy and communication, problematic anger management is often a relevant factor for couples seeking treatment for marital distress. Anger can build over time for a variety of reasons. It can develop as a result of an aversive control system, when couples no longer use positive control strategies to attain desired ends. Anger often serves instrumental purposes, leading to immediate compliance with requests (and thus being maintained by positive reinforcement), or terminating aversive stimuli (thus being maintained by negative reinforcement). Also, anger can result from poor communication and problem-solving skills, leading both partners to feel misunderstood, invalidated, or flooded by emotional arousal, unable to resolve differences or have their needs met. And certainly, relationship-focused cognitions can fuel angry feelings, as distressed partners attribute negative intent and blame to each other's actions, attend more to each other's negative qualities and deeds, and pine for the ideal and unrealistic relationship standards that are not being met. Outside stress, such as the loss of a job, can also contribute to anger directed toward a partner. Overall, patterns of either overly expressed or overly inhibited anger can contribute to the deterioration of both communication and conflict resolution attempts, and to the deterioration of contentment in the relationship.

RATIONALE FOR TREATMENT TARGETS

The problem for discordant couples, of course, is that none of the above-described marital problems occurs in a vacuum; rather, each problem tends to exacerbate the others and they become deeply intertwined, as illustrated in each section above. In a nutshell, behaviors, cognitions, and emotional states all affect one another, as do rewards, punishments, communication and problem-solving attempts, relationship cognitions, and angry outbursts. CBMT aims to untangle this web into its separate components and to address each systematically. Although treatment addresses the components separately, the impact of each intervention can affect several areas simultaneously.

Lack of Pleasing Behaviors

Since partners in distressed marriages experience few rewards and many punishing behaviors in the relationship, CBMT attempts to shift this ratio, both by increasing the positive behaviors and by reducing the aversive behaviors partners exchange. This is a particularly important point of intervention, since distressed couples not only report unfavorable ratios of pleasing to displeasing behaviors, but in their daily satisfaction ratings are also more influenced by the quality of their daily interactions than nondistressed couples are. Therefore, the CBMT therapist targets the couple's behavior exchanges early in treatment. Positive behaviors are increased directly through the institution of *positive tracking, caring gestures, shared pleasurable activities, and behavioral contracting procedures,* following models developed by such marital therapy innovators as Jacobson (Jacobson and Margolin 1979), Patterson (Patterson and Hops 1972), Stuart (1969), and Weiss (1980, 1984, Weiss et al. 1973, 1974, Margolin et al. 1975). Positive behaviors are also increased indirectly through other components of treatment, such as communication training.

One might suppose that an increase in rewarding behaviors toward a spouse would emerge naturally as anger subsides and intimacy grows as a result of other aspects of therapy. While this may be true in part, putting into place a specific plan of increasing rewarding behaviors is important for several reasons. First, partners may need such positive experiences to keep them motivated to remain in the marriage and work

to improve it while many negative marital events are still occurring. Since distressed partners are highly reactive to immediate relationship events, rapid positive behavioral changes may
bring accompanying positive shifts in satisfaction. Second, early
treatment experiences with pleasing events can instill hope
where hopelessness had predominated. Third, implementing
positive behaviors can lead to quick and relatively easily won
changes, giving couples a sense of mastery in a situation in
which they may have felt powerless. Fourth, spouses may simply not know the gestures that are most pleasing to a partner.
Partners may need a focused intervention to learn which events
their partner finds reinforcing.

Excess of Displeasing Behaviors

Although CMBT emphasizes an increase in positive behaviors, it tends to result in decreased negative or punishing behaviors in marriage as well. This occurs in many ways in
CBMT. One way involves the fact that reducing negative behaviors can be the flip side of increasing positive behaviors.
For example, partners can eliminate the irritating behavior of
leaving laundry on the floor with the positive gesture of putting laundry in the hamper. CBMT also reduces negative
spouse behaviors through communication and problem-solving training, allowing for the expression of feelings about negative situations and developing solutions satisfying to both
partners. In addition, through modifying distorted cognitions,
partners often alter their negative appraisals of behaviors. For

example, a wife's habit of working late, initially viewed as neglectful of the family, might come to be seen as dedication to earning a more secure future for her family. Finally, targeting the dysfunctional expression of anger can reduce a spouse's experience of negative marital events when anger expression itself has become a central negative marital event.

While working to increase pleasing and decrease displeasing behaviors, the CBMT therapist addresses the reciprocity of negative behaviors as well. A variety of elements in CBMT serve to reduce the reciprocation of punishing behaviors through encouraging noncontingent exchange of positive behaviors, teaching the acknowledgment and reinforcement of such behaviors, improving communication skills to reduce verbal negative reciprocity, teaching problem solving to replace aversive control strategies, and altering cognitions to reduce the tendency to perceive behaviors as negative and thus evoke a reciprocal negative response. Since the mutual exchange of negative behaviors tends to become self-perpetuating, the CBMT therapist attempts to break this destructive cycle and replace it with a self-sustaining positive one.

Despite the focus on marital behaviors in CBMT, clinicians and researchers operating from this perspective acknowledge the important *affective and cognitive correlates* of such behaviors. For example, receiving fewer rewards from one's partner may lead to sadness and negative appraisals about the viability of the relationship. Thus, behavior exchange techniques are aimed at producing accompanying cognitive and emotional shifts as well as behavior change for its own sake.

Deficits in Communication Skills

Distressed couples tend to have problems in communication and with problem-solving skills. In fact, couples and therapists highlight problems with communication as the most common and destructive difficulty for discordant couples (Geiss and O'Leary 1981). To help couples with communication, CBMT first provides training in both expressive and receptive communication skills, following methods pioneered by marital clinician-researchers including Gottman (Gottman, Notarius, Gonso, and Markman 1976), Bernard Guerney (1977), K. Daniel O'Leary (O'Leary and Turkewitz 1978), and Weiss (1978). Because distressed couples exhibit high rates of both verbal and nonverbal negative communication behaviors, *communication training* teaches couples to replace destructive speaker skills with constructive ones, such as replacing character assaults with "I" statements and global complaints with behaviorally specific requests. This intervention also targets the process of negative verbal reciprocity, as positive messages replace initial negative stimuli. Further, refined speaker skills increase chances that messages will be received clearly.

Since the impact of a partner's communication effort often fails to match the partner's intent in distressed relationships, partners are also taught *listener skills*, including how to paraphrase each other's statements and "check in" to ensure the correct understanding of a message. After checking on the intent of a communication, partners are taught to validate each other's feelings, replacing the tendency to register cross-complaints. Various forms of nondefensive listening are emphasized, as research indicates that partners are less likely to react with criticism or contempt when met with open-minded, accepting listening. As explicated in Guerney's (1977) relationship enhancement approach, providing the partners with a constructive set of speaker and listener skills not only equips them to tackle conflicts but also provides a new means for establishing intimacy, shared understanding, mutual validation, and trust.

Problem-Solving Skill Deficits

Because all couples have disagreements, CBMT also teaches a regimented set of problem-solving skills. Even when couples have mastered techniques for communicating about their different viewpoints, they may reach a stalemate when it comes to *resolving* these differences. Understanding each other and reaching a solution involve two separate sets of skills. In fact, research has shown that communication interventions that focus on insight and understanding alone fare less well than those that focus on problem resolution.

Thus, following a procedure tailored for couples by Jacobson and Margolin (1979), partners learn to define a problem in objective terms and to brainstorm solutions. Next, couples work together to eliminate unreasonable solutions and focus on feasible ones. They then construct a trial solution and agree to implement, evaluate, and revise the solution as necessary. With mastery of problem-solving skills, couples change their view of disagreements as a cause for alarm and reevaluate them as a normal aspect of relationships. They can then focus on resolving opposing views with less blame, anger, and coercion.

Dysfunctional Relationship-Linked Cognitions

Because people in discordant relationships hold negative cognitions about their partners and the relationship, CBMT directly targets their thoughts and beliefs (Epstein 1982). Although one might expect appraisals to improve as a by-product of increased rewards and improved communication, cognitions are by nature self-perpetuating and resistant to change. For example, if a husband assumes his wife does not care for him, he will attend more to behaviors that confirm his view and less to behaviors that disconfirm it. He will also be more likely to make causal attributions of ambiguous stimuli, such as his wife coming home late, that support his fundamental assumptions. Further, he may behave in ways that lead his assumption to become self-fulfilling, such as making unreasonable demands, in response to which his wife will likely become rejecting. Thus, his distorted cognitions might undermine even his wife's genuine affection for him.

Such cognitive biases can directly influence the impact of therapeutic interventions. Marital therapists may find that increases in positive behaviors or improvements in communication do not produce the expected positive results, or might even yield negative results, as skeptical spouses discount these changes as not genuine or unlikely to endure. In fact, Baucom and his colleagues (1984) have reported that daily marital satisfaction ratings are much more strongly predicted by looking at attributions for particular behaviors than by simply monitoring which behaviors occurred. Consequently, a spouse working to improve a relationship may often be punished rather than reinforced for efforts to change.

CBMT thus includes a focus on educating clients about various cognitive phenomena and their role in maintaining marital dysfunction, and teaches clients to identify their cognitive distortions and unrealistic standards, and to learn to challenge distorted cognitions or alter problematic standards. Beyond directly targeting cognitions, CBMT also builds in techniques of tracking the partner's positive deeds, which forcibly shifts attention to events that may have otherwise gone unnoticed. Also, because distressed couples tend to negatively frame qualities they once found desirable in their partners, they are encouraged to recall the favorable aspects of problematic partner characteristics, to enhance acceptance of partners as they are.

Destructive Expression of Anger

The successful application of the various CBMT treatment components can substantially reduce anger. Once couples are engaging in more rewarding and fewer punishing behaviors, sharing their viewpoints through improved communication, resolving their differences through problem-solving skills, and viewing each other through more positive cognitive "lenses," they will be likely to find less about which to feel angry. However, anger does not simply evaporate; in cases of severe marital discord, anger might linger and need to be addressed even with improved communication and negotiation skills. In fact, a strong dose of anger might override behaviors and cognitions and hinder progress in these areas. The emotional flooding often experienced during marital conflict precludes the ability to engage in constructive interaction; thus, the over-aroused client must learn strategies for self-calming and apply them before resuming a problem discussion. It should be noted that CBMT does not seek to eliminate anger totally (an unreasonable expectation), but rather to teach clients to manage the destructive expression or inhibition of anger while learning to use the emotion as a constructive signal for attending to a problem.

HOW TREATMENT COMPONENTS ATTEMPT TO REMEDIATE RELATIONSHIP DISTRESS

Orientation to Treatment

The orientation to treatment takes place in the first session (see Chapter 2). It informs couples about the theoretical orientation of the therapy approach and briefly highlights the methods and procedures of the therapy. The purpose is to familiarize couples with the treatment components and structure, and thereby attain their informed commitment to engaging in the therapy.

Assessment

The assessment process (Chapter 2) serves several purposes, including providing information for both therapist and clients and ascertaining that a couple is appropriate for CBMT. First, assessment provides information for the therapist on the specific problems the couple brings to treatment, allowing the therapist to form a conceptualization and consider ways in which the treatment might be individualized. Many practitioners hold the misconception that working with a manualized treatment means sacrificing an intervention tailored to a particular client's needs. This perception is understandable since, by definition, treatment manuals serve to standardize interventions. However, although treatment manuals provide structure and dictate method, they simultaneously allow for a tremendous amount of individualization. After all, each couple has a highly specific set of relationship cognitions, communication strategies, reinforcing activities, and areas of conflict.

For the couple beginning treatment, the assessment process can provide valuable information that can serve as an initial step in the intervention process. Often couples will report finding the assessment session eye-opening in helping them to label or recognize problems, provide insight, or frame difficulties in a novel way. Therapist feedback from the assessment materials can also put the couple at ease when what has seemed like an overwhelming morass of problems becomes framed within a coherent conceptualization. When the therapist uses assessment information to normalize the couple's problems and convey an initial understanding of them, couples may feel their first sense of hope for improvement and a simultaneous connection to their therapist.

Finally, assessment is the means through which the therapist determines whether the problems of the couple warrant a conjoint approach to treatment. Should assessment indicate the need for another type of treatment, the therapist must immediately discuss this conclusion with the couple and make the appropriate referrals. We will address this issue later in this chapter.

Goal Setting

Setting goals occurs through a collaboration between the clients and the therapist (Chapter 2). Although treatment goals can be expressed as mutual goals for the marriage, such as "improved communication," goal setting is best broken down into goals each partner selects for the partner and for him- or herself. Not only does this process focus treatment and reduce the magnitude of seemingly overwhelming problems, but it also initiates communication training by beginning to prompt clients to state problems in behaviorally specific terms. Encouraging clients to articulate what they would like to achieve from therapy prompts them to envision a healthier version of the relationship, and can generate hope and optimism. Setting goals for one's own behavior changes can shift the focus from blaming the partner to one of shared responsibility, diffuse anger as partners look to themselves for contributions to difficulties, and empower spouses with the belief that relationship improvement rests in part in their own hands.

Modes of Therapist Intervention

The various intervention strategies in CBMT are delivered through the general strategies of psychoeducation, modeling, behavioral rehearsal, coaching, feedback, and reinforcement. Throughout each component of the treatment, the cognitive-behavioral marital therapist includes psychoeducation, consisting of a description of and rationale for the particular aspect of treatment, often accompanied by a brief description in lay terms of relevant research findings. Typically, the therapist models new skills, through methods such as providing an example of a challenge to an automatic thought, or demonstrating effective communication in a role-play with a partner. Since couples are not expected to master skills simply by learning about them and watching them demonstrated, a critical aspect of this intervention involves couples' rehearsal of new skills, both in session and at home. The therapist reviews in-session practice and homework exercises in detail and provides coaching and specific corrective feedback. Coaching in the moment will be most helpful for strengthening skills, and this may involve frequent interruptions or interjections by the therapist. A therapist might coach a couple through a discussion by inserting comments such as, for instance, "That's good so far, John; now keep going, and remember to stay focused on your feelings," or "Hold it a second, Karen, can you go back and paraphrase what Bernie just told you?" Feedback then consists of detailed and balanced evaluations of attempts at new skills, so couples learn what they are doing well and where they need continued practice. Finally, the therapist provides ample reinforcement in the form of praise, encouragement, and support for efforts to change, compliance with assignments, and approximations toward improved skills. Reinforcement from the therapist should immediately follow adaptive moment-to-moment behaviors (e.g., head nodding and a smile when a client makes a loving gesture toward a partner), and should also reward larger increments of progress (e.g., "You both did a great job today of staying calm in the session and really making an effort to listen to each other").

Two additional strategies enhance the impact of these procedures. The first involves applying new skills to conflicts the couple identifies as being of low to moderate emotional intensity, rather than those they identify as the most heated. Extreme levels of emotion may impede attention and learning; in this state couples will find it difficult to assimilate new modes of interacting. With more manageable conflicts, couples will more readily master the didactic material and experience success in employing new skills. Once couples demonstrate reasonable proficiency with a set of skills, the therapist should encourage them to apply the skills to conflicts of greater magnitude, since progressively more challenging applications will enhance generalization. One would not want couples to learn only how to address low-intensity problems. The second strategy that enhances the impact of the modes of intervention described above entails balancing feedback between the partners so that one partner does not become targeted for predominantly negative or positive feedback. Even if one partner appears to contribute a greater degree of destructive behavior to the relationship, the therapist will want to devote extra effort to (1) searching for ways to empathize with this partner, and (2) reinforcing this partner's improvements, no matter how small. This balance strengthens the therapeutic alliance with the couple while reducing the likelihood of the therapist appearing to side with one partner.

In order to accommodate the introduction and intensive use of in-session skill acquisition and rehearsal, we recommend a seventy-five to ninety-minute session length. For Sessions 1 and 8, we schedule an additional hour to allow time for completion of assessment materials.

Behavior Exchange Techniques

Positive Tracking

Positive tracking, or the monitoring of positive experiences in the relationship, serves several purposes. First, it creates positive feelings as couples shift their focus from the negative aspects of the relationship that brought them into treatment. Additionally, by having partners express the positive aspects of their interaction, the therapist begins to change the nature of communication from being disproportionally negative. As partners begin to provide verbal reinforcers for each other, the ratio of pleasing to displeasing behaviors begins to change. Finally, spouses receive encouragement for their pleasing behaviors, whereas prior to this monitoring their positive deeds probably went unnoticed or unacknowledged. Thus, the cycle of negative reciprocity shifts to positive reciprocity as mutually rewarding interactions increasingly control behaviors.

Caring Gestures

Caring gestures, a variant of Stuart's (1980) "caring days" procedure; Weiss, Hops, and Patterson's (Weiss et al. 1973) "love days" approach; and Jacobson and Margolin's (1979) "positive exchange" methods, involve increasing rates of discrete, low-cost behaviors with the aim of improving a partner's relationship satisfaction (see Chapter 3). The therapist asks the couple to carry out gestures personalized to please the partner several times weekly on an ongoing basis. Caring gestures are intended to increase mutually pleasing behaviors, focus couples' attention on day-to-day relationship quality, and set in motion a positive chain of reciprocity. Caring gestures can also provide initial hope as quick, visible changes occur. Such early changes can challenge all-or-nothing cognitions involving the pervasive lack of rewards in the relationship or the lack of control one has over relationship quality.

Sharing Pleasurable Activities

Encouraging couples to increase their rates of shared pleasurable activities similarly increases relationship rewards, particularly for couples who have grown distant and find little in common (Jacobson and Margolin 1979) (see Chapter 3).

Communication Training

Communication training, developed by behavioral marital therapy pioneers including Gottman (Gottman, Notarius, Gonso, and Markman 1976), Stuart (1980), and Jacobson and

Margolin (1979), involves teaching partners how to master the roles of both speaker and listener by enhancing positive communication skills and at the same time reducing destructive communication efforts (see Chapters 4 and 5). Communication training also renews intimacy, builds empathy, de-escalates conflict, reduces defensiveness and withdrawal, and sets the stage for problem solving.

Problem-Solving Training

Problem-solving, as developed for couples by Jacobson and Margolin (1979), teaches positive attitudes toward problems as normal components of intimacy and systematizes a method for negotiating solutions (see Chapter 6). This technique both focuses the problem and creates distance from it as partners unite as a team to battle the problem. The systematic approach to disagreements reduces negative behavior exchanges as partners redirect anger and blame into brainstorming solutions. As couples work together, they shift dysfunctional relationship beliefs into hopeful ones while experiencing mastery in handling relationship difficulties.

Contingency Contracting

Contingency contracting was introduced as a component of behavioral marital therapy by Stuart (1969, 1980) and by Weiss and his associates (1974). It is an optional technique that boosts couples' motivation to follow agreements made during problem solving by developing contracts with built-in contingencies for compliance or noncompliance with contract terms (see Chapter 6). This strategy is particularly effective when clients are too angry, disengaged, or unmotivated to exchange pleasing behaviors on faith. Contracts specify the return on partners' behavioral investments and so provide motivation and create an external structure of positive reciprocity.

Cognitive Restructuring

Beck and his colleagues (1979) have suggested that distortions in thinking maintain negative moods while changes in cognitions lead to improvements in mood and behavior. Accordingly, clinicians work with spouses to determine the various cognitions that are contributing to marital distress and help them modify inaccurate cognitions by teaching them to challenge their validity (Baucom and Lester 1986) (see Chapters 7 and 8). By identifying and altering specific errors in information processing, partners can learn to be more accurate interpreters of marital events. In turn, negative emotional states and destructive relationship behaviors will tend to decrease.

Anger Management

Employing strategies developed by Novaco (1975), Neidig and Friedman (1984), Deschner (1984), and others, CBMT teaches partners to mitigate the destructive expression of anger toward a partner while expressing thoughts and feelings fueling the anger through constructive communication skills. Partners are taught to recognize physiological, cognitive, behavioral, and environmental warning cues, use such cues to employ coping skills, and identify the communicative function of their anger in a given context (see Chapter 9).

Relapse Prevention

Attaining relationship satisfaction differs from riding a bicycle; over time, improved relationship skills may fade if not practiced and reinforced. For example, Jacobson and colleagues (1987) found that 25 percent of couples receiving behavioral marital therapy, consisting of behavior exchange techniques and communication training, deteriorated considerably in satisfaction at a two-year follow-up evaluation. Although issues of maintenance have been addressed in behavior therapy since its inception, relapse prevention as an independent treatment package was originally developed by Marlatt and Gordon (1985) for use with substance abusers following intervention. Relapse-prevention strategies involve specific therapeutic activities geared toward maintaining treatment gains by helping clients learn to detect slides toward dissatisfaction and enhancing the successful application of skills to future difficulties. In this volume we suggest relapse-prevention strategies specifically applicable to the marital relationship (see Chapter 10).

WHEN COUPLES TREATMENT IS
NOT INDICATED

Several situations or conditions that commonly co-occur with marital discord are inappropriate for CBMT. These in-

clude the presence of marital violence or abuse, current involvement in an affair, and a diagnosis of substance dependence.
In these cases, we would recommend separate treatment targeting the specified problems as the primary treatment. The
therapist might, however, offer CBMT once the couple re-
solves these additional problems.

Marital Violence

The topic of marital violence has received increased attention and sparked much controversy since University of New
Hampshire researchers Murray Straus and Richard Gelles
(1990) published the results of their large-scale national sur-
veys in 1980 and 1986, reporting that one in six couples reported acts of physical aggression over the previous year.

The presence of spouse abuse poses a dangerous situation
for a couple-focused treatment for several reasons. First,
couple-based interventions typically espouse the family systems
model, which assigns shared responsibility for couple difficulties, viewing problems such as violence as stemming from mutually reinforced interactional sequences. For a husband battering his female partner, implicating both partners in the
women's victimization would further disempower the wife
while possibly supplying justification for the husband's violent actions. Second, the marital therapist may inadvertently
place the women in danger by eliciting content in session that
angers the abusive husband, who may take his anger out on
his wife later in the privacy of their home. Third, certain
marital problems or abuse-related issues, such as feelings of

safety, might remain unvoiced in therapy sessions due to the wife's fear of retaliation. Fourth, couple-based interventions stress the preservation of the marital relationship when, in some cases of abuse, the most helpful goal might be termination of the relationship. Because of these dangers, the therapist might refer couples who present with violence to treatment specifically targeting the violence. For perpetrators, this typically consists of psychoeducational and skill-based group treatments. For victims, this might consist of individual or group therapy focused on support and empowerment (or information on shelters, in the case of severely dangerous violence).

Proponents of couples treatment where marital violence is present have argued that a conjoint approach is useful because (1) conjoint therapy can alter dysfunctional interaction patterns that serve as the context for violence; (2) violence-reduction strategies, such as time-out, may backfire when taught to one partner only; (3) therapy can create a safe environment for tackling issues not broached at home; (4) the presence of both partners may reduce the tendency to minimize reports about ongoing levels of abuse. Based on these premises, O'Leary and Neidig (1993), from the State University of New York at Stony Brook, have developed a conjoint group treatment program for maritally violent couples. To be admitted to the program, aggression levels must be mild to moderate and the wife must report an absence of fear of her partner. Although this program contains some strategies that overlap with the CBMT approach, it also contains additional elements specific to stopping violence, including the use of "no-violence" contracts and psychoeducation regarding the potential justification for anger but the lack of any justification for a violent response to that anger. Thus, for adherents to a conjoint approach for violent couples, we stress that it is essential that the therapist assess violence severity, perceived danger, and fear in an individual interview before proceeding. As a rule, however, we would recommend that conjoint treatment should proceed only when the violence (and the threat of violence) has ceased.

Active Affair

When a spouse reveals an affair, the therapist must explain that proceeding with marital therapy will be pointless and even destructive unless the spouse ends the affair. Involvement with a competing partner strongly stacks the odds against treatment success; not only will the affair serve as a distraction from the hard work required in therapy, but one's spouse almost always appears unfavorable compared with the outside partner. Extramarital affairs typically carry an unrealistic halo, since this new relationship comes with the exhilaration of a budding romance without the years of adversity accumulated in a distressed marriage. Even gains in the marital relationship based on newly learned strategies from therapy will likely appear lackluster to a spouse engaged in an affair. Further, when a client reveals an affair to the therapist in confidence, continuing to work dyadically places the therapist in the position of holding an extremely awkward secret throughout therapy. This position would both compromise the therapist's effectiveness and do an injustice to the naive spouse. It is not the therapist's job to preach moralistic admonitions about an active affair, but simply to explain to the involved spouse why therapy cannot continue unless the spouse agrees to stop the affair.

Substance Dependence

If one or both partners enter treatment with an addiction to drugs or alcohol, we recommend that the therapist refer the addicted partner to a substance abuse program before beginning treatment. Like marital violence, addiction to substances is often one partner's problem, which the therapist can misguidedly address as an interactional issue. Moreover, an addicted spouse, accustomed to depending on a substance to cope with problems, will be less likely to engage in and master the new relationship-based coping strategies taught in CBMT. Substance dependence is difficult to treat on its own, and can add a vast additional layer of difficulties to a marriage. Thus, a relationship complicated by substance abuse would not be amenable to the brief treatment described in this volume.

Other Conditions

There are several presentations of marital discord the marital therapist is likely to encounter that might be appropriate for a couple-focused treatment, but that require a somewhat different format than that presented in this book. These include specific marital problems such as sexual dysfunction, issues of past infidelity, and cases of marital discord co-occurring with individual psychopathology (e.g., Beach et al. 1990). Appendix II contains an annotated bibliography listing various scenarios of this kind and recommended readings for treating these specific problems.

The present chapter has introduced the cognitive-behavioral model of marital relationship distress, provided a rationale for treatment targets, and explained how treatment components remediate relationship distress. We now invite the reader to join us in a session-by-session illustration and elaboration of the concepts addressed in this chapter.

2

Session 1: Assessment

In this chapter we present the first of an eight-session intervention program for maritally distressed couples. The eight-week format includes all of the components of the CBMT intervention; however, the clinician may opt to allocate session time differently, or to meet with a couple over a longer time frame, depending on the particular couple's problems.

THE INITIAL PHONE CONTACT

The initial phone contact is typically brief and focused on business such as scheduling times, gathering phone numbers and other contact information, providing directions to the office, and answering the clients' questions regarding session length and format, fees, insurance, or other issues. Despite its brevity, however, the therapist can also use the initial contact to gather some important information and begin the process of orienting the couple to treatment.

For example, one spouse typically desires marital therapy to a greater extent than the other. This spouse's partner likely falls into one of three categories: (1) not viewing the relationship as troubled enough to warrant therapy, (2) viewing the relationship as troubled yet not seeing couples therapy as the optimal way to address the problem, or (3) not feeling committed enough to the relationship to participate in therapy. In any case, this partner might be lacking in motivation and require extra attention to form a therapeutic alliance (this is-sue will be addressed later in the chapter). Most of the time, the partner who makes the initial phone call for treatment is the treatment-seeking partner, and more often than not, this is the woman. Thus, it can be useful to assess over the phone whose idea it was to seek treatment, and whether both part-ners desire treatment, in order to gauge the expected motiva-tion level from each partner.

The therapist can also use the initial phone call to gain a brief explanation of why the couple is seeking treatment. This information can be important in several ways. First, it gives the therapist a preliminary awareness of the marital difficul-ties, which enhances the mutual sense of comfort and famil-iarity when the couple arrives for treatment in person. Second, it allows the therapist to be sure the referral is appro-priate. For example, the couple may desire services other than straightforward marital therapy, such as divorce mediation, parent training, or sex therapy. In such cases, the therapist would be able to determine before the first meeting whether he or she would be able to work with the couple, using CBMT or another appropriate treatment modality, or would need to suggest an alternative referral. Third, the phone contact allows the therapist to begin planting the seeds of a therapeutic rela-tionship by responding in an understanding, validating man-ner to the problems the client briefly conveys. Fourth, it pro-vides an opportunity for the therapist to begin orienting the couple to treatment by explaining in brief the structure of the therapy.

THE INITIAL MEETING

Setting the Agenda

Each week, CBMT begins by setting an agenda for the session. An agenda simply involves a basic plan for what will be covered in the therapy session for a given day. Although in this brief therapy format the agenda regarding the structure of the sessions is guided primarily by the therapist, the client will provide input concerning the specific content, making agenda setting a collaborative process. The session agenda will generally consist of (1) tracking of positive events from the previous week, (2) review of homework, (3) a brief review of the week, (4) didactic presentation and practice of new skills, and (5) a session review and assignment of homework. Clients may offer input regarding events from the previous week in need of discussion, selection of problems on which to sample new skills, or other items in need of critical attention.[1]

When the clients first arrive, setting the agenda for the first session should follow introductions and any small talk concerning finding the office, difficulty parking, and so on. In the following excerpt from a first session, the clients were asked to schedule two and a half hours for the initial session to allow time for the therapist to conduct a series of questionnaire, interview, and behavioral assessments. Alternatively, this ses-

---

1. While this brief and structured treatment format precludes routine, lengthy discussion of "crises of the week," the therapist may elect to break from the format when circumstances warrant it.

sion could be split into two sessions, with the written assessments, individual interviews, a behavioral observation task, and a brief conjoint interview conducted the week prior to beginning treatment. In either case, setting the agenda in a first meeting might consist of a discussion such as the following:

Therapist: Well, I'm glad you two were able to make it in today; it's nice to finally meet you. What I'd like to do is just take a moment and go over with you how I thought we'd use the session time today. Then, if you have any questions or any different ideas, you can let me know.

Dave and Rosalie: (in unison) Okay.

Therapist: All right. First, as I mentioned over the phone to you, Rosalie, I had you two come in early tonight to leave time for you to fill out some forms and go through an assessment procedure before we jump in and start the process of therapy itself.

Dave and Rosalie: (both nod)

Therapist: So, first, I'll set one of you up here in the waiting room with some forms and a clipboard. In the meantime, I'll meet with the other one of you in my office. Then, after about thirty minutes or so, we'll switch, so that I'll meet with the other person while the one I just interviewed will fill out forms. That way, I'll get the chance to meet with both of you individually and get each of your perspectives on the problems that brought you here; it seems that most people find it less inhibiting to meet alone with the therapist as a way of starting to talk about problems in the relationship. When that's

finished, I'll collect all of the forms and have both of you
in together. At that time, I'll tell you a bit more about
how I work and about the cognitive-behavioral approach
to relationship problems. I'll then ask you to discuss
some specific problems that you're having and help you
to translate those problems into some concrete things we
can work on here. I'd also like to hear about the history
of your relationship. Then, before you go, we'll come
up with something for you to work on during the week.
How does that sound?

Here, the therapist informs the clients of exactly what they
can expect, and elicits their input about the agenda. This brief
explanation of the session structure reduces anxiety and sets
the tone for collaboration.

ASSESSMENT

Assessment at treatment outset has two purposes. The first
is to provide information to the therapist that can be used to
inform treatment goals and content.   Serendipitously,the assessment process often provides valuable information for the couple
as they gain insight or consider issues in novel ways. The second purpose is to provide a baseline measure of functioning
against which to compare outcome, or response to treatment.

Paper and Pencil Measures

The following sample intake form (Table 2–1) provides the
type of information we find useful to ask clients.

Table 2-1
Couples' Therapy Intake Form

Date: _____

Name: _____   Spouse's Name: _____

Address: _____

Phone: (Home) _____   (Work) _____

If employed outside the home:

Employer _____

Title/Position _____

Length of employment: _____

Family:

Describe your current relationship status (check one):

_____ Married   _____ Dating, not living together   _____ Other (explain):

_____ Living together   _____ Separated or divorced   _____

Length of relationship: _____

Children:	Name	Age	Living with you?	
	_____	___	___ Yes	___ No
	_____	___	___ Yes	___ No
	_____	___	___ Yes	___ No
	_____	___	___ Yes	___ No
	_____	___	___ Yes	___ No

Mental Health and Medical History:

List previous or current mental health services received:

Year(s)	Service (e.g., outpatient psychotherapy):	Type of practitioner: (e.g., psychologist, psychiatrist social worker)	Condition: (e.g., depression)
___	_____	_____	_____
___	_____	_____	_____
___	_____	_____	_____

Have you ever received inpatient hospitalization for a mental/psychiatric condition? If yes, please state year, condition, and length of stay: ___ Yes   ___ No

_____

_____

Do you have any medical problems or chronic medical conditions?   ___ Yes   ___ No
If yes, please describe: _____

_____

Intake Form Page 1

Mental Health and Medical History, continued:

Are you on any prescription medications?   ____ Yes ___No
If yes, please list any medication, and condition for which it
was prescribed:

_____

_____

Have you ever been hospitalized for a medical condition?   ____ Yes ___No
If yes, please state year(s) and reason for hospitalization:

_____

_____

Have you ever had a problem with drug or alcohol abuse
or dependence?   ____ Yes ___No
If yes please describe, including year(s) of problem, substance used:

_____

_____

Present Visit:
Why are you seeking therapy at this time? _____

_____

Please list your three major marital problems, indicate the length of time each has been a
problem, and rate how distressing they are to you using the scale below:[2]

                                                          Length of Problem
1._____   ____ yrs ___ mos

    0   1   2   3   4   5   6   7   8   9
Not at all   Extremely
distressing   distressing

2._____   ____ yrs ___ mos

    0   1   2   3   4   5   6   7   8   9
Not at all   Extremely
distressing   distressing

3._____   ____ yrs ___ mos

    0   1   2   3   4   5   6   7   8   9
Not at all   Extremely
distressing   distressing

_____   Intake Form Page 2

2. This item and the following two items (three major marital problems, desired partner change, and desired self change) are adapted
   from intake questions presented in O'Leary and Arias (1987) and
   used with permission.

Please list 3 things you would like **your partner** to change to improve the relationship:

1. _____

2. _____

3. _____

Please list 3 things you feel that **you** might change to improve the relationship:

1. _____

2. _____

3. _____

Please list 3 **positive qualities** of your partner or your relationship:

1. _____

2. _____

3. _____

Any other information you feel it is important for the therapist to know: _____

_____

_____

_____

_____

Intake Form Page 3

In addition, we recommend use of several standardized paper-and-pencil measures that assess both global perceptions of relationship satisfaction and specific areas of relationship functioning. Such self-report measures are especially useful with a time-limited treatment format, since they provide a wealth of information in an efficient format. Each partner should fill out all measures independently and not share answers, to increase freedom to answer honestly. Couples should

Table 2-2

Self-Report Measures for Assessment of Marital Functioning

Topic	Measure	Description	Reference
Global Satisfaction	Marital Adjustment Test (MAT)	Brief, widely used measure. Fifteen items cover frequency of disagreement over a range of content areas (e.g., finances, in-laws), shared leisure-time activities, regrets over marrying, and a global happiness rating.	Locke & Wallace (1959)
Global Satisfaction	Dyadic Adjustment Scale (DAS)	Thirty-two items assess dyadic cohesion, dyadic consensus, dyadic satisfaction, and affection. Well-researched, this scale reflects more contemporary attitudes than does MAT.	Spanier (1976)
Behavior	Daily Checklist of Marital Activities (DCMA)	Adapted from the Spouse Observation Checklist (Weiss et al. 1973), this scale contains 109 items (half positive, half negative). Spouses rate presence and impact of each behavior on a daily basis.	Broderick and O'Leary (1986)
Behavior	Individualized Checklist of Marital Activities (ICMA)	Each partner selects 10 positive and 10 negative items from the DCMA (described above) considered most related to personal marital satisfaction. The presence and impact of each behavior are then rated over a specified period of time.	Johnson and O'Leary (1996)

Table 2-2, continued:

Topic	Measure	Description	Reference
Communication	Primary Communication Inventory	Twenty-five items assess couple verbal and and nonverbal communication in a variety of contexts.	Navran (1967)
Communication	Problems in the Style of Communication	This brief checklist assesses problematic communication styles and negative beliefs about communication with a partner.	Beck (1988)
Cognitions	Relationship Belief Inventory (RBI)	This inventory measures dysfunctional relationship assumptions and standards. Five 8-item scales include: (1) Disagreement Is Destructive, (2) Mind Reading Is Expected, (3) Partners Cannot Change, (4) The Sexes Are Different, and (5) Sexual Perfectionism.	Eidelson and Epstein (1982)
Cognitions	Relationship Standards Sentence Completion Form	This 21-item measure provides qualitative information about standards and expectations in marriage.	Epstein (1983)
Affect	Positive Feelings Questionnaire	Seventeen items assess the level of positive affect toward the partner.	O'Leary et al. (1983)
Physical Aggression	Conflict Tactics Scale (CTS)	This is an 18-item self-report measure that assesses couples' use of verbal and physical aggression to resolve disputes.	Straus (1979)

be told that the information on these questionnaires will remain confidential; the therapist will review the measures but no specific responses will be shared with the partner. Table 2–2 presents an overview of common self-report measures used for couple assessment.[3]

In the next section we present several questionnaires, to assess global satisfaction (Marital Adjustment Test, Locke and Wallace [1959], Table 2–3); cognitions (Relationship Belief Inventory, Eidelson and Epstein [1982], Table 2–4) Relationship Standards Sentence Completion Form, Epstein [1983], Table 2–5), and affect (Positive Feelings Questionnaire, O'Leary et al. [1983], Table 2–6). These may be included as part of a basic assessment battery. The Relationship Standards Sentence Completion Form may be used either at treatment outset or later in treatment when addressing marital cognitions (i.e., Session 7 or 8).

After the couple completes these measures (before the conjoint interview), the therapist should invite the couple to take a break for several minutes, during which time he or she can briefly look over their measures. Although time will not allow scoring the measures yet, the therapist can at least scan the instruments and intake form to get a feel for the couple's responses. The therapist may wish to become familiar with the items on the instruments ahead of time and choose particular items of interest to look at briefly before meeting with the

---

3. For in-depth discussion of couple assessment and additional assessment instruments, we refer the reader to O'Leary (1987).

Table 2-3

MARITAL ADJUSTMENT TEST (Locke and Wallace [1959])

1. Check the dot on the scale below which best describes the degree of happiness, everything considered, of your present marriage. The middle point, "Happy," represents the degree of happiness which most people get from marriage, and the scale gradually ranges on one side to those few who are very unhappy in marriage, and on the other, to those few who experience extreme joy or felicity in marriage.

O   O   O   O   O   O   O

Very Unhappy	Happy	Perfectly Happy

State the approximate extent of agreement or disagreement between you and your mate on the following items. Please check each column.

	Always Agree	Almost Always Agree	Occasionally Disagree	Frequently Disagree	Almost Always Disagree	Always Disagree
2. Handling family finances	____	____	____	____	____	____
3. Matters of recreation	____	____	____	____	____	____
4. Demonstrations of affection	____	____	____	____	____	____
5. Friends	____	____	____	____	____	____
6. Sex relations	____	____	____	____	____	____
7. Conventionality (right, good, or proper conduct)	____	____	____	____	____	____
8. Philosophy of life	____	____	____	____	____	____
9. Ways of dealing with in-laws	____	____	____	____	____	____

Table 2-3, continued:

10. When disagreements arise, they usually result in:

    Husband giving   Wife giving   Agreement by mutual
    in_____   in_____   give and take_____

11. Do you and your mate engage in outside interests together:

    All of them_____   Some of them_____
    Very few of them_____   None of them_____

12. In leisure time do you generally prefer:

    To be "on the go"_____   To stay at home_____

    Does your mate prefer:
    To be "on the go"_____   To stay at home_____

13. Do you ever wish you were not married?

    Frequently_____   Occasionally_____   Rarely_____   Never_____

14. If you had your life to live over, do you think you would:

    Marry the same   Marry a different   Not marry
    person_____   person_____   at all_____

15. Do you confide in your mate:

    Almost never_____   Rarely_____
    In most things_____   In everything_____

Note: From Locke, H. J., and Wallace, K. M. (1959). Short marital adjustment and prediction tests: their reliability and validity. *Marriage and Family Living* 21: 252. Copyright 1959 by the National Council on Family Relations, 3989 Central Avenue N.E., Suite 550, Minneapolis, MN 55421. Reprinted with permission.

Table 2–3, continued:

SCORING KEY
MAT

SCORING DIRECTIONS: Add the appropriate numbers (which correspond to the items circled); the total of all items is the scale score. Scores range from 2 to 158; scores of 100 and below indicate a distressed marriage.

0	2	7	15	20	25	35
O	O	O	O	O	O	O

Very Unhappy	Happy	Perfectly Happy

State the approximate extent of agreement or disagreement between you and your mate on the following items. Please check each column.

	Always Agree	Almost Always Agree	Occa- sionally Disagree	Fre- quently Disagree	Almost Always Disagree	Always Disagree
2. Handling family finances	5	4	3	2	1	0
3. Matters of recreation	5	4	3	2	1	0
4. Demonstrations of affection	8	8	4	2	1	0
5. Friends	5	4	3	2	1	0
6. Sex relations	15	12	9	4	1	0
7. Conventionality (right, good, or proper conduct)	5	4	3	2	1	0
8. Philosophy of life	5	4	3	2	1	0
9. Ways of dealing with in-laws	5	4	3	2	1	0

Table 2-3, continued:

---

10. When disagreements arise, they usually result in:

0	Husband giving in
2	Wife giving in
10	Agreement by mutual give and take

11. Do you and your mate engage in outside interests together:

10	All of them
8	Some of them
3	Very few of them
0	None of them

12. In leisure time do you generally prefer:

_____	To be "on the go"
_____	To stay at home

Does your mate prefer:

_____	To be "on the go"
_____	To stay at home

Both "stay at home" = 10
Both "on the go" = 3
Disagreement = 2

13. Do you ever wish you were not married?

0	Frequently
3	Occasionally
8	Rarely
15	Never

14. If you had your life to live over, do you think you would:

15	Marry the same person
0	Marry a different person
1	Not marry at all

15. Do you confide in your mate:

0	Almost never
2	Rarely
10	In most things
10	In everything

Table 2-4
RELATIONSHIP BELIEFS INVENTORY
(Eidelson and Epstein 1982)

The statements below describe ways in which a person might feel about a relationship with another person. Please mark the space next to each statement according to how strongly you believe that it is true or false for you. *Please mark every one.* Write 5, 4, 3, 2, 1, or 0 to stand for the following answers.

5. I *strongly* believe that the statement is *true*.
4. I believe that the statement is *true*.
3. I believe that the statement is *probably true,* or more true than false.
2. I believe that the statement is *probably false,* or more false than true.
1. I believe that the statement is *false*.
0. I *strongly* believe that the statement is *false*.

_____ 1. If your partner expresses disagreement with your ideas, s/he probably does not think highly of you.

_____ 2. I do not expect my partner to sense all my moods.

_____ 3. Damages done early in a relationship probably cannot be reversed.

_____ 4. I get upset if I think I have not completely satisfied my partner sexually.

_____ 5. Men and women have the same emotional needs.

_____ 6. I cannot accept it when my partner disagrees with me.

_____ 7. If I have to tell my partner that something is important to me, it does not mean that s/he is insensitive to me.

_____ 8. My partner does not seem capable of behaving other than s/he does now.

_____ 9. If I'm not in the mood for sex when my partner is, I don't get upset about it.

_____ 10. Misunderstandings between partners generally are due to inborn differences in psychological makeups of men and women.

_____ 11. I take it as a personal insult when my partner disagrees with an important idea of mine.

_____ 12. I get very upset if my partner does not recognize how I am feeling and I have to tell him/her.

Table 2-4, continued:

5. I *strongly* believe that the statement is *true*.
4. I believe that the statement is *true*.
3. I believe that the statement is *probably true*, or more true than false.
2. I believe that the statement is *probably false*, or more false than true.
1. I believe that the statement is *false*.
0. I *strongly* believe that the statement is *false*.

_____ 13. A partner can learn to become more responsive to his/her partner's needs.

_____ 14. A good sexual partner can get himself/herself aroused for sex whenever necessary.

_____ 15. Men and women probably will never understand the opposite sex very well.

_____ 16. I like it when my partner presents views different from mine.

_____ 17. People who have a close relationship can sense each other's needs as if they could read each other's minds.

_____ 18. Just because my partner has acted in ways that upset me does not mean that s/he will do so in the future.

_____ 19. If I cannot perform well sexually whenever my partner is in the mood, I would consider that I have a problem.

_____ 20. Men and women need the same basic things out of a relationship.

_____ 21. I get very upset when my partner and I cannot see things the same way.

_____ 22. It is important to me for my partner to anticipate my needs by sensing changes in my moods.

_____ 23. A partner who hurts you badly once probably will hurt you again.

_____ 24. I can feel OK about my lovemaking even if my partner does not achieve orgasm.

_____ 25. Biological differences between men and women are not major causes of couples' problems.

_____ 26. I cannot tolerate it when my partner argues with me.

_____ 27. A partner should know what you are thinking or feeling without you having to tell.

_____ 28. If my partner wants to change, I believe that s/he can do it.

Table 2-4, continued:

5. I *strongly* believe that the statement is *true*.
4. I believe that the statement is *true*.
3. I believe that the statement is *probably true*, or more true than false.
2. I believe that the statement is *probably false*, or more false than true.
1. I believe that the statement is *false*.
0. I *strongly* believe that the statement is *false*.

_____ 29. If my sexual partner does not get satisfied completely, it does not mean that I have failed.

_____ 30. One of the major causes of marital problems is that men and women have different emotional needs.

_____ 31. When my partner and I disagree, I feel like our relationship is falling apart.

_____ 32. People who love each other know exactly what each other's thoughts are without a word ever being said.

_____ 33. If you don't like the way a relationship is going, you can make it better.

_____ 34. Some difficulties in my sexual performance do not mean personal failure to me.

_____ 35. You can't really understand someone of the opposite sex.

_____ 36. I do not doubt my partner's feelings for me when we argue.

_____ 37. If you have to ask your partner for something, it shows that s/he was not "tuned in" to your needs.

_____ 38. I do not expect my partner to be able to change.

_____ 39. When I do not seem to be performing well sexually, I get upset.

_____ 40. Men and women will always be mysteries to each other.

Note: The Relationship Belief Inventory is described in Eidelson, R. J., and Epstein, N. (1982). Cognition and relationship maladjustment: development of a measure of dysfunctional relationship beliefs. *Journal of Clinical and Consulting Psychology* 50:715–720. Scale reprinted with permission of the authors.

Table 2-4, continued:

RBI Scoring

SCORING INSTRUCTIONS: Add scores for appropriate items to determine subscale scores. Add scores for each subscale to obtain total score.

Subscale	Positive Items[a]	Negative Items[b]
Disagreement Is Destructive (D)	1, 6, 11, 21, 36, 31	16, 36
Mindreading Is Expected (M)	12, 17, 22, 27, 32, 37	2, 7
Partners Cannot Change (C)	3, 8, 23, 38	13, 18, 28, 33
Sexual Perfectionism (S)	4, 14, 19, 39	9, 24, 29
The Sexes Are Different (MF)	10, 15, 30, 35, 40	5, 20, 25

---

[a] Positively keyed items are scored same as subject's response. A response of "5" is scored as "5," a response of "4" is scored as "4," etc.

[b] Scoring on negatively keyed items must be reversed. See the following chart.

Subject's Response		Scoring
5	=	0
4	=	1
3	=	2
2	=	3
1	=	4
0	=	5

Table 2-5
RELATIONSHIP STANDARDS SENTENCE COMPLETION FORM
(Epstein 1983)

Directions: The following questions are intended to elicit your expectations and desires regarding a close relationship. Answer each in the space provided, using a phrase or one or two sentences. Try not to dwell too long on any one item.

When I have a close romantic relationship:

(1) The amount of time spent per week sharing our feelings and thoughts would be

(2) The way we handle our individual interests and hobbies would be

(3) The way we decide how to spend vacation time would be

(4) The amount of direct, open communication about our sexual relationship would be

(5) Our involvement with our respective families of origin would be

(6) The roles of work and careers would be

(7) The way we'd fight would be

(8) We'd show our appreciation for each other by

(9) We'd keep the relationship interesting over time by

(10) We'd spend time apart when

Table 2-5, continued:

(11) The amount of information about our relationship that we would share with others would be

(12) We'd end our relationship if

(13) We'd help raise each other's self-esteem by

(14) We'd exhibit tolerance for each other by

(15) We'd demonstrate commitment to each other by

(16) We'd decide on how to spend money by

(17) The degree to which we would protect each other from the world would be

(18) The extent to which we would have a "healthy competition" between us would be

(19) If there were something that one of us would like the other to change about himself or herself, we would

(20) We would handle any differences in our personal values by

(21) We would handle daily chores by

Note: Reprinted with permission of the author. Since this is a qualitative and not a quantitative measure, there is no scoring system.

Table 2-6
POSITIVE FEELINGS QUESTIONNAIRE (O'Leary et al. 1983)

Below is a list of questions about various feelings between married people. Answer each one of them in terms of how you *generally* feel about your spouse taking into account the last few months. The rating you choose should reflect how you *actually* feel, not how you think you should feel or would like to feel.

Please answer each question by choosing the best number to show how you have generally been feeling in the past few months. Choose *only one number* for each question.

1	2	3	4	5	6	7
Extremely Negative	Quite Negative	Slightly Negative	Neutral	Slightly Positive	Quite Positive	Extremely Positive

1. How do you feel about your spouse as a friend to you?   1 2 3 4 5 6 7
2. How do you feel about the future of your marital relationship?   1 2 3 4 5 6 7
3. How do you feel about having married your spouse?   1 2 3 4 5 6 7
4. How do you feel about your spouse's ability to put you   1 2 3 4 5 6 7
   in a good mood so that you can laugh and smile?
5. How do you feel about your spouse's ability to handle stress?   1 2 3 4 5 6 7
6. How do you feel about the degree to which your spouse   1 2 3 4 5 6 7
   understands you?
7. How do you feel about your spouse's honesty?   1 2 3 4 5 6 7
8. How do you feel about the degree to which you can trust   1 2 3 4 5 6 7
   your spouse?

The following 9 items are in the form of statements rather than questions. However, please complete them in the same manner, remembering to base your responses on how you *generally* feel about your spouse, taking into account the last few months.

1. Touching my spouse makes me feel   1 2 3 4 5 6 7
2. Being alone with my spouse makes me feel   1 2 3 4 5 6 7
3. Having sexual relations with my spouse makes me feel   1 2 3 4 5 6 7
4. Talking and communicating with my spouse makes me feel   1 2 3 4 5 6 7
5. My spouse's encouragement of my individual growth makes   1 2 3 4 5 6 7
   me feel
6. My spouse's physical appearance makes me feel   1 2 3 4 5 6 7
7. Seeking comfort from my spouse makes me feel   1 2 3 4 5 6 7
8. Kissing my spouse makes me feel   1 2 3 4 5 6 7
9. Sitting or lying close to my spouse makes me feel   1 2 3 4 5 6 7

Note: The Positive Feelings Questionnaire is described in: O'Leary, K. D., Fincham, F. D., and Turkewitz, H. (1983). Assessment of positive feelings toward spouse. *Journal of Clinical and Consulting Psychology* 51:949–951. It appears in O'Leary, K. D. (1987). *Assessment of Marital Discord*. Hillsdale, NJ: Lawrence Erlbaum. Scale reprinted with author permission.

	Mean	Standard Deviation
Table 2-6, continued:		
Means and standard deviations to assist clinicians and researches in interpreting scores on the PFQ:		

	Mean	Standard Deviation
Community Sample		
Men (n = 46)	100.52	12.44
Women (n = 46)	104.26	9.73
Clinic Sample		
Men (n = 58)	83.98	18.16
Women (n = 56)	73.86	22.40

couple together (e.g., physical violence on CTS). In this way, the therapist may not only conduct the interview from a more informed position, but also become aware at a very early point of any factors for concern or for special consideration in setting goals or structuring treatment. Should the therapist detect an important inconsistency between a partner's responses in the individual interview and the assessment forms, the therapist can ask to speak again briefly with him or her for a clarification of the information.

Interviewing

There are two basic approaches to conducting initial interviews with couples. One involves meeting with the partners only as a couple. The other, as alluded to in the clinical example above, involves meeting with each partner individually before (or just after) meeting with them as a couple. Each approach has benefits and shortcomings. Interviewing the couple together makes sense, since relational problems form the basis for seeking therapy. Meeting together provides the opportunity for the couple to begin building the therapeutic relationship on an equal footing, without wondering what complaints the partner has registered in private. It also sets a tone of mutual responsibility and collaboration, as partners together tell their story and set goals. A conjoint assessment interview also prevents the therapist from becoming the holder of secrets.

However, conducting only a conjoint interview risks limiting partners' opportunity for disclosure. With a spouse present, partners may not be able to reveal information critical to understanding relationship problems or to making an informed choice regarding the intervention approach. Examples of such revelations include a desire to end the relationship, an ongoing affair, or the occurrence of marital violence. The positive side of learning, for example, the presence of an affair is the ability to speak with the partner about the fruitlessness of proceeding in marital treatment while conducting a simultaneous extramarital relationship. Knowledge of a particular secret might prompt the therapist to either recommend a different or adjunctive treatment or, depending on the nature of the secret, to urge the partner to disclose it with the support of the therapist. Without such knowledge, treatment may be doomed from the outset, with the therapist never fully understanding the factors impeding progress. Moreover, asking partners about sensitive issues, such as the presence of marital violence, may be harder to broach in a conjoint context. Even when a therapist raises such topics, spouses may constrict their responses in the presence of a menacing partner. The therapist might then proceed as usual, secure in the knowledge that critical issues were addressed, but missing the fact that the responses were provided under coercion.

Therefore, we prefer to conduct separate interviews before meeting with the partners as a pair. We prefer the risk of being privy to sensitive information to the risk of missing information that could sabotage treatment or prove dangerous to clients. Even if individual interviews reveal nothing of concern, the therapist can request individual meetings at a later point in therapy should new issues emerge or should the therapist suspect that important information is being withheld.

The Individual Interview

The individual interview with each partner should last approximately thirty minutes, barring any content necessitating a longer meeting. Because we allocate two and a half hours for the first session, this structure leaves ample time for conducting a conjoint interview assessment and beginning therapeutic interventions. In this first session, the therapist should bring up the issue of confidentiality. As in any therapy, the therapist should inform the clients about limits of confidentiality (i.e., if the client poses a danger to him- or herself or others, or if ongoing physical or sexual abuse of a child is revealed). However, the therapist should tell clients that any other information shared during this individual meeting will remain confidential. This means that the therapist must be willing to maintain confidentiality, even if he or she believes a particular issue is destructive to the relationship (e.g., an affair). Having said this, since it is preferable to avoid holding secrets between partners, the therapist may check with the client whether certain information is private or can be discussed openly. For example, a client may report that sex with a spouse has become too infrequent, and feel perfectly comfortable allowing the therapist to acknowledge this complaint with the partner. Many of the issues mentioned will be familiar to each partner, since both members of the couple know all too well what they have been arguing about. The therapist will want to encourage an environment of openness while protecting information a client does not feel comfortable discussing in front of a partner. The therapist can also inform clients that information may emerge that precludes CBMT, and that he or she may make recommendations for individual therapy or other treatment alternatives based on assessment findings.

Once the issue of confidentiality is covered, the therapist can ask each partner why he or she is seeking therapy now, what problems are occurring in the relationship, and when the problems began. The therapist can also take this opportunity to ask the client if there is anything else that would be important to know at this time to understand the relationship or that spouse's position with regard to the relationship. This can be a time to learn about extramarital relationships or other issues that weigh heavily on the marriage but are difficult to raise in the presence of the partner.

Assessing Specific Behaviors

Ordinarily, clients will initially describe the problems in the relationship in vague terms such as "he doesn't care about this marriage" or "we never communicate." Clients also tend to editorialize as they discuss the relationship issues, letting the therapist know that their wife is "just like her mother" or that their husband is "a terrible influence on the kids." Many clients see relationship problems as stemming from their partner's deficiencies, and are hoping the therapist will repair the partner. Like someone who brings a lemon of a car to a mechanic's shop, marital clients often expect to explain what isn't running properly, have an expert go in and take a look, and fix whatever's wrong. Meeting with partners individually can further this partner-blaming tendency, since the spouse is not present to counter with another perspective. Generalizations such as "he doesn't care about this marriage" may reflect important, emotion-laden relationship themes (e.g., partners' closeness versus distance-seeking styles), which may be manifested through fifty different behavioral exemplars (e.g., works long hours, engages in independent leisure activities, withholds physical affection). However, such generalized descriptions of relationship dissatisfaction portray intractably ingrained problems, dissuade discussion of collaborative behavior change, and obfuscate discovery of important themes (i.e., a vague statement may mean five different things to five different couples or therapists).

Therefore, the therapist will need to encourage clients to *describe problems in nonjudgmental, behaviorally specific terms.*

This involves reporting "just the facts," without editorializing, deriding the partner's character, or speaking in generalizations. Rather, the therapist should prompt the client to describe the exact nature of the troublesome behaviors (i.e., *what happens*, and then what happens next, and so on) and the impact of these behaviors on the client. For example, if a husband says, "She's inconsiderate and irresponsible," the therapist would prompt him to discuss the exact things his wife does that lead him to that conclusion. A more specific translation of "inconsiderate and irresponsible" might include coming home late from work without calling, not returning phone calls, or leaving important bills unpaid. Table 2–7 offers a selection of prompt questions that the therapist can use to gather more specific information.

Table 2-7
Therapist Prompts for Gathering Behaviorally Specific Information

▸ Can you give me a specific example of *behavior x*?

▸ In what situations does this usually happen?

▸ Tell me what tends to lead up to *behavior x*

▸ What happens when your partner does *behavior x*?

▸ Could you tell me what you mean by *characteristic x*?

▸ How would I know your partner was being *characteristic x*?

▸ How would you define *characteristic x* when it comes to your partner?

▸ If I were observing your interaction, what exactly would I see that would tell me your partner was being *characteristic x*?

In the following vignette, the therapist determines the behavioral specifics of a wife's complaint about her husband, remaining focused on one problem at a time.

Sarah: Part of the problem is that Bruce is just a cold person.

Therapist: Could you tell me what you mean by "cold"?

Sarah: You know, I mean just really cold and distant sometimes. It's like he doesn't have a warm bone in his body. I almost never feel close to him anymore.

Therapist: Could you tell me exactly what Bruce does that you consider cold or distant?

Sarah: Well, he'll never kiss me goodbye in the morning or when I get home from work. I'll walk in and he'll mumble "hi" without even looking up from his paper. If I try to put my arms around him, he'll stiffen up, or he'll push me away and say he's hot or something. I haven't even tried recently. We just pass each other in the apartment and we never touch.

Therapist: Oh, so a lot of what you're talking about involves affection; he doesn't kiss you or embrace you, and he doesn't greet you warmly. It sounds like he doesn't satisfy your need for that type of closeness.

Sarah: Yes, that's it. But there's more than that, too. He's distant in other ways. Like he never really talks to me about his day; I feel like I'm pulling teeth to find out how his job is going.

Therapist: All right, we'll get to that next, but let's just stay with the issue of affection for a moment. If Bruce were to express affection toward you in a way that you would consider warm and close, rather than cold and distant, what would that look like?

Sarah: You know, just a lot more touching and stuff, I guess.

Therapist: Try to tell me exactly what you would want to be different, so that if I were in your house observing I could tell right away if he were acting warmly toward you.

Sarah: Well, the first thing would be that he would give me a kiss on the mouth when we said goodbye in the morning. Then, when I walked in at the end of the day, I guess I'd like it if he got up from the couch, walked over to me, and gave me another kiss. Then *(smiles)*, I guess my favorite thing of all would be if we could curl up together as we fell asleep. As it is, we're usually on opposite edges of the bed.

Note that the therapist accomplishes many tasks. First, she comes to understand what Sarah means by the vague labels "cold" and "distant," by breaking these labels down into discrete behaviors. Second, rather than moving on to another complaint (i.e., Bruce's not talking about work), the therapist remains focused on one topic at a time (i.e., affection). This helps to obtain a more thorough understanding of one particular issue while keeping a large number of marital problems from overwhelming either the client or the session focus. Third, in specifying these behaviors, she develops ready targets by which to monitor change. While "coldness" might be too nebulous to track over treatment, behaviors such as kisses and embraces provide objective means to follow progress. Fourth, she begins to alter Sarah's definitions of (and thereby perceptions of) the problems from Bruce's character flaws to a shortage in the number of times he engages in particular behaviors, which would appear less intractable. Fifth, by asking what Sarah would want to be different, she begins to shift her pessimistic stance of focusing on negatives to the more hopeful stance of envisioning the relationship in a more positive light. This strategy also prepares Sarah to begin conceptualizing behaviorally specific treatment goals, which the therapist will address later in this session and throughout treatment.

Conducting Functional Analyses

Part of understanding the nature of a couple's interactions involves conducting a functional analysis. The goal of a functional analysis is to uncover the antecedents and consequences of problematic marital behaviors in order to understand their environmental context. As explained in Chapter 1, partners are constantly influencing each other through interaction sequences, and understanding the exact progression of events in these sequences can lead to knowledge of factors that precipitate, reinforce, or punish important marital events. In the following example from a therapy case, the therapist finds out more about a husband's disappointment at his wife's failure to call and touch base from work during the day as she used to as an example of the increasing distance in their marriage.

Therapist: You said she used to call during the day. How did those conversations go?

Luis: Some were okay, but a lot of times we'd end up in an argument.

Therapist: How would they lead to an argument?

Luis: Well, I would want to really talk to her, tell her about things going on at work, or get her input on something. And she'd sometimes be distracted, and want to keep it brief, you know, just "what's the plan for dinner," and that kind of thing. So I'd get mad.

Therapist: And what would happen when you'd get mad?

Luis: I'd say to her, "What's the matter with you; you're not even paying attention!" A couple of times she even hung up on me 'cause she said she didn't want to be heard having a fight on the phone during work.

With this line of questioning, the therapist quickly uncovers the punishing consequence for the wife of speaking with her husband during the day (i.e., getting pulled away from her work and encountering an argument).

In this next example from another couple, a wife bemoans her husband's inability to soothe her when she is upset or to support her feelings.

Graciella: I can't talk to him. He gets so moody, and he puts me down for having feelings. Like this week . . . I was upset and tried to talk with him, and he ended up criticizing me and leaving the room in a huff.

Therapist: Could you tell me how the conversation went? What feelings were you talking with him about?

Graciella: I was saying I was upset because I was feeling

uncertain about our relationship, and then he cut me off
and began yelling at me, "Why are you always doing
that? Things are going fine and then you have to say
those things!" Then he says, "I'm not going to talk about
this" and got up and went into the other room and shut
the door. It's like I'm not allowed to say what I feel!

As Graciella's husband was especially sensitive to criticism and
rejection, what for her was an honest expression of feelings
was experienced by him as a threatening attack. Thus, much
of his bothersome moody behavior was precipitated by her
own comments, which were hurtful to him. Here, the therapist identified what turned out to be a common antecedent
to the husband's nonsupportive behavior and moodiness—the
wife's expression of negative feelings about the relationship.
Note that a functional analysis may also be conducted with
both partners present and involved in a description of the relevant events.

In both of the previous examples, understanding the pre-
cipitants and consequences of a behavior through functional
analysis led to a discovery of interactional factors that were
influencing the behaviors of interest. The therapist later helped
the couple use the knowledge of these patterns when coaching them through communication, problem solving, and other
skills to address the problematic interactions.

Although there will not be time in the first interview to
obtain a full understanding of every marital problem, this type
of questioning, along with prompting clients to use behaviorally specific terms, will prove helpful throughout therapy.

Assessing Marital Violence

Importantly, the therapist can use the individual interview to assess for the presence of physical aggression in the relationship. It is often useful to broach this topic with questions such as, "How is conflict handled in your relationship?" or "How does your partner handle anger?" The therapist can then probe for specific examples by asking for a description of the sequence of events during a recent, prototypical, or worst-case dispute. This helps the therapist avoid labeling particular behaviors as "abusive" or "violent" when the clients themselves might not define them that way. For example, asking a woman the question, "Is your partner ever abusive toward you?" might yield a defensive response such as, "No, of course not!" The topic is now dismissed and it may be difficult to gain specific information about aggressive interactions at this point. However, an alternative dialogue with the same woman might unfold as follows:

> *Therapist:* One of the things that would be helpful for me to understand is how the two of you handle conflict or disagreement. Could you give me an idea of how that usually goes?
>
> *Elizabeth:* Well, it depends. I've learned that the easiest thing is to try to avoid conflict with Alan altogether, so I usually try to fix problems with the kids or the house or that kind of thing myself and not even tell him. Or, when he's in a *mood*, I usually just back off and let him have his way.

Therapist: What do you mean by "in a mood"?

Elizabeth: I mean that you could definitely say he has a problem with anger. He just explodes sometimes, and he can be a little frightening to be around. Sometimes you can see it coming because he gets withdrawn and tense. When he's like that, he has the kids and me walking on eggshells.

Therapist: What happens when he explodes?

Elizabeth: Sometimes he just starts yelling at everyone and making hostile accusations. Once in a while, he'll start slamming doors or pounding his fists on the table. Last week he was pointing at me with a pencil when he was yelling at me and then he took the pencil and snapped it in half right in front of my face.

Therapist: It sounds like that can get pretty frightening for you and the kids.

Elizabeth: Well, maybe a little, sometimes.

Therapist: Can you tell me about the worst it's ever gotten, that is, the most explosive or frightening?

Here, the therapist follows Elizabeth's lead with follow-up questions, which glean increasingly specific information, allowing her to simply describe events without filtering what she reports through labels. Whether the client regards her husband's behavior as abusive or not, it is important for the therapist to make a realistic determination of the presence of dangerous or intimidating behaviors. Once the therapist has raised this topic, if it remains unclear whether physical aggression has occurred, he or she can follow up with specific probes such as, "Do things ever get physical?" or "Has there been any pushing, grabbing, shoving, or that type of thing?"[4] The therapist should also assess whether the woman feels intimidated or threatened about discussing marital issues with her husband present. As stressed in Chapter 1, should a picture of intimidation or violence emerge, the therapist will want to assess for the client's safety and consider treatment other than marital therapy.

Building an Alliance with the Less-Committed Partner

The individual meeting also provides a chance to connect with a partner who may have been pressured into attending therapy by his or her mate. If one partner has been reluctant to seek couples treatment, it will be helpful to ask the less motivated partner how he or she feels about being there, and to validate his or her view, whether it involves not seeing a need for treatment, seeing marital difficulties but not viewing marital therapy as the way to solve them, or seeing the relationship as too deteriorated to benefit from treatment. In the first case, it can be helpful to point out that a marital problem in the eyes of one partner inevitably becomes a problem for the other, and to ask the client about ways in which this has already occurred. In the second case, the therapist can ask

---

4. The Conflict Tactics Scale (Straus 1979) may provide additional information about specific violent behaviors occurring in the relationship.

the client about his or her objections to couples therapy. Objections may include factors such as culturally based misgivings about seeing a therapist, skepticism about the effectiveness of therapy, misunderstandings about the nature of therapy, or a belief that only one's partner needs treatment. Talking about a client's particular concerns allows the therapist to support the client and respond to specific hesitations. Sometimes simply expressing concerns to a validating therapist will in itself be sufficient to increase motivation to participate in therapy. In the third case, when a partner sees a relationship as too distressed to be helped by treatment, it may be helpful to remind the partner that there may be little to lose from attending treatment. If nothing else, CBMT can provide helpful training in communication and problem-solving skills, which should be helpful no matter what course the relationship takes. The therapist can also encourage thinking of ways therapy can be useful to a client, to reframe the view that "I'm just doing this for my partner." It is important to obtain a commitment from this client to actively participate, at a minimum giving treatment a chance for a specified number of sessions and then reassessing. If the client cannot make even a minimal commitment, it will be pointless to proceed with couples therapy. However, being sensitive to this partner's position and addressing the reluctance openly will help the formation of a therapeutic alliance and may lead to greater receptivity to treatment. Although initial reluctance in one partner is common, it is usually possible to overcome the reluctance by validating, reframing, and contracting for a specified number of sessions.

The Conjoint Interview

The conjoint meeting combines additional assessment with initial intervention. This first meeting with the couple consists of an orientation to treatment, a problem discussion, an assessment of the relationship history and strengths of the relationship, goal setting, and assignment of homework for the following week. In cases in which the assessment has revealed the need for an alternative treatment approach, this meeting can be used to discuss other treatment options and make recommendations.[5]

Orientation to Treatment

Assuming the couple and therapist agree to proceed with CBMT, the therapist should use this first conjoint meeting to orient the couple to the therapeutic approach. This orientation will consist of briefly explaining the various components of treatment (i.e., focus on behaviors and cognitions, as outlined in Chapter 1), as well as the structure of treatment (e.g., directive teaching of new skills, role-plays, homework assignments). The therapist can also take this opportunity to confirm telephone agreements about payment of fees or scheduling, and the clients can use this time to ask any questions

---

5. When physical abuse has been uncovered, the therapist may need to meet individually in a more extended fashion with each client to assess the level of danger and fear, and to develop, if necessary, a plan to ensure safety. Appendix II lists additional readings on this topic.

they might have at this point. Finally, the therapist should go over the agenda for the remainder of the session time for that day, briefly outlining the session content that will follow (i.e., continued assessment and arriving at treatment goals), and checking that the couple understands and accepts the session plan.

Problem Discussion

The problem discussion involves assessment through behavioral observation in which the therapist observes the couple as they discuss a problem exactly as they would at home. The purpose of this task is to provide the therapist with a close analogue of the couple's interactions as they naturally occur, rather than relying solely on their reports of such interactions (Weiss and Heyman 1990). By having the couple discuss a true area of contention in the office, the therapist can learn a great deal about the couple's communication and problem-solving style.

In order to begin this exercise, the therapist tells the couple that they will be asked to discuss an area of conflict with each other for five to ten minutes as the therapist observes, so that the therapist can observe firsthand their style of communicating and handling disagreements. The therapist then asks the couple to select an area about which they frequently argue or disagree. It is important that the therapist clarify that the couple must select an area of disagreement, that is, an area in which the partners differ, rather than simply a problem on which the partners agree (e.g., a husband and wife may both feel that financial worries create stress in their marriage, but they may agree on a strategy for remedying their financial strain). It is helpful to ask couples to select a conflict of moderate severity, rather than their most extreme or heated issue, to reduce chances of an uncontrolled, explosive battle occurring during the task.

Once the couple has selected a topic, the problem discussion task can begin. The simplest way is for the couple to discuss the problem in front of the therapist, with the therapist as a passive observer. The discussion should be stopped after ten minutes, but, depending on the remaining session time and on the intensity of the conflict, therapists may wish to preempt arguments after a shorter period of time. However, unless the conflict is escalating severely, we recommend allowing the couple to continue for the full amount of time set; while the therapist may feel uncomfortable witnessing an argument without intervening, it is helpful to remember that one is simply seeing what likely occurs at home, and that observations from this interaction will help later in stressing those aspects of communication that most apply to this couple. Another option is to seat the couple alone in the office (or separate room) and audiotape or videotape their problem discussion (the therapist should remain in earshot in case the discussion escalates enough to warrant interruption). This is typically done in research settings where the tape is then coded for various aspects of communication. Leaving the couple to interact alone reduces the reactivity that might occur in the therapist's presence. The therapist can later listen to or view the taped discussion.

Regardless of the chosen alternative, the partners are instructed to sit facing each other and begin a discussion of their chosen conflict exactly as they would discuss it at home. They should speak only to each other, as if they were alone, and should be told that they will be stopped by the therapist when the agreed-upon time is up. After the discussion is over, the therapist can ask the couple about their feelings and thoughts during the interaction to gain additional information about the couple's characteristic affect and cognitions during conflict. To get a sense of the representativeness of the discussion, he or she can also ask to what extent this was a prototypical problem-solving interaction. Primarily, this exercise can expose the therapist to strengths and weaknesses in the couple's communication, as well as to roles played by each partner in handling conflict (e.g., initiating topics, interrupting, making suggestions). Such discussions will vary from being calm and pleasant or neutral in affective tone to heated and filled with anger, frustration, or pain. Depending on the tone and intensity of the interaction, couples may need a "debriefing." This may consist of the therapist helping clients to calm down (see Chapter 9 for strategies on handling anger), asking clients about their experience with the task, validating their reactions, pointing out global observations from the exercise, and explaining that observations from the task will be revisited and incorporated into interventions throughout therapy.

Assessing the Relationship History

When assessing the history of the relationship and for the

remainder of this first session, the therapist will balance discussion of relationship problems with *positive* aspects of the relationship. It can be helpful to inform the clients of this attention to positives with a statement such as the following:

> *Therapist:* I've now heard from each of you individually a bit about what you see as problems in the relationship, and I've also had a chance to observe you differing on a real problem that concerns you. In the rest of the time today I'm going to be asking you to let me in on some of the *positive* things in your relationship, in addition to the negatives.

Asking clients about the history of their relationship has three major purposes. The first involves learning the general context of the relationship and its deterioration. The second involves assessing the potential of the relationship by learning of its strongest historical points. The third involves beginning to shift the couple's focus from the most negative aspects of their interaction to the more positive aspects that led to and maintained their union.

Because the overall treatment follows a brief format, and because this first session is packed with several tasks to accomplish, the relationship history gathering must remain brief, highlighting a few essential points. The basic information needed includes the length of time the couple has been together, including the landmark dates in their relationship (e.g., year of moving in together, marriage), the number and ages of children, any previous marriages or significant long-term relationships, as well as a description of when and how they met, what first attracted each partner to the other, what the best time(s) were in their relationship, and when and why things started to go downhill. Table 2–8 provides sample questions for assessing relationship history.

Table 2–8
Prompt Questions for Relationship History

▸ How long have you been together? (When did you marry, move in together?)

▸ When and how did you meet?

▸ (To each partner in turn) What first attracted you to (partner's name)?

▸ What were the best times in your relationship? When were you the happiest together?

▸ When did things begin to deteriorate? To what do you attribute the deterioration?

▸ What stressors were you experiencing around the time things began turning for the worse (e.g., birth of a baby, move, new job)?

One useful technique when assessing relationship history is to ask each partner to provide a succinct description of his or her parents' relationship. This can be beneficial in that it (1) offers the therapist immediate data on potentially significant variables affecting the relationship or individual (e.g., death of a parent, history of marital betrayal, witnessed abuse), (2) allows for a potential empathic connection from the spouse when hearing the spouse's report, (3) provides information on relationship beliefs derived from the family of origin that may not be effective in the context of the present relationship.

In assessing the positive aspects of the relationship and part-

ner, couples in distress will often move the interview in a negative direction, finding fault with the relationship and their
partner. It is as though couples believe that to be understood
they must convince the therapist that they are, and always
were, miserable. With perceptions colored by anger and nega-
tivity, they may make disparaging remarks such as, "There were
no really good times; we fought constantly right from the
beginning," or "I only dated him because he was good-look-
ing. I should have known better." Because of this tendency,
in addition to simply learning more about a couple, the purpose of asking about good times in their relationship is to shift
their sole negative focus to a more positive one. Recalling the
virtues of the relationship may be a motivating factor in working to recapture the better times. It is useful, therefore, to help
the couple keep the focus positive by gently and frequently
guiding them back on the course of speaking from a positive
perspective. This might involve interrupting a client when
necessary, and reminding him or her that there will be ample
opportunity to address problems, but for now you would like
them to focus on some of the positives in the relationship.

In the following vignette, the therapist encounters initial
resistance in staying focused on the positive:

Therapist: I'd like to get a sense of the history of your relationship. Could you start by telling when you met, and
how long you've been together?

Anthony: We met in our first year of college; we were in
the same dorm. We got married the year after college,
and that was twenty-two years ago.

Therapist: That's a long time. Okay, so how did it go once you met? Did you start dating right away?

Monique: Actually, we were friends for about a year first. I wanted to go out with him, but he didn't pick up on it for a while, and so we were just friends.

Therapist: (to Anthony) Is that true? You didn't pick up on it?

Anthony: Yeah, that's right. I was just a shy kid, you know? I think I was afraid to even think about a relationship when I was a freshman.

Therapist: Sure. *(to both)* How was it when you were just friends?

Monique: Things were okay then, I guess. We weren't living together or anything, so there weren't any problems. We would just hang around together. There would usually be other people around, too.

Therapist: Monique, you mentioned you wanted to go out with Anthony. What first attracted you to him?

Monique: I don't know . . . I think I probably liked the fact that he wasn't pursuing me. It made it a challenge. Little did I know that to this day I'd have to pull teeth just to get him to . . .

Therapist: (interrupts) Hold it; let me stop you for a moment. Let's just try to stick with this topic a bit. What else attracted you to him? There were probably other young men who were not pursuing you, right? What made you pay attention to Anthony?

Monique: Well, I thought he was cute, for one thing. But I didn't know that you can't build a marriage on looks. It was foolish to focus on that; if I'd had any idea about his temper . . .

Anthony: *(to therapist)* See, I'm just sitting here not saying anything and she's putting me down!

Therapist: Monique, let's focus on only your early *positive* feelings about Anthony for now; next I'll be asking him the same questions, and you'll both have plenty of time to let me know about the problems. All right?

Monique: (nods)

Therapist: Good. So you said you thought he was cute— you were attracted to him?

Monique: Yeah.

Therapist: Great! Okay, so what was "cute" about him?

Monique: Well, he had this thick curly black hair, and a nice smile, and a really athletic build. You can see, he still has that build.

Therapist: Boy, that's a nice description! *(to Anthony)* Did you know she thought that about you?

Anthony: Well, in the past, yeah, but I didn't know she thought I still looked that way.

Therapist: So you're learning something new already! *(to Monique)* What else now . . . what did you like about Anthony as a friend that made you more interested in him?

Monique: *(pauses to think)* I think one of the best things was that I could talk to him about anything—really be myself. We used to have these marathon phone conversations *(smiles)* . . . I'd say, since we're talking, why don't

you just come over? And he'd say, no it's too late, I
should get to bed soon, and then we'd stay on the phone
all night, till it got light out. *(to Anthony)* Remember
those conversations?
Anthony: (smiling a little) Of course I do.
Therapist: That was a wonderful example, Monique. I really get this sense of the closeness, like best friends.

Note that rather than making an interpretation of derail-
ing comments, the cognitive-behavioral marital therapist instead repeatedly guides the discussion back toward a positive
focus. The therapist does not assume that the partners wish,
consciously or unconsciously, to sabotage a warm interaction,
but attributes the derogatory remarks to clients' learned
patterns of talking about the relationship, negative cognitive
"filters" on accessing mood-congruent information about the
relationship, and assumptions that therapy is the appropriate
setting to vent such complaints. The task, then, is to shape
clients toward expanding their repertoire to allow favorable
thoughts and comments about their partner. In the above
vignette, note the therapist's reinforcing comments as Monique
ventures more complimentary remarks, and the therapist's
checking in with Anthony, to include him in the discussion
and to gauge the impact of Monique's positive statement. With
the therapist's persistence, Monique is finally able to generate
positive memories of her courtship with Anthony. When successful, this process can leave a couple warmly reminiscing and
even laughing together, providing them with what may be
their first such encounter in a long time.

Assessing Positives in the Relationship

After learning the history of the couple's relationship, the next area of assessment is asking about the current positive features of the relationship. In particular, the therapist can ask the couple what they see as the strengths of their relationship, and ask both spouses what they appreciate in their partner. These questions prime the couple for *the technique of positive tracking*, which will be explained in the beginning of Chapter 3 on Behavior Exchange. As with assessment of relationship problems, clients should use behaviorally specific terms when discussing relationship strengths. For example, if a woman allows that her husband is considerate, the therapist might prompt her to explain what she means by "considerate." The woman might then offer that her husband regularly helps her do laundry and prepare dinner. This specificity gives her husband concrete feedback on which aspects of his behavior are pleasing to his wife.

This technique not only provides the therapist with useful information about the couple's strengths (including the observation of whether the couple can even identify positive aspects of the relationship), but also serves as a stimulus for producing warm feelings between partners early in treatment. It invites partners to share rewarding feedback with their mates, who may have come to believe they are no longer valued by their spouses. Whereas couples may normally interrupt or not listen to each other, a spouse reciting virtues of the relationship and partner often commands rapt attention by the partner.

This area of inquiry taps the antithesis of the couple's focus when entering treatment, and the partners are sometimes surprised by the positive focus of the questions. Like reporting on favorable times in the relationship during history taking, reporting on current positive features often generates an opportunity for devaluing the relationship. If this occurs, it will again be important to steer the couple back on course.

At times the therapist may encounter couples who enter treatment with such an extreme degree of anger and hostility that they absolutely cannot (or will not) come up with any positive relationship history or current relationship strengths. The therapist might first try to encourage such a couple to discriminate between *more* and *less* problematic relationship attributes or historical periods (e.g., a husband might admit that a wife's family hasn't been a source of conflict, even though he is not ready to say anything positive about them). Even admitting that some areas are neutral or not cause for extreme concern may provide some hope and begin to challenge the perception that "everything in this marriage is awful."

If this attempt fails to elicit anything positive and the couple appears demoralized, the therapist might then normalize the partners' experience, explaining that this negative outlook is a common occurrence for distressed couples. To generate hope, the therapist might offer that couples therapy can help to increase the number of positive events in the relationship, as well as help them to become more cognizant of positive relationship features that may already exist.

Setting Goals

The last part of the conjoint interview consists of setting treatment goals. These goals will be important in focusing the treatment and will be considered during each component of the intervention. Each client should state goals for (1) *changes in the partner* that would improve the relationship and (2) *changes in him- or herself* that would improve the relationship. The therapist's job here will be to direct the couple to set goals in positive, behaviorally specific terms. That is, instead of generalizations about what the partner doesn't do, goals should be framed in specifics that the partner could do more of. For example, the goal of "not being so distant" could be reworded into the goal of "spending more leisure time with me and increasing the frequency of sexual intercourse." *Wording goals in positive terms of change* rather than terms of deficits or put-downs both reduces defensiveness in the partner and sets up a definable target. Table 2–9 lists prompt questions that the therapist can use to elicit specific and positive goals:

Table 2–9
Prompt Questions for Setting Treatment Goals

- ▸ What would be different?
- ▸ What would you like to see more of?
- ▸ How would things look if this were to be satisfactory to you?
- ▸ How would I be able to tell that your partner was (or you were) being more *characteristic x*?

It is likely that there will not be enough remaining session time to articulate treatment goals fully. Thus, additional goals may be generated and worded positively as part of the homework.

Session Review and Homework Assignment

In reviewing the session, the therapist should summarize the major relationship difficulties expressed, apparent relationship strengths, and central goals for therapy. The therapist can also begin to offer a general sense of how the cognitive behavioral approach will address the couple's relationship difficulties, and inform them that in the next session, after looking over their assessment information, he or she will provide more specific feedback.

For homework, if session time did not permit completing the generation of treatment goals, clients should each generate at least three written treatment goals for themselves and three for their partner. As instructed in session, these goals should be specific and positively worded and be completed by each partner independently.

In addition, the therapist should ask each spouse to write down at least one thing that his or her partner does over the next week that he or she appreciates or finds pleasing in some way. This will be discussed in the next session and linked with one of the initial intervention strategies.

3

Session 2: Behavior Exchange Techniques

By the time a couple returns for Session 2, the therapist has already made substantial strides in becoming familiar with the case. After gathering the assessment information in the previous week's session, the therapist has had the week to review all of the materials, including carefully reading through and scoring self-report measures, watching or listening to the problem discussion, and reflecting on the interview material. In addition to getting an overall picture of the case, the therapist can compare responses between spouses and between written and interview assessment materials, noting any important discrepancies. If the therapist observes a discrepancy between the written materials and the interview information, he or she can begin this session by noting the discrepancy and getting clarification from the couple.

Occasionally, the nature of the assessment material (e.g., an ongoing affair reported on forms but not revealed in the interview) may lead the therapist to request a brief individual meeting with each client. In such a case, the therapist should clarify the situation, make appropriate treatment recommendations (e.g., not continuing in marital therapy while one partner is engaged in an affair, as discussed in Chapters 1 and 2), or discuss the need for additional or alternative treatment as necessary. When a therapist feels repeatedly compelled to separate spouses and speak with them individually, this should be a signal that the brief CBMT format described in this volume is not the appropriate treatment.

Setting the Agenda

Session 2 will consist of a brief review of the week, feedback from the assessment materials, a review of homework and an introduction to positive tracking, an introduction to behavior exchange techniques, and assignment of homework. The therapist should briefly lay out the agenda for the session with the clients, checking that they agree with the session plan' and asking if they have anything to add.

Brief Review of the Week

The review of the week should be used to inform the therapist of any major events (including major setbacks, improvements, or anticipated problems) that the couple feels are important for the therapist to know. The therapist will also want to check with couples about their reaction to beginning treatment or their thoughts about the first session.

In rare cases (e.g., crises) a couple's weekly report will alter the session agenda; however, typically the therapist would suggest working the reported problem into the skill focus of the day's session. For example, if a couple reports that a lack of time together led to conflict in the previous week, the therapist can offer the couple the chance to focus on that issue as part of the work on behavior exchange techniques. The therapist could easily address the issue at other points in the therapy as well, depending on the focus of the particular session. For example, conflict over too little time together could be handled as part of communication training, problem-solving, cognitive restructuring, or managing anger.

If the couple brings up an issue that clearly does not fit in with the planned agenda (e.g., a clear communication problem when the agenda is behavior exchange), the therapist can choose one of several options. If the topic has already been covered in therapy, session time can be devoted to reviewing it. If it relates to a topic that will be covered in the coming weeks, the therapist can explain that future sessions will be more geared toward addressing that problem, and ask if the couple feels comfortable waiting until then to handle the issue. If the therapist or couple feels that the matter absolutely cannot wait, then the order of treatment components can be modified to accommodate the emergent topic.

Providing Feedback from Assessment Materials

Based on reviewing the previous week's assessment materials, the therapist should broadly summarize all observations and initial formulations, tying these together with the clients' stated treatment goals. This part of the homework assignment can be reviewed at this time and incorporated into the discussion. The review will include delineation of particular conflict areas, identification of the couple's strengths, a conceptualization of the central problems based on models of development of relationship distress presented in Chapter 1, a reiteration of the clients' stated personal contributions to the problem, and a proposal for treatment. Relationship strengths and treatment targets should now include data from reviewed self-report inventories. While not reporting actual scores, the therapist can comment on areas that seem to be going well, areas that will need particular attention, or noted areas of agreement between partners. The therapist should relate this feedback in a confident yet open-minded manner, frequently checking in with the partners to ask if they agree, or if they have anything they would like to add. Since there will likely be several issues the couple wishes to address in therapy, and since this will be a brief therapy format, the therapist might help the couple narrow these to the most pressing or distressing difficulties. These selected problems will then be the primary targets for change, remembering that treatment teaches skills intended to foster continued improvement after therapy and generalization to other problem areas. Finally, while it is essential to be genuine and to respond realistically to the couple's problems, it is also helpful to convey optimism and hope where possible.

Review of Homework and Introduction to Positive Tracking

Typically, the couple's homework is reviewed in the early part of each session, independent of the introduction of new material. Homework assignments are normally designed to review and strengthen the skills taught in a given session, and so are covered before moving on to a new component of treatment. The first homework assignment, however, relates directly to the new material on *positive tracking*, so it will be reviewed in conjunction with the introduction of this topic.

Positive tracking is monitoring and reporting on positive relationship events and characteristics. This is an important part of shifting interchanges between partners from an aversive to a positive control system, building in verbal reinforcers for each partner and adding communication that is not solely complaint-centered. Further, it helps to shift perceptions toward positive events that might otherwise go unnoticed. The technique is introduced at the outset of therapy and used throughout. In the first session (Chapter 2), partners are asked to convey to the therapist the pleasing characteristics about each other and the relationship, as well as to report on the positive attributes that initially attracted them to each other. These constitute the global and long-term forms of positive tracking. Now we will turn our attention to positive tracking in the short term.

For homework, clients are asked to record at least one positive partner behavior. The therapist can ask the couple to take out their written assignments at this time and provide a rationale for and description of positive tracking, such as the following:

> *Therapist:* I'd now like to turn to a discussion of the events from the previous week that went well. Now, I know that if, each week, I asked you to tell me about what went *wrong* between you two over the previous week, it would surely be effortless for you to give me a laundry list of problems. But instead, I'd like to challenge you every week we work together to begin the session by reporting on what went *well* between you in the past week. Today, it will be easy, since you already recorded at least one thing you were pleased about since last week. You

can use what you recorded, or you can tell me about a good thing or two that you didn't write down but that still had a positive impact.

Amy: But we didn't come to therapy to tell you about what's going well between us. Isn't that missing the point of why we're here?

Therapist: Now of course, you came for therapy because you had problems and wanted help in handling those problems. We'll get to those soon enough. The issue, though, is that all too often distressed couples become so focused on *troubling* marital events that they neglect to notice or give their partners any credit for positive events.

Bob: (skeptically) What positive events? I can tell you, there aren't a lot of positive things to talk about at this point when it comes to Amy and me.

Therapist: I know it feels that way now. But I can tell you from experience, when you begin to look for some positives you can usually find them. I'd like to help change your focus a bit so that you're noticing the pleasing things Amy does as well as the bothersome things. Not only that, but if Amy gets some recognition or feedback for the things you appreciate about her, it will help her learn what's important to you, and she may be more likely to do more of those things. *(turning to Amy)* And of course, Amy, it will work the same way with you reporting on the things you appreciate about Bob.

Note that Amy and Bob did not easily accept the notion of recounting each other's positive deeds. While some couples will participate in positive tracking readily, others will need some urging. For some, feelings of anger or hurt may be coloring their perceptions to the point that they truly remember no positive events whatsoever, or may leave them reluctant to utter even the most tersely expressed words of praise. Others may believe that by applauding their partner's behavior in any way, they will somehow let their partner off the hook for more troublesome behaviors. Others may genuinely have no positives to report (e.g., the couple was separated for a week). Whatever the case, once the couple's hesitations are understood, the therapist can more effectively address them by prompting them with examples, repeating the rationale, and assuring them their problems will not be neglected.

Now that positive tracking has been explained, the couple is asked to turn to the behavior(s) they recorded during the week. The therapist can restate the assignment and then ask each partner, in turn, to relate the two or three behaviors they most appreciated during the previous week. For this interaction, the partners should shift their chairs toward one another and look directly at each other when speaking. They should direct their remarks toward each other, speaking in the second person (i.e., "*You* pleasantly surprised me when you . . ."), rather than directing them toward the therapist and speaking in the third person (i.e., "*He* pleasantly surprised me when he . . ."). This tends to increase the impact of the feedback and can enhance generalization of the interaction by practicing it as it would take place outside the therapy session. Also, as in discussing all marital events, the couple should give the feedback in behaviorally specific terms. Finally, the couple should avoid disguising a criticism as a compliment (e.g., "You weren't as sloppy this week as you usually are"), but instead keep the feedback truly positive ("You had your work all spread out in the living room and I noticed that you made an effort to clean up everything when you were finished").

After one partner voices positive sentiments about a recent event, the therapist should ask the other partner if he or she knew that this behavior had been appreciated, and if so, how he or she knew. If not, the therapist can ask how it feels to receive the positive feedback for the behavior. Presumably, the partner receiving the feedback will feel good about it. With these questions, the therapist reinforces the message that it benefits the partners to verbalize their positive reactions.

The following example continues with Amy and Bob and illustrates how a first attempt at positive tracking might unfold:

Therapist: So why don't we give it a try by looking over the behaviors you recorded from the last week. First, I'd like you to turn your chairs so that you are facing each other . . . that's it. Now, either by taking an item from what you wrote, or mentioning something that wasn't from the list, I'd like you each to come up with two things that pleased you. Who wants to start?

Amy: I guess I can start. What I appreciated this week was that Bob helped me . . .

Therapist: Hey, just a minute! What I'd like you to do is to tell Bob, not me. Face him, and let *him* know what you appreciated this week.

Amy: All right. *(looks at Bob)* What I appreciated this week was that you helped me around the house more.

Therapist: Now be more specific.

Amy: For instance, you helped me fold and put away the laundry.

Therapist: Okay, good. Bob, did you know that Amy appreciated it when you helped her with the laundry?

Bob: Yeah, I knew it.

Therapist: How did you know?

Bob: I know she always appreciates it when I do my share of the chores.

Therapist: Did she say anything to you at the time?

Bob: I don't think so.

Therapist: How does it feel to hear her say she appreciates it now?

Bob: To tell you the truth, not very good. I mean, so what? I did the laundry. Is that such a big deal? Is that the best thing she can come up with?

Amy: It was a big deal! When you help me like that it frees me up to spend more time on things that are important to me.

Bob: I know, but it seems so mundane. Is that all I'm good for now? Folding laundry?

Here, Bob exhibits the common reaction of devaluing a partner's comments. As part of the cycle of discordant interaction, even compliments can elicit conflict or hurt feelings. When this occurs, it can be helpful to have the partner who made the comments explain more about the positive impact of the events, and to explain to the couple that each partner will mention different things from week to week. This is not a contest, and what happens is not meant to be judged; it is simply an exercise to begin getting them used to noticing and expressing positive elements of the relationship. While sometimes clients will feel uplifted from the feedback, at other times they may simply have to accept that, given the state of the relationship, their partner may not be ready or able to report on anything more substantial than folded laundry. However, often what may seem trivial to one partner may be highly significant to the other. Thus, it can be enlightening to learn that even mundane acts can have a notable impact on a partner.

After the therapist discusses this with Bob, the dialogue continues:

Bob: All right, so let's hear what else she has to say.

Therapist: *(to Amy)* Why don't we go on to your next observation?

Amy: Okay. *(looks at Bob)* What I also appreciated this week was that you weren't as moody. You didn't lose your temper and start yelling like you usually do.

Bob: *(rolls his eyes).* See? There she goes. She's always accusing me of things!

Therapist: Okay, wait a minute. Amy, it seems like you experienced something positive this week, and yet do you see how it ended up sounding like somewhat of a put-down?

Amy: Yeah, I guess so.

Therapist: Good. So why don't you think about how you

could express the same thing in a positive way, telling Bob what you liked that he *did* do.

Amy: Well, let's see . . . I guess what I'm saying is that he was . . .

Therapist: (interrupts) Tell Bob.

Amy: I guess you were kind of calm this week. You were in a pleasant mood. I liked that.

Therapist: Good, that's much better. *(to Bob)* Does that sound better? Easier to hear?

Bob: Yes. It feels better. I don't feel like she's attacking me!

Therapist: Right. Now, Amy, can you tell Bob a bit more specifically what you mean by "calm" or "pleasant"?

Amy: Well, like when the kids were going wild in the restaurant on Sunday. You just looked at me and shook your head and smiled.

Bob: Oh, yeah. They were completely out of control.

Amy: Anyway, you let it go, and even seemed to find it almost funny. That made the dinner more pleasant and relaxing for me.

Bob: (smiles) If you found three kids running around and screaming relaxing, you have the patience of a saint! *(to therapist)* They're never letting us back into that restaurant.

Amy: (chuckles)

Therapist: Bob, did you know Amy liked the way you let that go and even smiled at her about it?

Bob: No, actually, I really didn't give it any thought.

Therapist: How does it feel to hear now that she appreci-

ated that, and that she had a nice time with you that
evening?

Bob: It feels good.

Here, the intervention quickly results in the desired effect.
Both partners briefly relive an enjoyable evening, and Bob
learns that his acting calmly in a trying situation resulted in a
pleasant evening for his wife. Thus, through this technique,
partners increasingly dwell on their pleasing interactions, learn
which behaviors are reinforcing for their partners, and receive
praise for their pleasing gestures. Although this intervention
may feel overly methodical to some therapists, it is important
to realize that discordant couples, as shown in Chapter 1, typically will not recall positive experiences on their own, even
though, as the above vignette illustrates, positive events do
occur in discordant relationships.

Note that the therapist makes ample use of in vivo coaching with Amy, until she masters the skills. Interrupting the
partners and having them rephrase their statements to each
other is more effective than relying on their memory and
waiting until they are finished. Also, jumping in and helping
a partner word statements during the interaction reduces the
magnitude of destructive messages that might be conveyed,
while enhancing the immediate positive impact of the intervention. Had Amy had trouble, for example, conveying Bob's
decreased moodiness in a positive way, the therapist might
have modeled a statement for her and then asked her to try
saying it to Bob.

In the session, the therapist would next prompt Bob to report on pleasing events from Amy over the previous week.
After a couple of weeks, couples become more adept at positive tracking, since each session begins this way. Thus, they
begin to arrive prepared with their feedback and need less
prompting and coaching in the session.

When the Couple Doesn't Do the Homework

Once engaged in therapy and familiar with the routine,
most clients will complete their assignments. However,
whether for tracking a partner's behaviors or other weekly
assignments, therapists will inevitably encounter clients who
appear for the session with their homework undone. There
are many possible reasons for this, including not understanding the instructions, not seeing the relevance of the assignment,
not having time, and not being motivated to facilitate therapeutic gains. The most useful therapist response involves both
discovering why the couple did not complete the assignment
and using session time to complete it.

Once the therapist understands the reason for the incomplete assignment, he or she can often remedy the situation by
providing clarification or repeating the rationale. If the reason involves not having time, the therapist should remind the
client that CBMT involves more than a one-hour-a-week commitment. Unless working on the relationship (including the
out-of-session work) is a priority, therapy can be of little value.
If undone homework continues to be a problem, the therapist might offer that since the couple seems unable to make

working on the marriage a priority, this may not be an appropriate time for them to be in therapy. If the clients seem unmotivated (a common scenario given pessimistic views of the relationship), it can be helpful to ask them to temporarily suspend their passive stance toward the relationship. Instead, they might try "going through the motions" of engaging in the various components of treatment, since there will be little to lose. If after the eight weeks of therapy they still feel unmotivated, they may then feel free to return to their state of inactivity.

It is important to finish uncompleted homework in session, regardless of the time cost. This sends couples the clear message that the therapist is serious about the homework assignment, and that it is crucial to further practice last week's skills before introducing new ones. Therapists will also want to take care not to assign homework hesitantly or apologetically, as some therapists new to behavioral approaches are prone to do. It may help to remember simply that the couple's relationship takes place predominantly at home, without the therapist present; skills must be practiced in that setting to enhance generalization. A confident presentation of homework plus a policy of devoting session time to undone assignments will typically result in rapid compliance with homework. Clearly explaining the rationale of the homework, asking couples to indicate whether they understand the task, having them write down the assignment, and obtaining their verbal commitment to doing the assignment can all increase the likelihood of homework completion.

CARING GESTURES

Rationale

Since distressed couples experience an unfavorable ratio of negative to positive exchanges, and marital satisfaction ratings are intimately tied to these exchanges, CBMT attempts to bolster the positive interactions between partners. Positive tracking initiates increased positive interactions, and caring gestures, which consist of pleasurable behaviors directed toward a partner, continue this trend. Caring gestures can produce rapid, low-cost improvements in relationship satisfaction, and may be crucial to increasing motivation, instilling hope, and providing a sense of mastery over relationship outcomes. In addition to these short-term benefits, caring gestures can stimulate a pattern of long-term, noncontingent investments upon which protracted relationship satisfaction will depend.

Establishing such positive interchanges between partners is the rationale offered couples for this therapeutic strategy. The therapist can also point out to the couple that when couples are newly together, such behavioral exchanges are at a premium and contribute to relationship satisfaction; however, for distressed couples, these crucial building blocks of contentment have typically languished. Caring gestures will involve increasing the daily attention needed for a satisfying relationship.

Developing Caring Gestures Lists

The technique of caring gestures involves asking each partner to develop a list of small, specific gestures that meet the criteria of being (1) reasonably simple and realistic to execute (i.e., low-cost), (2) likely to please the partner and enhance the partner's relationship satisfaction on the day they occur, and (3) not central to core conflict areas. Although generated early in therapy, these inventories of personalized rewards serve as a stimulus for expanding positive exchanges throughout treatment. Expressions of acknowledgment and gratitude for these gestures, initially prompted by the therapist, will serve to enhance the spiral of escalating rewarding exchanges. Thus, like positive tracking, caring gestures contribute to increased positive reciprocity. The procedure is intended to support a fragile system of mutual reinforcements; ideally, the ritualized nature of the exercise will ultimately become unnecessary as the couple's positive interactions increase, maintained by natural contingencies.

After providing the rationale of compiling a list of caring gestures, the therapist can continue by asking the couple to develop some hypotheses about current or past gestures of affection or caring that have contributed to each partner's happiness in the relationship. These might include displays of intimacy or companionship, such as writing love poems, taking a walk in the rain, going cycling together, or saying "I love you" before bed. Others might be more mundane, such as putting one's clothes in the hamper or taking out the garbage without being asked. No event is too mundane to be a caring gesture, for successful partnerships depend on each spouse doing his or her share of commonplace tasks. In fact, aversive control strategies such as coercion often center on everyday, practical tasks. When partners voluntarily increase these actions, strategies of aversive control yield to those of positive control. It may be helpful to point out to clients that the impact of showing such routine consideration cannot be underestimated.

Once partners have begun to consider such gestures, the therapist can then ask them to each begin writing a list, in session, of fifteen to twenty items they see as potentially pleasing to their partner, without input from the partner. Listing the items on paper is not intended to limit each partner to the written gestures alone but may initially spur a greater number of ideas for caring behaviors, and may later serve as a reminder to carry out the gestures.

Items on the caring gestures list should be small, specific, and objective. For example, an item such as "show interest in Kate" would be global and imprecise. Presumably, it would take more than one discrete behavior to show interest, and what would constitute a reasonable definition of "showing interest"? Would a kiss on the cheek count? Bringing a gift? The therapist should spend a few minutes working individually with each partner on his or her list (without revealing specific content to the other partner—the partner can simply continue to generate items for his or her own list during this time), and in this case would prompt the partner to define "showing interest" in more specific terms, such as: "ask her how her day went," "pay her a compliment," or "take her out for breakfast." If the partners need help in generating items or making them specific, the therapist might provide them with a sample list such as that in Table 3–1. Ideally, items will constitute a balance of practical gestures, companionship activities, and romantic indulgences. At this point it will probably be most helpful if partners do not share their lists with each other. However, even if this happens, the important restriction is that each partner refrain from providing input into the other's list. The goal at this point is that partners concentrate on their *own* abilities to enhance the relationship and to break the pattern of coercive methods of influence and of blaming.

Table 3-1
Couple's Caring Gesture Lists

Felice's List:	*Mario's List:*
Sit with Mario while he watches the news	Give Felice a back rub
Go with Mario to the supermarket	Read the kids a story at bedtime
Kiss Mario goodbye in the morning	Go for a walk with Felice
Call to say "hi" during the day	Hold hands while driving
Ask about Mario's day	Go to a baseball game together
Do the crossword puzzle together	Suggest having wine with dinner
Pay Mario a compliment	Get the car washed
Do gardening or yardwork together	Bring home flowers
Go for a bike ride together	Balance the checkbook
Go to the movies	Plan a social event with friends
Call Mario's parents	Straighten up the living room
Help sort the laundry	Go for a jog together
Cuddle on the couch together	Share thoughts with Felice
Make pancakes on the weekend	Help the kids with homework
Call if coming home late	Take the family out for ice cream

Carrying Out Caring Gestures

Once partners have generated several items, the therapist can instruct them to begin engaging in these behaviors throughout each week of therapy. The particular behaviors selected and their frequency are to be of the partners' own choosing, but aiming for five of the behaviors per week is a good guideline. Rather than a one-time assignment, caring gestures are presented as an ongoing and integral aspect of the couple's interactions. Importantly, each partner must be instructed to carry out caring gestures independently of the other partner's caring behaviors, so that the specified behaviors occur freely and noncontingently. This method (1) encourages each partner to focus on his or her own role in improving relationship satisfaction; (2) prompts partners to put thought and effort into expanding their repertoire of reinforcers (in an environment where many reinforcers are likely to have eroded); (3) allows for a sense of free will, which eliminates the resistance to acting in response to a partner's demand; and (4) enables the receiver to recognize that the gestures were chosen willingly, which reduces the tendency to attribute the behavior to a therapist's directive or some other external motive.

An alternative method of carrying out caring gestures is asking partners to construct lists of behaviors that are pleasing to themselves and to exchange these lists; each spouse is then instructed to increase the frequency of the behaviors his or her partner has requested. The advantages of this approach are that each partner specifies the behaviors he or she would like (which

increases the accuracy of the behavior selections as reinforcers), and that communication of wants to the partner is encouraged (which reduces the expectation that the partner
should "just know" what one likes). However, the disadvantages of this approach include perpetuating the stance that "my
partner is responsible for improving this relationship"; eliminating a forum for partners to consider expanding their own
reinforcement capabilities; adding an additional set of partner
"demands," which spouses may be inclined to resist; and devaluing a partner's caring gestures because they were requested.
In order to incorporate partner input about what each finds
reinforcing, the therapist can later, in future sessions, encourage partner feedback about the impact of any gestures carried
out. Further, in the next session, the therapist can ask both
partners if they would like to add several behaviors to their
spouse's list, *provided there is an atmosphere of mutual collaboration.* If partners appear competitive or resistant, the therapist will want to wait for a more opportune time to suggest
that they expand each other's lists with personal requests. This
allows caring exchanges to be established on the basis of self-
focused attention to giving, but to be revised with the partner's
proposals for additional reinforcers. Couples will have further
opportunity to practice making requests during the sessions
in which communication skills are taught.

   In future sessions, the therapist can periodically check in
with clients about their use of the gestures as part of the positive tracking exercise that takes place early in each session. Continually bringing the clients' attention to these behaviors helps
defeat the perception of the relationship as devoid of rewards.

Moreover, having partners acknowledge and reinforce each other for their displays of caring is crucial in maintaining the behaviors.

Over time, the effects of following the caring list often generalize, and couples begin to independently expand their demonstrations of caring. In one of our favorite examples, a wife in marital therapy, whose marital satisfaction was closely tied to her husband's demonstrativeness, came to the session beaming one week. She reported that one of her husband's caring gestures that week involved awakening extra early and quietly leaving a trail of notes saying "I love you" along the path of her entire morning routine, so that she would discover the notes from the moment of waking until leaving the house for work. His creative placements of the notes included her alarm clock, the bathroom mirror, her shampoo bottle, her shoes, the coffee maker, and her car keys. Not only was the impact on the client's wife tremendous, but her exuberant response to the gesture was extremely reinforcing for him, and spurred him to concoct additional inventive ways of showing his affection.

What Not to Put on Caring Gesture Lists

Certain items are best left off the caring gesture list, since engaging in them can feel coercive or disturbing for the partner. A simple rule can be that if the item feels uncomfortable for the partner or marks a sore spot in the relationship, leave it off the list. Sexual intercourse is the most common example of this type of caring gesture. While distressed couples frequently report some type of problem in the area of sexual relations, we find sex life is best addressed after other areas of intimacy are restored.[1] It might place a partner in a compromising position, for example, to feel pressure to increase sexual frequency in an environment of hostility, rage, or mistrust. Sensitive issues, such as the companionship activity of going to a bar together when a husband sees his wife's drinking as a central marital problem, are best excluded as well. Finally, gestures are best if they are reasonably easy to accomplish. Major or unrealistic demands, such as selling the house and moving to another part of the country or having another child, may be topics for discussion in therapy but do not belong on the list of caring gestures. Essentially, the best caring gestures consist of small demonstrations of caring acceptable to *both* partners (although not necessarily enjoyable to both—for example, a husband's gift of his wife's favorite chocolate dessert, even though he doesn't like chocolate, would be pleasing and probably not make him feel compromised in any way).

Shared Pleasurable Activities

Engaging in shared pleasurable activities with a partner can be a critical part of increasing a relationship's mutual rewards and recapturing positive feelings, particularly for couples whose

---

1. An exception occurs when couples with relatively low levels of discord present with some form of sexual dysfunction as their primary problem. In this case, we would advocate addressing the sexual problems from the outset, employing treatment strategies designed specifically for such problems (see Appendix I).

presenting complaints include growing distance, lack of intimacy, or few common interests. Distressed couples have often experienced a decline in companionate activities because
of altered life circumstances, increasingly disparate interests,
or routine shared activities losing reinforcement value. Although couples may include such activities on their caring
gestures lists, the therapist can introduce shared activities as a
strategy related to but separate from the caring gestures list.
In session, the therapist can ask clients to brainstorm about
prior activities they enjoyed together or new activities they
believe they might both enjoy. These can be one-time activities, such as going as "dates" to a street fair, or long-term
avocations, such as investing in scuba gear and taking diving
lessons, or studying a foreign language together. Couples can
begin their list together in session; they can expand it for
homework. Table 3–2 contains a sample list of shared pleasurable activities.

CONTRACTING FOR BEHAVIOR CHANGE

Contracts are written and signed agreements for behavior
change. Their benefit lies in the fact that making formalized,
specific, and public commitments increases the chances of
adhering to these commitments. Contracts are an optional
component of CBMT, and are generally not advocated this
early in treatment as their utility hinges to some degree on
the partners' ability to define problems and negotiate solutions
(skills are covered in Chapters 4 through 6; contracts are discussed further in Chapter 6). However, formalized agreements

Table 3–2
Couple's Shared Pleasurable Activities List

Skiing
Camping
Playing cards
Yardwork
Going to museums
Learning French
Entertaining
Antiquing
Preparing dinner together
Trying new restaurants
Planning ways to redecorate the house
Reading the newspaper together
Eating by candlelight
Getting up before dawn and taking a walk outside as the sun rises

can offer a useful and even essential form of behavior exchange when the couple presents with a situation that needs immediate resolution,[2] and so we will briefly review them here. Two types of such situations are those posing potential danger, such as domestic violence, or those with the potential for spurring

2. The placement of this topic in this chapter follows from its relation to behavior exchange procedures. Note, however, that such situations may arise at any point in treatment; thus, contracts may be implemented at any time. In later sessions, however, enhanced communication and problem-solving skills will permit a more thorough approach to addressing problems that may be temporarily handled through a contract.

rapid deterioration in the relationship if not handled promptly (e.g., one partner's ex-lover, now a friend, will be visiting over the next few days; the last visit resulted in arguments so extreme they resulted in a temporary separation). In such situations, contracting can provide a means of crisis intervention before the couple has learned the multitude of communication and problem-solving skills taught in the ensuing weeks. Contracts developed in this type of climate should be as specific as possible and should address an immediate and limited period of time (i.e., it would not be appropriate to contract for changes to last a lifetime; contracts are best used as a "band-aid" with the full therapy content providing skills for enduring change).

Contracting around domestic violence should occur rarely because, as explained in Chapter 1, we recommend a format other than brief CBMT for such cases. However, exceptions to this recommendation are cases that may still be deemed appropriate for this brief, conjoint approach because of physical aggression determined to be low in intensity and impact. For example, in one such exception where we saw a couple reporting domestic violence, there had been a recent, brief, mutual exchange of shoves, which, as a first-time occurrence, left both partners shaken (they had not seen themselves as having the potential to become physically aggressive) and strongly determined not to repeat the behavior. Thus, they sought therapy primarily to stop the potential for further occurrences through improving communication and negotiation skills. Because they both expressed remorse, they voiced a commitment not to engage in further violence, there was not an entrenched pattern of violence, and neither partner reported fear or intimidation, couples therapy proceeded. However, a contract was collaboratively developed in the first session. This contract served to equip the couple with an alternative strategy to handle a severe conflict, quell the couple's own anxiety about having lost control to the point of engaging in physical aggression, and send a "no tolerance" message concerning violent behavior in the relationship. The contract contained the following provisions:

1. Neither partner will use any sort of physical aggression toward the other between now and the next session.[3] This includes not only direct physical contact (e.g., shoving) but also other physical means of expression (e.g., breaking or throwing things).
2. If either partner senses an uncontrolled escalation of conflict (as defined by subjective perception), this partner will identify this escalation and then call a "time-out,"[4]

---

3. To increase the probability of compliance (which increases couples' sense of mastery and therapist credibility), short-term contracts are usually best. This strategy also allows for evaluation of the contract's effectiveness in the following week, with the possibility of renewal or revision if needed. This method follows the process of developing a trial solution during problem solving (Chapter 6), to be implemented and then evaluated, allowing for further input based on experience with the proposed solution.
4. Chapter 9 provides further discussion of the time-out procedure. However, couples can be briefly taught this technique as a crisis intervention strategy by prearranging the signal for the time-out,

and the couple will go into separate rooms for forty-five minutes and attempt to calm down.

3. If and only if both partners agree, the discussion may be resumed after this forty-five-minute period. If one or both partners do not feel willing or able to resume the discussion calmly, the couple will either resume at a mutually agreeable time, or bring the issue to the next therapy session.

4. If the second attempt at discussing the topic leads to a similar escalation, one or both partners will phone the therapist for additional help.

5. If the therapist cannot be reached, the couple will separate for an additional forty-five minutes and then refrain from discussing the topic before the next therapy session.

Such an agreement is then signed and dated by both partners and the therapist. This type of contract provides the couple with a sense of control over the problem and thereby a sense of relief; seldom in our experience has such a contract been broken.

For a different type of problem warranting a contract, the therapist would work with the couple to develop a plan of action that satisfies both partners and endeavors to contain conflict escalation. For example, in the earlier-mentioned scenario in which the impending visit of a partner's former lover poses a threat, a contract might include provisions delimiting

---

the duration of the separation, and the way in which the time-out period will be spent.

the amount of time spent with the visitor, including both partners during all contact, and bringing along additional friends to diffuse the intensity of the situation and lend support to the concerned partner. Regardless of the subject matter, the more precise the conditions of the contract, the more likely it will serve its purpose of forging a settlement on an urgent issue while minimizing conflict.

It should be noted here that in contrast to behavior exchange for the purpose of increasing positive behaviors, contracting is used as a direct means of decreasing negative behaviors. Contracting for behavior change in crisis situations is best viewed as a strategy to address extreme circumstances; in the absence of these situations, therapy should proceed without them at this point.

SESSION REVIEW AND HOMEWORK ASSIGNMENT

After reviewing the major session points and answering any of the couple's questions, the following homework should be assigned:

1. Couples will likely not have had time to finish their caring gestures lists in session. Often, after being coached on the nature of the items during session, they will need to generate more behaviors to develop a broad list of behaviors from which to choose. This, then, will constitute part of their homework assignment, and they are to bring in their expanded lists the following week. The next part of their assignment will involve choosing be-

haviors from the list at will and beginning to increase the frequency of the chosen behaviors. The therapist should remind the couple that they should each choose independently which behaviors to engage in, and inform them that they will be asked about these behaviors in the next session.

2. Couples should also work together to expand their list of shared pleasurable activities; eight to twelve activities is a good target. In addition to carrying out caring gestures, the couple should agree on one activity from this list and engage in the activity before the next session.

3. In the event that the therapist introduced contracting with the couple and devised a particular agreement with them, then abiding by the contract would also be assigned.

4

Session 3: Enhancing Communication: Basic Communication Skills

Before Session 3, therapy has primarily targeted increasing positive exchanges, through both verbal feedback and behavioral gestures. In this session, couples will begin to learn skills to improve their communication, an area of difficulty for most couples seeking treatment.

Setting the Agenda

The agenda for Session 3 will include positive tracking, reviewing the homework on caring gestures and shared pleasurable activities, a brief review of the week, and the introduction of communication training. Specifically, communication skills taught will consist of speaker and listener skills, including identifying feelings, using "I" statements, paraphrasing, and validating.

Positive Tracking

In every session, the therapist asks the partners to review favorable events from the previous week, telling each other directly what they found pleasing. This week, since caring gestures were implemented in the prior session, clients may report on gestures from these lists. Regardless of what behaviors partners report, the therapist should have them speak directly to each other, determine whether they had exchanged feedback on the matter previously, ask how it feels to hear the feedback now, and reinforce the clients for their positive behaviors.

Sometimes, partners will be vague or terse in providing feedback to a partner. For example, a husband might say to his wife, "I was glad you came to the baseball game with me on Sunday." In order to let the wife know what exactly her husband appreciated about this, the therapist might coach the husband with the following prompts: "Could you tell her *what* you appreciated about it?" and "Can you let her know *why* you were glad she came," or "How did it make you feel that she came?" As a result, the husband might expand his statement to: "I was glad you came to the game because it was a chance for us to spend an afternoon doing something fun together. I enjoyed it, and it made me feel cared about because you made an effort to participate in something you know I really enjoy." Here, the feedback becomes much more specific and instructive for the wife. Remember that in addition to shifting partners' focus to positive marital events, the purpose of tracking appreciated events is to increase positive reciprocity through (1) educating partners about which behaviors are rewarding and (2) reinforcing such behaviors through feedback. Further, it will be helpful to continue to stress speaking in terms of specific behaviors and their impact for both pleasurable and problematic behaviors.

Review of Homework

The previous week's homework involved completing both the caring gestures lists and the list of shared pleasurable activities, and engaging in selected behaviors from the lists. With regard to the caring gestures list, homework review will begin with the therapist checking over each partner's caring list for items that are low-cost and behaviorally specific. Should the clients still have trouble developing items in this way, the therapist can spend a few minutes working with clients to edit their items.

Once the lists have been checked over, the therapist can ask the partners directly if they engaged in any of the caring gestures from their lists. If clients have already reported on their partner's caring gestures during the positive tracking exercise, the therapist can reinforce the use of those behaviors again now, and then inquire about any gestures attempted other than those mentioned by the partner:

> *Therapist:* Chris, which caring gestures did you try this week?
>
> *Chris:* Well, like Les said a few minutes ago, I did all of the shopping and straightened up the house on Sunday.
>
> *Therapist:* Yes—and it clearly seemed to have a positive impact on Leslie. You really seemed to hit the nail on the head with that gesture; it brought Leslie a lot of relief. That was a thoughtful choice—one that really took Leslie's needs that day into account.
>
> *Leslie:* Yes, it was.
>
> *Therapist:* Good! Now were there any other behaviors you attempted, Chris, to please Leslie?

The therapist should inquire about any caring behaviors implemented, and how they were received. It is important to ask both clients about their own observations of the impact of their gestures on the other's apparent relationship satisfaction; in this way, the therapist prompts clients to stress those behaviors that are most reinforcing for their partners and helps enhance clients' ability to determine the effect of their own contributions to relationship quality. In addition, as in the positive tracking exercise, the therapist should then ask clients to give feedback to their partners about which gestures they found particularly pleasing. Remember, the principal message is that making even small and simple changes in behavior can directly influence the marital climate.

When partners have exchanged positive feedback, and if both partners have made efforts to initiate pleasing behaviors, this may be the appropriate time to have partners share their lists and ask each other to suggest several additional items. A collaborative and friendly spirit is necessary for allowing partners' input; in a hostile environment, behavior requests will likely sound coercive or critical and will undermine the benefits of this procedure. If tensions arise during the caring gestures review in this session, the therapist should postpone eliciting partner input into the lists and attempt to understand the source of the tensions, as elaborated below.

If one or both partners have not performed any caring gestures, it will be important for the therapist to find out what prevented completion of the assignment. The therapist will want to praise clients for any attempts to implement the caring gestures (even if not completed or not executed as planned), and also take care to address what problems, if any, the couple encountered with this assignment.

Two main difficulties commonly arise when couples first attempt to perform behaviors from the caring gestures lists.

First, partners will often report that although they tried performing gestures from the list, they felt uncomfortable because executing the gestures felt "artificial," "unnatural," or "forced." Some will cite this feeling as a reason for not even trying the behaviors (e.g., "I went to buy him a card and it just didn't feel right; it wasn't from the heart. So I left the store"). In response to this difficulty, the therapist should first validate the partner's experience; after all, referring to a written list of caring gestures *does* impose an artificial structure on the couples' interactions. The therapist can also remind clients that the variety of items on the list is designed to provide choices comfortable for the giver (e.g., perhaps a romantic card felt unnatural and too intimate this week, but getting the car washed would have been a sufficiently neutral gesture). Thus, the therapist can work with a partner to select items or devise new ones that feel more comfortable for the partner to do.

Moreover, the therapist can help a partner *relabel* the sense of artificiality or discomfort as "novel" or "different." Recall the trap of negative reciprocity and the state of reinforcement erosion that together plague discordant couples. Behavior exchange techniques in CBMT attempt to eradicate these patterns by spurring mutual investments of positive behaviors. Such behaviors are then likely to yield both reciprocal positive behaviors and more positive emotions and cognitions about the relationship. Like anything new, such behaviors *are* likely to feel unnatural, and we often feel we should "follow our heart" and be ourselves. Yet most behavior change, by definition, cannot be natural or feel "like ourselves." CBMT thus essentially asks clients to act unnaturally, and not be themselves, at least until new behavior patterns become second nature. Rather than viewing the associated feelings as undesirable, clients can reinterpret their sense of behaving "differently" as a positive indication of making needed changes.

The second common difficulty arising from initial attempts at caring gestures involves a tendency for the recipient to discount a partner's pleasing behaviors, assuming the partner engaged in the behavior only because it was a homework assignment, or to impress the therapist. In this case, it can be helpful to remind the client that the partner did in fact have a choice about whether to engage in a behavior, regardless of whether it was on a list devised in therapy. The partner could easily have not engaged in the behavior at all; the fact that he or she attempted a caring gesture might be taken to indicate an effort toward improving the relationship. Even if the behavior was in part an attempt to gain the therapist's approval, caring about the opinion of the marital therapist might be seen as a sign of involvement with therapy and, by extension, investment in the relationship. Furthermore, devaluing a change because it was assigned by the therapist places the partner in a Catch-22 situation: whether or not the partner makes improvements, his or her stance will be criticized. Such a position leaves no way for a spouse to exhibit commitment to working on the relationship.

The second part of the homework assignment involved asking couples to expand their list of shared pleasurable activities and participate in one activity from the list. The therapist can inquire about the couple's experience with this part of the assignment and ask partners to relate how they felt as they shared a pleasurable activity.

In continuing the review of homework, in cases in which the therapist worked with the couple to generate a contingency contract during the previous session, the therapist will want to review this assignment with the couple at this time. The therapist can review with the couple the terms of the contract, and inquire about whether they abided by these terms. If both partners complied with the agreement and the contract proved a success, the therapist should praise the couple's efforts and determine with the couple whether a continuation of the contract's terms is needed. If the couple reports a problem in following the terms of the contract, the therapist should attempt to understand what went wrong and remedy the problem with the couple's input. With complex difficulties, it may be best to ask the couple to put off an immediate solution and address it through the communication and problem-solving skills they will be learning over the next several weeks.

INTRODUCTION TO COMMUNICATION TRAINING

Rationale

The role that communication between partners plays can be thought of as similar to that of the spinal cord between the brain and the other body parts: it is essential for the transmission of messages and without it all interactive functions are lost. Thus, one can expect marital dysfunction if communication between partners is severed, and little progress in therapy if communication is not addressed.

It should not be difficult to explain the need for improving communication to a couple in therapy; since most couples report communication as a central problem in their relationship (Geiss and O'Leary 1981), communication training will often map directly onto their goals for therapy. When communication is not a specific therapy goal for the couple, the therapist can point out that learning communication skills will help provide the couple with the tools to address their treatment goals, whether those involve increasing intimacy, improving mutual understanding, resolving specific differences, or reducing hurtful interactions. The therapist can offer the rationale that communication skills will not only help a couple with their communication problems, but will also give them abilities that will improve their interactions regarding all the other problems they face. Like learning a common language, learning communication skills will help each partner both understand and be understood by the other.

As discussed in Chapter 1, research on the interactions of distressed couples reveals that, compared to nondistressed couples, they exhibit higher rates of negative communication behaviors, are more likely to reciprocate negative communication, and make statements that have a more negative impact on their partners (despite comparably positive intent). Further, distressed partners often exchange messages tainted by criticism, contempt, defensiveness, and withdrawal. The following communication interventions thus target each of these problematic areas of communication.

Speaker and Listener Skills

Typically, couples find themselves frustrated by their efforts to communicate, experiencing escalations of conflict while not feeling heard. The initial point to convey to clients about interacting effectively is that communication can be divided into a set of "speaker" skills and a set of "listener" skills (Guerney 1977). The speaker role involves the task of sending a message, and the listener role involves the task of receiving a message. When partners are discussing a topic, they must each assume one of these roles until they agree to switch. When bringing up a complaint, the speaker has the floor, meaning that although the listener will interact with the speaker, the speaker's topic remains the focus until the speaker feels it has been satisfactorily addressed. The listener should check in with the speaker before changing the topic, voicing his or her own gripe, or moving on to problem solving. While switching speaker and listener roles typically occurs quite fluidly in conversations once couples master the skills, partners must become familiar with the two roles and recognize which role they are playing at a given moment. Each part has its own set of skills that makes the role most effective.

Distressed couples often abandon the listener role either by competing for the speaker role (e.g., with interruptions) or by withdrawing. Even when partners covet the speaker role, they often express themselves in ways likely to reduce the chances that the partner will listen, as the following example illustrates:

Jose: You were so selfish and inconsiderate tonight! You

didn't sit with me at the dinner, you left me alone, and you know I'm uncomfortable in those situations.

Theresa: I was selfish! You humiliated me! You sat there and sulked around all of the people from my office! You didn't even try to mingle, or make an impression.

Jose: Make an *impression*? You only care about how you look to other people. You don't give a damn about how I was feeling!

Theresa: And did you care about how I was feeling when you were sitting in the corner pouting like a 2-year-old?

Jose: You don't even appreciate the fact that I came with you, even though I had plenty of other things I would have preferred to be doing!

Theresa: Fine, so stay home next time!

Jose: You're damned right I'm staying home next time!

Note that Jose began his communication with an insult. Although he had a complaint, and was looking for recognition of his feelings, he instead received an attacking response to his inflammatory opening. Note also that Jose and Theresa stole the floor with each new statement, focusing on their own complaints rather than addressing the speaker's agenda before moving on. This resulted in a rapid escalation in which neither one felt heard and nothing was resolved. In this and the next session clients will learn specific strategies for improving both speaker and listener skills.

Basic Speaker Skills

To learn effective speaker skills, couples will need to identify their feelings and express them in a fashion that assumes responsibility for their own emotions and behaviors. When voicing a complaint, partners will also need to provide specific and nonjudgmental references to the behavior to which they are reacting.

Identifying Feelings

A central aspect of communication involves accurately recognizing one's feelings. Simply teaching clients a format to express feelings will have limited value if they cannot accurately identify their own emotions. Sometimes, we simply do not know precisely what we are feeling, but may experience being "upset," "down," "fine," or "strange." A related problem, which we revisit in Chapter 9 on controlling the destructive expression of anger, is that when upset, we are often aware only of the strong, dominant feelings we experience, such as rage, frustration, or resentment. Although "softer" emotions, such as hurt, sadness, jealousy, and worry, typically underlie these "tougher" emotional states, it feels safer to express emotions that do not leave us feeling as vulnerable. As Christensen and colleagues (1995) point out, the problem with expressing only these more dominant emotions is that they usually send the listener the message that he or she did something wrong, and thus are harder to empathize with and more likely to evoke defensiveness. In unstable relationships, couples may feel especially reluctant to show vulnerability, and therefore rely on more dominant messages, receive unsupportive responses, and escalate their complaints. Hence, a vicious cycle can develop in which "stronger" communication further weakens the relationship.

The therapist can point out this pattern to couples, and elicit examples of times when dominant statements led to escalations of conflict, or when more vulnerable communication worked. To enhance couples' ability to discern their emotional states, the therapist can give the couple copies of Table 4–1, which contains a list of positive and negative emotions. The therapist can ask partners to read through the list, and have each partner give examples of a softer emotion on the list that might accompany a more dominant emotional state on the list (e.g., shame might underlie disgust). Couples can be encouraged to review this list before communicating about an important topic. The therapist can also ask partners to choose several emotions and generate scenarios in which they might experience them (e.g., the therapist might ask, "In what kind of situation might you feel unloved?").

"I" Statements

"I" statements express one's emotions, thoughts, preferences, needs, or reactions. These statements differ from other types of statements because they focus on conveying a personal perspective rather than implying that one's view represents objective truth. Because they reveal thoughts and feelings while avoiding blame or judgments, "I" statements promote intimate self-disclosure while minimizing chances for debating reality. In fact, "I" statements are nearly impossible to debate; one can contest an accusation such as "you were

Table 4–1	
Feeling List	
Positive Emotions	*Negative Emotions*
Happy	Sad
Interested	Depressed
Excited	Disappointed
Glad	Hurt
Pleased	Miserable
Attracted	Threatened
Turned on	Anxious
Inspired	Upset
Relieved	Angry
Alert	Ashamed
Ecstatic	Furious
Enthusiastic	Guilty
Proud	Hostile
Exhilarated	Betrayed
Satisfied	Hopeless
Content	Frustrated
Energetic	Resentful
Cared for	Scared
Fulfilled	Envious
Gratified	Empty
Confident	Bored
Cheerful	Jealous
Delighted	Agitated
Special	Irritated
Inspired	Bothered
Thrilled	Dejected
Aroused	Let down
Calm	Sorrowful
Secure	Lonely
Loved	Unloved

being selfish and inconsiderate," but not the disclosure "I felt hurt." Thus, "I" statements often have much greater credibility than their "you"-focused counterparts. Table 4–2 lists several examples of "I" statements as alternatives to "you-" or "other"-focused statements.

Table 4–2 "I" Statements	
Original Statement	*"I" Statement*
"You should drive more slowly."	"I feel frightened when you drive at that speed on this road."
"Your parents should call more often."	"I'd prefer it if your parents called more often."
"Both partners need to work for a couple to survive financially."	"I think it would help our financial situation if you got a job."
"Taking the train is ridiculous for such a long trip."	"I think I'd be more comfortable flying than taking the train."
"It was wrong that you forgot our anniversary."	"I felt hurt that you forgot our anniversary."
"It's important that married people save money for a house."	"I would like it if we could start saving money for a house."

A specific form of the "I" statement follows what is known as the *XYZ formula* (Gottman, Notarius, Gonso, and Markman 1976), which conveys the impact of another's behavior in a nonblaming manner. The XYZ formula is:

"When you do X in situation Y I feel Z."

In this XYZ formula, X refers to a specific behavior, Y refers to the situation, setting, or conditions under which the behavior is of concern, and Z refers to the emotions or thoughts linked with the behavior of concern. Consider the above argument between Jose and Theresa addressed with Jose using an "I" statement:

> *Jose:* When you didn't sit with me *(X)* at your work dinner tonight *(Y)* I felt hurt *(Z)*.

This opening is more effective than the one in the earlier example in several ways: Jose, as speaker, describes his feeling, being specific about the troubling behavior and situation. He does not attack Theresa or hold her responsible for his reaction; he merely expresses it to her. In response to this tempered approach, Theresa will be less likely to become defensive or to counterattack, and more likely to hear Jose's message. In session, the therapist can ask each partner to practice making an "I" statement using the XYZ formula, coaching clients as necessary.

Partners can use the XYZ formula to communicate positive feelings as well as negative ones; they should not feel compelled to reserve this strategy for complaints. Examples of positive XYZ statements include, "When you remembered to ask me how my meeting went, I felt pleased," and "I felt really cared for when you brought me dinner while I was studying." The therapist can encourage couples to express positive sentiments using "I" or XYZ statements, since they offer a chance to practice behaviorally specific communication, and positive statements always make a valuable contribution to marital interactions.

Basic Listener Skills

Paraphrasing and Validating

Once one partner brings up an issue, that partner automatically becomes the speaker and the other partner becomes the listener. The listener's first task is to *paraphrase* the speaker's statement and *validate* his or her feelings.

Paraphrasing involves simply summarizing or repeating the speaker's message. After paraphrasing the speaker, the listener checks with the speaker to see that the paraphrased version of the sentiment was accurate. Paraphrasing thus prompts the listener to pay close attention to the message and ensures correct reception of the message. Continuing with the above example, Theresa might paraphrase Jose's statement as follows:

> *Jose:* I felt hurt when you didn't sit with me at your work dinner tonight.
> *Theresa:* You felt hurt when I didn't sit with you tonight?
> *Jose:* That's right.

Notice the completely different tone this conversation takes from the outset, compared with the earlier example; Theresa does not become defensive or change the topic. By paraphrasing Jose, she conveys that she is listening to him, and allows the conversation to follow its original trajectory—the issue of Jose's feelings at Theresa's work function.

Paraphrasing provides the opportunity to clarify intent as well; when the impact of a message differs from the speaker's intent, the restated message will often reflect this discrepancy. In a climate of anger and dysfunctional communication, constructive attempts might still be filtered by the partner as provocative. Consider the following route this conversation might have taken:

> *Jose:* I felt hurt when you didn't sit with me at your work dinner tonight.
>
> *Theresa: (angrily)* So you're saying I ruined your evening because we weren't sitting together?

Theresa's attempted paraphrase allows her to check the intent of Jose's message. He responds:

> *Jose:* No! That's not what I'm trying to say! Yes, it wasn't the greatest evening for me, but I wanted us to talk about it so you can understand what these things are like for me. That way, maybe we can plan some better strategy for the next time.
>
> *Theresa: (calmer, but still skeptical)* So, you're just bringing it up so you can tell me your feelings about it and we can maybe see to it that we handle it differently at my next work party, say the Christmas party?
>
> *Jose:* Exactly.
>
> *Theresa:* Because it sounded to me like you were looking to start something . . .
>
> *Jose:* That's not my intention at all. I just want us to discuss it so we can *avoid* fighting about it in the future.
>
> *Theresa: (relieved)* Okay, so let's talk about it. So you were saying you felt hurt . . .

After the listener has paraphrased the speaker's statement, the next task is *validation* of the statement. Validation is an expression of empathy or understanding that basically conveys: "I can see why that feeling makes sense from your vantage point." Continuing with the scenario between Theresa and Jose, Theresa follows her now accurate paraphrasing of Jose's message with a validation:

Theresa: So you were hurt that I didn't sit with you.
Jose: Right.
Theresa: I guess I can understand why you might've been hurt that I didn't sit with you at the party.

Note that validation does not necessarily imply that the listener *shares* the speaker's vantage point, but only that, envisioning him- or herself in the speaker's position, the listener could imagine having such feelings. The listener does not have to agree with the partner's feelings or evaluation of a situation, but merely to accept that, given the way the partner perceived the situation, the partner's feelings were valid. At times, the listener will feel unable to empathize with the speaker's point of view, even following a clear "I" statement. That is, the listener may simply not understand why a particular behavior or situation was upsetting to the speaker. In such a case, the listener can ask the speaker to explain the problematic situation further, so that it makes sense to the partner in the role of listener. The listener can then go on to paraphrase and validate the new information. Let's examine the interaction between Theresa and Jose when Theresa cannot see Jose's point of view right away:

Theresa: So you were hurt that I didn't sit with you.

Jose: Right.

Theresa: Why were you hurt? I can't really see why that would bother you so much. We always mingle a lot in social situations.

Jose: Yeah, but in this case I didn't know anyone, and everyone was talking about work-related things, and it was uncomfortable for me. I just felt kind of abandoned and hurt that you didn't seem to be thinking about my feelings.

Theresa: So, it was uncomfortable for you because all of these strangers were talking about work, and you felt abandoned and hurt because I didn't seem to be thinking about your feelings?

Jose: Yes, that's it, exactly.

Theresa: Well, I guess I can see how that would be uncomfortable, and I can understand your feeling abandoned and hurt if you thought I wasn't considering your feelings.

Here, Theresa asked Jose to expand on his explanation until his feelings made sense to her. As long as this inquiry is handled in a way that conveys an earnest desire to understand (as opposed to conveying a derogatory reaction to the speaker's feelings), it will help the interaction progress and send the message of being interested in the speaker's feelings. By validating Jose's experience, Theresa provides an empathic response to Jose's complaint, keeping the conversation focused and preventing escalation.

Theresa may not feel there was anything wrong with sitting separately at the dinner, and may not agree with Jose's conclusion that she was not thinking of his feelings (e.g., she may indeed have considered his feelings, but simply misinterpreted how he would react to the situation). However, it would be hard to argue with Jose's *experience* of the various events: he felt uncomfortable with her colleagues, he felt abandoned being left with them, and, given his perception that Theresa didn't consider his feelings, he felt hurt.

In session, the therapist can guide couples through trying basic speaker and listener skills by applying them to a specific conflict. As always, the therapist should model and coach liberally and remember to reinforce the couple in their attempts.

Session Review and Homework Assignment

The therapist should devote a few minutes to recounting the basic content of today's session, making explicit links between the concepts introduced and their application to the couple's specific difficulties. The therapist might also "quiz" the couple on the basic communication premises, perhaps by asking them to explain the speaker and listener roles, or asking them to give an example of a validation. Throughout therapy, this type of drilling following the introduction and rehearsal of new skills will help in solidifying the concepts.

Homework will consist of practicing the speaker and listener roles by identifying feelings, sending messages using the XYZ formula, and responding to messages with paraphrasing and validating. As speakers, partners should first use the XYZ formula to communicate a positive message, and next use it to communicate a complaint; the partner in the listener role will paraphrase and validate each communication. Guidelines for the assignment include (1) beginning with a positive message (to endorse the practice of communicating positive feelings to balance negative ones), (2) voicing a complaint (preferably of low or moderate intensity, to increase chances for success without escalation), and (3) switching roles until the speaker indicates that the listener has accurately paraphrased and validated the sentiments expressed. Before using the XYZ formula, the speaker should review the emotions list in Table 4–2.

In addition, the therapist should ask clients to continue engaging in caring gestures as part of their homework. These gestures are intended to continue throughout the course of therapy.

5

Session 4: Enhancing Communication: Advanced Communication Skills

Setting the Agenda

The agenda for Session 4 will consist of positive tracking, reviewing the communication homework on basic speaker and listener skills, a brief review of the week, and continuing communication training by learning to identify (and avoid) destructive communication methods while further enhancing adaptive communication skills.

Positive Tracking

Beginning the session with positive tracking, the therapist should inquire about what went well over the past week in the relationship. The couple may report on caring gestures, or, with exposure to communication training, may now report on positive experiences of conversing with each other. In any case, as always, the therapist should have the partners speak directly to each other, check in with each partner about the impact of receiving the positive feedback, and praise the couple for carrying out this exchange.

Review of Homework

The homework was to practice identifying feelings, using the XYZ formula, paraphrasing, and validating. When reviewing the homework, ask the couple to discuss both the content and the process of the exercise. If the couple was able to carry out the assignment flawlessly, praise them, discuss the impact on each partner of employing this different type of communication, and move on. More likely, the couple will report some difficulty with the exercise. This presents an opportunity to address any misconceptions about basic speaker and listener skills. Often, the problems will lie in the misapplication of an "I" statement (e.g., unintentionally disguising a criticism or attack as an XYZ-formatted statement), or in the misunderstanding that validation means agreement with a partner's position rather than an understanding of it. It is the job of the therapist to gather a detailed report of how the interaction went astray, coach the couple as they venture the interactions again in session, and praise the couple for their efforts in attempting the assignment.

Some couples (and therapists) feel uncomfortable with the rigidness of distinct speaker and listener roles, complete with nearly scripted lines. Therapists can assure such clients that this protocol need not characterize their conversations for life.[1] Although the formal structure of conversation advocated in this and the previous session may fade as communication be-

---

1. As Baucom and Epstein (1990) have pointed out, couples typically drop paraphrasing from their everyday communication quite rapidly, although they recommend particular situations where it remains highly facilitative (e.g., to indicate careful listening, to clarify intent). Furthermore, as Linehan (1993) explains, various forms of validation exist, ranging from the act of listening intently itself to the verbal communication that one understands another's position. Gottman's (1994) research has even demonstrated that not all couples in stable marriages communicate alike (e.g., they may not use "I" statements all of the time). Thus, while we hold that noncritical feeling expression, listening, and validation remain essential

tween partners becomes more fluid, the distinctions between speaker and listener roles nevertheless are instructive for couples trapped in destructive communication patterns. As with studying a new language, acquisition requires rote recitation and memorization of exemplars; once the rules are mastered, students of the language become able to create their own sentence combinations in a way that feels natural.

CONTINUATION OF COMMUNICATION TRAINING: CHANGING DESTRUCTIVE COMMUNICATION METHODS

Rationale

Although expressing a gripe using an "I" statement and learning to validate a partner's feelings are important first steps in improving speaker and listener skills, many more specific strategies will truly enhance a couple's interactions. In today's session, the couple will learn to identify the various destructive elements of communication in which they may be engaging, remove these from their repertoire, and replace them with more helpful strategies. The strategies to be presented were developed primarily by Gottman in his skills-training manual for couples (Gottman, Notarius, Gonso, and Markman 1976) and by Jacobson and Margolin (1979) in their problem-solv-

---

components of constructive communication, once couples have mastered the regimented format taught here, they may feel free to adapt these strategies to a style that feels more natural for them.

ing manual, and have been presented in workbook form by others (Fincham et al. 1993).

An important point for clients to understand is the centrality of communication in their relationship. After all, it is only through verbal and nonverbal communication that partners can share their inner worlds; when this mechanism fails, distance and isolation prevail. It can be helpful to explain that research has identified many communication tactics that differentiate distressed from nondistressed couples as they try to work out their problems, and that difficulty with communication is the most commonly reported problem among couples seeking treatment. Moreover, distressed couples frequently get caught in communication traps, where time after time disagreements lead to escalations or withdrawal, with no problem resolution. In fact, the longer these destructive patterns continue, the more difficult it is to break out of them, as increasingly minor signals of conflict lead to rapid emotional arousal. The partners are likely to recognize themselves in many of the problematic communication styles they will learn about in this session.

Maladaptive Communication

After providing the rationale, the therapist can ask the partners to think about their own communication pitfalls, and to offer some examples of traps into which they have fallen when attempting to resolve problems. In keeping with the spirit of mutual responsibility, the therapist should be certain this does not turn into an opportunity for blaming, but that partners stay focused on reciprocal interaction patterns or on their own destructive tendencies.

Once clients have begun considering the nature of their communication difficulties, the therapist can move into a didactic mode. The therapist should explain that destructive communication falls into two categories: provocative or self-defeating tactics, committed primarily by the partner in the speaker role, and defensive tactics, committed primarily by the partner in the listener role (note, however, that for distressed couples the speaker–listener distinction tends to blur, and some tactics, such as getting off track, also reflect a mutual interaction process). The therapist should also explain that provocative and defensive styles will obstruct communication, increasing the likelihood of conflict escalation while reducing the likelihood of resolution.

The destructive strategies that follow are summarized in Tables 5–1 (below) and 5–2 (see page 174), which the therapist should copy ahead of time and hand out to couples at this point in the session. While reading through each item with the couple, the therapist can elicit examples from their repertoire, or share his or her own observations of styles that particularly characterize the couple. The therapist can take time to review and discuss each item with the couple, avoiding presenting them in a judgmental manner, but instead explaining how each can be self-defeating. Most couples will recognize many examples of their own interactions, and will have had the experience of finding them frustrating and damaging.

Table 5-1
Communication Errors I:
Provocative and Self-Defeating Speaker Practices

---

1. *Getting Off Track:* You wander off the topic, rambling from one issue to another without sticking to one problem; this overwhelms the listener and hinders problem solving.

2. *Kitchen Sinking:* Your discussion of one issue escalates to bringing in other gripes, leaving the partner feeling overwhelmed with complaints.

3. *Bringing Up the Past:* You bring old resentments or prior examples of a problem behavior into current discussions, complicating the current issue and likely leading to useless debates over the details of past problems. It is more helpful to stay focused on the impact of the current behavior in question.

4. *Mind Reading:* You assume what your partner is thinking or feeling without asking, or you expect your partner to know what you are thinking and feeling without stating it. The trouble is that this can result in an ill-informed emotional, cognitive, or behavioral response, such as one spouse's withdrawing based on an inaccurate presumption that the other partner is angry. In the case of expecting your partner to infer your thoughts and emotions, you may inhibit your communication and then resent it when your partner does not accurately read your mind.

5. *Character Assassination:* You verbally attack your partner's character through insults and put-downs ("You're a lazy slob") rather than specifying the behavior you have a problem with. This will invariably invoke a defensive response rather than resolving the problem.

6. *"Should" Statements:* You impose your values on your partner by using "shoulds" and "oughts" ("You should have . . . ") rather than stating what you would prefer. These messages of "I know better than you" are another form of communication likely to feel like a put-down and elicit a defensive response.

7. *Generalizing:* You begin statements with "always" or "never" rather than pointing out a specific instance of a problem. Such generalizations tend to evoke defensive responses consisting of exceptions to the generalization ("What about the time when . . . ?") rather than replies to the issue at hand.

8. *Threatening or Demanding:* You attempt to get your way by using threat statements ("If you don't stop that I'll walk out of here") or demands ("Don't

---
Table 5-1, continued:
---

you EVER do that!") rather than making a request. These aversive attempts to control a partner will likely elicit a defensive response (e.g., counterattack or withdrawal). However, even compliance with the demand comes at the cost of wearing away the loving feelings in the relationship.

9. *Whining:* Using a whiney tone of voice to get one's way not only annoys the partner and conveys impatience and entitlement, but also tends to lead to a negative response from the partner.

10. *Blaming:* You attribute fault to your partner with the implication that if only your partner changed, there wouldn't be any problem ("If it weren't for you, we'd have money in the bank!"). Blaming will likely evoke a defensive response or a blame-containing counterattack.

11. *Showing Contempt:* Contemptuous behavior is characterized by insults, mockery, sarcasm, or hostile body language, and is intended to hurt, put down, or express disgust toward the partner. One of the most extreme forms of destructive communication, contemptuousness often signals a serious deterioration in the relationship.

Provocative and Self-Defeating Speaker Practices

Getting Off Track

Getting off track means drifting off the topic rather than sticking to the central complaint. This seems to happen as the speaker loses sight of the original point or becomes flooded with emotion. Like links on a chain, each complaint seems intertwined with a related one, and then another, and so on. The difficulty here is that the listener becomes barraged by problems and cannot possibly respond to the primary issue. The overwhelming nature of discussing several problems at once also contributes to a sense of hopelessness about ever solving even simple problems.

Kitchen Sinking

Related to getting off track, kitchen sinking involves the speaker's tendency to heap gripe upon gripe, often in an attempt to bolster a position when the speaker is feeling defensive. Like getting off track, kitchen sinking leads to the escalation of the original problem, leaving the partner feeling deluged with complaints.

Bringing Up the Past

This refers to introducing prior incidents of a problem behavior into a disagreement about a present issue. Partners may feel tempted to bring up past instances of the problem to provide additional evidence that the problem is serious ("What about when I was in the hospital for my surgery last winter? You spent less time with me than my parents did! That's another perfect example of when you weren't there for me when I needed you!"). However, like getting off track and kitchen sinking, bringing up past examples of the problem will likely derail the issue and lead to defensiveness or withdrawal in a partner who feels overwhelmed by the attack. In particular, citing prior instances often leads to fruitless arguing involving memory clashes over what actually happened. It is more helpful to stay focused on the impact of the current behavior of concern.

Mind Reading

Mind reading occurs when one partner assumes he or she knows what the other partner is thinking or feeling. The problem emerges when (1) such presumptions lead to ill-informed behaviors, emotions, or cognitions, or (2) the partner finds it annoying to be told what he or she is experiencing.

In the first case, consider the following example: Yolanda brings up a problem and, based on the look on her husband's face, concludes, "He thinks I'm being unreasonable." Yolanda then feels invalidated, thinks, "This is going nowhere; why bother?" and ends the conversation by saying, "Look, forget it. I can't talk to you about anything" and leaves the room. Her husband, Wayne, then feels attacked and bewildered. In fact, if Yolanda had slightly adjusted her thinking to remove the mind-reading component, and stated, "From the look on your face I feel like you think I'm being unreasonable," she might have found out that Wayne's look was in fact a look of guilt, confusion, or some other response.

In the second case, mind reading can derail constructive interaction if one partner makes a mind-reading statement to the other, such as in the situation where Wayne inaccurately makes the accusation, "You didn't come in when I asked you because you're angry about last night," and Yolanda, exasperated by the mind reading, emphatically exclaims, "I am not!" Wayne then responds, "Just listen to your tone! I knew you were angry!"

Another type of mind reading involves expecting one's partner to know what one is thinking and feeling without having to state it. This manifestation of mind reading can be problematic because it tends to inhibit one's communication and then results in blaming the partner for an unmet need. For example, one husband's conviction that his wife "should just know" that he would want a party for his fiftieth birthday prevented him from voicing this wish. When his wife failed to plan a party, he became angry and hurt, and accused her of not caring enough about him to give him what he obviously wanted on this significant birthday. Had he simply broached the topic of how he would like to spend his birthday, he could have gotten what he wanted and avoided an argument.

Mind reading can also occur in the listener role, in the form of a misconstrued paraphrase. That is, instead of reflecting accurately what the speaker has said, the listener may infuse his or her own interpretation into the summary of the message.

Finally, mind reading produces positive results at times, potentially coming across as empathic and sensitive.

Mark: You look preoccupied . . . are you worried about the doctor's appointment next week?

Rita: How did you know just what I was thinking? You're remarkable!

Mark: You know, I canceled my afternoon meetings that day so I could go with you. I figured that might make it easier for you.

Rita: It would make it a lot easier for me—thank you. You are being really sensitive about this whole procedure and it means a lot to me.

When used to anticipate a partner's needs or to supportively read a partner's emotional state, mind reading can promote intimacy. In these situations, even if the mind reading is inaccurate, the speaker is still making a supportive, even if unnecessary, statement. Provocative or destructive mind reading occurs primarily when a partner jumps to negative conclusions and acts without first checking them out, inaccurately accuses a partner of harboring particular feelings, or distorts a message that is being stated clearly.

Character Assassination

Character assassination is the use of insults to send one's partner the message that problems are due to his or her negative traits, rather than using neutral descriptive language to identify a particular problematic event, situation, or behavior. Through verbal assaults, a spouse communicates that his or her partner has character flaws that are deeply embedded and unlikely to change. For example, if a husband failed to fold the laundry as promised, a wife might say "You're lazy and undependable" rather than stating that she felt upset about the specific task left undone. The trouble with this type of communication is that it immediately *deflects* the attention from the problem (e.g., the unfolded laundry) by inevitably provoking a defensive reaction (i.e., likely a denial or a counterattack in response to being called "lazy and undependable"). It is more helpful to identify a particular problematic event and express its impact (e.g., "I was frustrated that the laundry wasn't folded because now the clothes will be wrinkled").

"Should" Statements

Making "should" statements involves judging or imposing one's values on a partner in a demanding way ("You shouldn't waste so much time," or "You ought to exercise more often," or "You should have put Taylor to bed by nine o'clock") rather than either directly stating a preference (e.g., "I like to have Taylor in bed by nine because otherwise she has a hard time waking up in the morning") or resisting the temptation to control the partner. Many people feel that the intimacy of the relationship justifies the right to tell a partner what to do. Yet, frequently barbing a partner with "shoulds" imparts messages implying that "I know better than you," or "My judgment is better than yours," or "You can't manage your life properly without direction from me." Thus, the "should" statement is yet another form of communication likely to feel like a put-down and elicit a defensive response.

Generalizing

Generalizing involves using the terms *always* and *never* when referring to a partner's problematic behavior rather than pointing out a specific instance of a problem. For example, a partner might say "You're always late," or "You never support me." Generalizations prove self-defeating, inviting defensive responses ("That's not true; what about last week when . . . ") or hurtful cross-complaints based on similar generalizations ("Well, maybe if you weren't always so cranky I'd feel like being more supportive!"). Partners will find it more helpful to focus on the impact of a specific behavior (e.g.,

"When you tell me I'm not patient enough with the kids, I feel unsupported").

Threatening or Demanding

The use of demands (e.g., "Put the paper down and set the table, NOW") or threats (e.g., "If you don't put that newspaper down now and set the table your dinner's going in the garbage!") represents a coercive attempt to get one's way. In addition to the self-evident aversiveness threats or demands evoke when one partner is being bullied by the other, such statements are likely to rapidly increase emotional arousal (and thereby increase the chance of a defensive response or withdrawal), or to elicit fear, if they are associated with past explosive outbursts.

Husbands and wives will sometimes report that they have resorted to threats or demands after previous, more mild-mannered approaches failed. The therapist can acknowledge past frustrations but point out that although threats and demands may lead to compliance, this often comes at the cost of wearing away loving feelings in the relationship. As noted in Chapter 1, this pattern may become strengthened over time as one partner learns that coercion works, and the other partner learns that compliance stops the aversive communication (and prevents the implicit or explicit consequence). If making direct requests repeatedly fails, a partner might try scheduling a communication discussion and use of the XYZ formula to bring up this problematic pattern in a positive, responsibility-sharing way (e.g., "It feels like when I ask you to help me before dinner, you don't respond and I end up raising my voice, which upsets me. I don't want it to be tense between us every night; do you think we can try to figure out a way to deal with this pattern?").

Whining

Speaking in a whiney tone of voice (e.g., using a high pitch, elongating certain words, and displaying a generally childish attitude, as in, "I wanted to go *nowww*—I don't see why we have to *waaait*") both annoys a partner and conveys disapproval. The response from the partner will usually be negative. Instead, even when impatient, partners will receive better results by using a neutral tone of voice to ask for what they want.

Blaming

Blaming sends a partner the message that he or she is at fault for a particular problem, in contrast to assigning responsibility to oneself or to the situation. A statement of blame usually implies that if the partner were fundamentally different, the problem would not exist (e.g., "If it weren't for the way you managed money, we'd have money in the bank!"). Blaming represents yet another style of communication likely to evoke a defensive response ("I managed my money fine all those years when I was living on my own!"), or a counterattack involving blame ("Well, if you worked a little harder maybe you'd earn more, and then you wouldn't have to be so worried about how I spend the few pennies we have!").

An accusation of responsibility not only causes hurt feelings but is much more likely to result in escalation or withdrawal than in productive problem solving. Even in cases where one partner is clearly at fault (e.g., parking a car illegally while alone and then having it towed), the problem will be more easily resolved if met with understanding (e.g., "Boy—you must feel terrible. Why don't we start calling places to try and figure out where to go pick it up?"). This type of support will actually be much more likely to lead to acknowledgment of responsibility from the partner.

If a spouse feels too upset to offer support, perhaps because a partner's errant behavior has serious ramifications or represents a troublesome pattern, then the spouse can most effectively respond by waiting for the appropriate time (e.g., not when the couple is in the midst of trying to locate the towed car) and using an XYZ statement to broach the topic.

Showing Contempt

Contemptuous behavior is characterized by insults, mockery, sarcasm, or hostile body language, all delivered with the intention of hurting, putting down, or expressing disgust toward one's mate. Examples of contempt may include statements (e.g., "What's the matter with you, you good-for-nothing moron!") or body language (e.g., pointing in the partner's face, glaring). Contemptuous styles of speaking include speaking slowly and deliberately, to patronize a partner; speaking menacingly, to threaten or control a partner; and speaking mockingly or sarcastically, to demean a partner.

Contemptuousness is one of the more extreme forms of destructive communication, and can signal an acutely deteriorated situation. Couples exchanging contemptuous communications have likely become caught in a vicious cycle in which harshly delivered demands result in a partner's defensiveness or withdrawal, which results in increasingly antagonistic demands, and so on. Even when extremely upset or frustrated, partners will inflict less harm by keeping communication more neutral, even if it means waiting until calming down to interact.

Defensive Listener Practices

Cross-Complaining

Cross-complaining involves voicing another complaint in response to a speaker's complaint (e.g., "Oh, you don't like the way the yard looks? Well, I haven't been so happy about how you've been maintaining the inside of the house!"), rather than responding to the complaint with an indication of interest in what the speaker has to say (e.g., "Really? What bothers you about it?"). It represents a defensive attempt to outdo the partner, as if bringing up a fault of one partner somehow will overshadow the other partner's original gripe. The difficulty lies in the fact that a cross-complaint almost always provokes an escalation, rather than helping to settle the issue. The partner who raised the initial problem will not only feel unheard and invalidated, but also attacked. Even if a seemingly related issue jumps to mind, a listener should acknowledge the

---

Table 5–2
Communication Errors II:
Defensive Listener Practices

---

1. *Cross-Complaining:* Each partner voices a complaint in response to a complaint, rather than responding to the initial issue. It is as though the listener wishes to get off the hook and outdo the speaker rather than settle the issue raised.

2. *Yes-Butting:* You respond to speaker's statements with "Yes, but . . . ," negating your partner's point and leaving your partner feeling invalidated.

3. *Interrupting:* You interrupt your partner's statements, or speak at the same time as (or over) your partner, rather than listening and waiting your turn. This ends the listening role, frustrates the speaker, and sidetracks a discussion (e.g., Partner 1: "You just interrupted me!" Partner 2: "Well, if you weren't going on and on . . . ").

4. *Shirking Responsibility and Making Excuses:* This involves denying responsibility for one's role in a problem or providing explanations intended to excuse a problematic behavior. The listener is putting more effort into dodging blame than into trying to understand the partner's feelings.

5. *Repeating Yourself:* This occurs when a partner states his or her own position over and over, rather than directly responding to the other partner's point. This leads to a communication standstill and sends the message, "I want what I want and your needs are not important."

6. *Negative Body Language:* Nonverbal messages can sometimes send stronger messages than verbal ones, conveying lack of interest, hostility, or the absence of a genuine response. Examples of body language undermining listening efforts include focusing on something other than the speaker, shifting impatiently, or rolling one's eyes.

7. *Stonewalling:* Stonewalling is a complete cessation of communication by the listener that typically follows the physiological overarousal that occurs when a partner is feeling overly upset, frustrated, or attacked. The listener may become completely unresponsive or may leave the situation. The speaker generally experiences this shutdown as a potent act of hostility and becomes even more upset.

---

speaker's concern and indicate some understanding of his or her perspective before voicing an additional complaint.

Yes-Butting

This tactic represents a pseudo-agreement with a statement, where what follows the word "but" negates support of the partner's point. Examples include statements such as "I agree with you, but . . . " or "Yes, I understand, but . . . " which have an impact equivalent to saying "I don't agree" or "I don't understand." Although the "yes" part of the statement represents a minor attempt to acknowledge the speaker's position, what follows the "but" typically contradicts or *invalidates* that position.

Interrupting

Interrupting is cutting in before the other person has finished, or speaking at the same time, often by trying to speak over the other person with a louder volume or more forceful tone of voice. Few behaviors provoke more frustration and arousal during a disagreement than being interrupted, particularly when it happens repeatedly. The listener often interrupts because of an urge to respond immediately to a perceived attack or inaccuracy, or an inability to get a word in edgewise with a rambling speaker. Although it is important for the speaker to avoid attacks and to speak concisely (see below on enhancement of speaker skills), the listener will be more effective by acknowledging the speaker's point before moving on. The very act of interrupting indicates the listener has stopped listening and become preoccupied with taking over the speaker role, and will likely focus the speaker's attention more on the disruptive process than on the content of the interruption.

Shirking Responsibility and Making Excuses

This style of defensive responding consists of denying responsibility for a role in a problem, or providing explanations intended to excuse a problematic behavior. When listeners engage in these tactics, they put more effort into dodging blame than trying to understand the partner's feelings. Thus, the discussion is likely to become sidetracked and escalate.

Repeating Oneself

This destructive strategy occurs when a partner states his or her own position over and over, rather than paraphrasing and validating the partner's point. This leads to a communication standstill and does nothing to propel the conversation forward, as in the following example:

Pat: I think we ought to talk about how we are going to spend our vacation. I would like it if we could do something different this year, maybe with friends.

Alex: I thought we'd spend it with my parents in Florida again.

Pat: Look, I think it's time we do something different—like maybe going in on a house-share on the shore.

Alex: I was counting on going down to Florida—when else do we get to see my parents?

Pat: For once we should do something else . . .

Alex: I don't know about you, but I'm planning on going to Florida!

In this case, neither partner responds to the other's communication, but instead both repeatedly summarize their positions. Rather than signaling a willingness to negotiate, this maneuver sends the message, "I want what I want and your needs are not important."

Negative Body Language

Nonverbal messages hold their own against verbal messages in their impact on a partner. Regardless of verbal content, negative body language can indicate hostility or lack of interest or insincerity. Samples of negative body language include looking at or engaging in something else when a speaker is talking (e.g., thumbing through the paper), shifting impatiently, putting on a fake smile, or displaying a facial expression that does not match the spoken theme (e.g., exclaiming, "Isn't that wonderful!" while rolling one's eyes). Such enacted messages will often evoke an intensified complaint from the speaker.

Stonewalling

Stonewalling is a complete shutting down of communication by one partner, and follows from extreme overarousal resulting from the escalating attack by the other. This extreme withdrawal can be manifested as a physical departure from the situation, or as an icy silence conveying an emotional departure from the situation. Although this withdrawal sometimes reflects an attempt at self-control over an extremely negative or explosive reaction, (and may feel virtually involuntary to the stonewaller), it can feel to a partner like a potent act of hostility.

CONTINUATION OF COMMUNICATION TRAINING: ENHANCING ADAPTIVE COMMUNICATION METHODS

Although limiting destructive communication will be helpful, couples will further benefit from learning constructive alternatives to the negative methods. The following speaker skills (see Table 5–3) are intended to increase the speaker's capacity to send a clear message without attacking the listener. The listener skills (see Table 5–4) that follow, primarily from Gottman and colleagues (Gottman, Notarius, Gonso, and Markman 1976), are intended to increase the capacity to respond in a way that thwarts a speaker's need to intensify the complaint. Remember that the speaker role involves sending a message and the listener role involves receiving it, and that the roles will alternate between partners throughout the course of a discussion.

Speaker Skills

Being Specific

As explained in Chapter 4, couples should follow the XYZ formula ("When you do X in situation Y I feel Z"), which

---

Table 5-3

Positive Communication Strategies I:

Speaker Skills

---

1. *Be Specific:* Don't speak in vague generalizations ("You never call me"). Use the XYZ formula: "When you do X in situation Y I feel Z." Example: "When you forget to call when you're coming home late I feel worried."

2. *Use "I" Statements:* Embedded in XYZ statements, "I" statements express the impact a behavior had on you, rather than criticizing your partner. Say "I felt hurt when you insulted me," rather than "You were mean to me at the party."

3. *Be Brief:* State your complaints clearly and concisely; don't expect to hold your partner's attention if you ramble on.

4. *Be Assertive:* State what you would like directly: "I would appreciate it if you called me when you were going to be late."

5. *Be Polite:* Talk to your partner as you would to an acquaintance. Avoid hostility, frowns, anger, or commands.

6. *Frame Desires Positively:* Frame requests positively, stating what you would like more of, not only what your partner is doing wrong. Say "I would really like it if we could spend more time together in the evenings," rather than "If you cared about me, you wouldn't work late all the time."

7. *Make Requests, Not Demands:* Ask your partner for what you would like; do not act like you are his boss or his parent. Say "Could you please clear off the table before dinner?" rather than "clean off the table, NOW!"

8. *Give Compliments:* Acknowledge the positive things your partner does. Even a complaint can be turned into a compliment and a request: instead of "You don't make a vegetable often enough with dinner," say "That salad you made last night was delicious. Why don't we include vegetables with dinner more often?"

9. *Express Feelings of Pleasure:* Express feelings of joy or excitement, letting your partner know when you are having a good time or feeling optimistic. Express appreciation and demonstrate affection.

10. *Use Humor:* Smiling and joking with your partner can cut tension and rekindle positive feelings. Just be certain the use of humor is appropriate (laughing at your partner's expense will not be helpful).

11. *Say What You Are Willing to Do to Help:* Offer to help, rather than expecting your partner to make the only changes. "We should eat more fresh vegetables.

Table 5-3, continued:

I can begin to stop at the market on the way home from work a couple of times a week." Also, acknowledge your own role in the problem: "I know I'm not always understanding about your job; would it help you feel comfortable sharing more about it if I made more supportive comments?"

12. *Edit Out Negative Content:* Eliminate unnecessary and unhelpful content from your messages, so that a statement like "I'm upset because you were late *for the millionth time*; what *the hell* happened?" becomes "I'm upset because you were late; what happened?"

13. *Metacommunicate:* When you are feeling stuck or noticing an escalation, *communicate about your communication* with your partner. This repair strategy helps to catch destructive processes as they are happening and demonstrates concern for the discussion outcome. Examples: "We're getting off track," "I can see we're both starting to get upset," or "I'm trying to understand but this is difficult."

14. *Stop the Action:* If you see your discussion escalating or heading nowhere, suspend it midstream, discuss the escalation or impasse itself (i.e., focus on process, not content), and take a break to calm down or try to redirect the conversation.

15. *Pick the Appropriate Time and Place:* Bring up important topics at mutually convenient times. Do not expect your partner to be willing to engage in an important discussion at bedtime, before an important meeting, and so on. For scheduled communication sessions, partners should prearrange a limited time period in a place protected from interruptions.

---

specifies the situation and behavior causing the problem. When making a request, being specific helps convey one's exact wishes and avoids confusion. For example, asking a partner "Could you please throw away those waste papers and file those bills?" will be less ambiguous than asking him or her to "Please straighten up in there."

Using "I" Statements

Embedded in the XYZ format, an "I" statement expresses

the impact of an event, and indicates that the speaker takes responsibility for his or her reaction rather than holding the partner responsible.

Being Brief

It is important for the speaker to state gripes clearly and concisely. A speaker may have several points to make, and may fear that pausing after making just one point may eliminate the opportunity for further expression. However, listeners will probably stop listening or interrupt if a speaker rambles on. A message will be more effective if delivered in small doses. In fact, the speaker is likely to have a greater opportunity to make the remaining points if the initial message keeps the conversation on track and the listener engaged.

Being Assertive

Being assertive means asking directly for what one wants or needs, or saying no directly to an unwanted request. When executed in the context of other positive communication strategies such as being specific, assertive statements increase the likelihood of getting one's needs met while combating mind-reading expectations and built-up resentments.

Being Polite

Distressed partners often treat each other much more rudely than they would an acquaintance or stranger. Partners may state that they are not capable of speaking to their spouses as they would to a stranger or acquaintance; they are not in conflict with most strangers or acquaintances. However, most couples will agree that there have been times they've acted politely toward a stranger in a problem situation, such as when billed incorrectly in a restaurant or pulled over by a police officer. With people we do not know well, most of us maintain a certain degree of civility, even in situations of adversity. Ironically, the avowed preciousness of the marital relationship provides a context in which intimacy seems to justify *mis*treatment of a partner.

By pointing out to couples their capacity to respond differently to conflict with others, they may come to realize they are capable of this with partners. Further, they are more likely to be met with receptive listening if they avoid hostility, frowns, anger, commands, or other impolite styles of communicating.

Framing Desires Positively

Framing desires positively means stating what one would like more of, rather than only mentioning what the partner is doing wrong. For example, instead of saying "I don't like it that you work late so many evenings," one could say, "I would really like it if you could spend more time at home in the evenings, so the kids and I could see more of you." This is a subtle yet powerful shift in communication, as it transforms a complaint into a compliment. The former remark about working late too often conveys, "You are doing something that bothers me," while the latter remark conveys, "I really like spending time with you." Positively framed requests delivered with similarly positive vocal tone and body language result in the most positive impact.

Making Requests, Not Demands

When asking one's partner for something, it is helpful to actually *ask* and not demand. For example, it will be more effective to say, "Could you please clear off the table before dinner?" than to demand "Clear off the table, NOW!" The latter, demanding way of communicating may lead to compliance but will surely engender hostile feelings as well.

As we discussed in the above section on communication errors, a spouse may report that it feels necessary to speak that way because it has become the only way to get an acceptable response from the partner. If this is the case, it is best to point out that treating one's spouse like one's servant or child will only increase distress. Instead, one should refrain from giving commands and schedule a time to discuss the pattern, using the XYZ format (e.g., "When you tune me out when I make requests I feel frustrated and ignored, and like I have to demand things of you to get you to listen").

Giving Compliments

By the time couples contact a marital therapist, they are typically focused on negative aspects of the relationship. Thus, they frequently interact about areas of displeasure but seldom about areas of contentment.

Even when couples report that many positive aspects of the relationship remain, they tend to either (1) take these aspects for granted and not think to compliment their partners for them, or (2) believe that acknowledging the positives will send the message that these behaviors are optional, and will therefore decrease their occurrence. For example, a distressed partner might offer the following rationale for withholding a compliment: "I'm not going to *thank* him for picking up the kids from their music lessons. After all, *he's their father*. Yes, I appreciate it, but there's no choice; I don't get home in time to do it. I don't want him to think that on a whim he could decide *not* to."

In this case, the therapist might ask the wife to express her positive feelings about the gesture, and then check out with the husband what message he takes from it. Spouses usually report simply feeling good that their gestures, even if mundane, are appreciated. In fact, feedback about the positive impact of such gestures can increase motivation to continue to carry them out (remember that praise tends to be reinforcing for most people and that *reinforcers increase the likelihood of a behavior*).

So, in addition to positive tracking during therapy sessions, the therapist can encourage couples to routinely acknowledge their partners' positive behaviors. In fact, the clinician might coach partners to balance requests for change with compliments: "I notice you've really been making an effort to speak more calmly with Ian, and I'm grateful for it. It still concerns me when you yell at Patti, though—she's too little to understand."

Even a complaint can be rephrased as a compliment with a request tagged on. For example, instead of saying "You don't make enough vegetables with dinner. Don't you care about our health?" one could say, "That salad you made last night was delicious. Why don't we make it a point to eat more fresh vegetables with our dinner?"

Expressing Feelings of Pleasure

Distressed couples too often voice only their *dis*pleasure, and keep positive feelings to themselves, almost as if they believe that expressing their happiness will spoil the moment. The result is that partners in distressed relationships often accurately perceive their partners as negative, complaining, or morose. Rather than ruining the mood, expressing positive feeling states to the partner will only increase the chances for a positive interaction (note, however, that initially, positive statements might be received with quizzical looks, as partners accustomed to negative comments may question their authenticity). Thus, clients should be encouraged to express feelings of joy or excitement, letting their partners know when they are having a good time or feeling optimistic. Related communication gestures include expressing genuine appreciation and engaging in verbal and physical signs of affection.

Using Humor

Smiling, joking, and keeping things light when possible and appropriate can cut through tensions and rekindle positive feelings.

Saying What One Is Willing to Do to Help

Here is where negotiation comes in. Too often, one partner in a conflictual relationship expects the other partner to make all the changes. Rather than focusing only on what one's partner should do differently, clients will elicit more cooperation when they first offer to change something themselves, or to help the partner carry out the change they are requesting.

For a one-time request, the negotiation might go something like this, "I'd love to go see that science fiction movie tonight, and I know it's not your first choice. How about if next weekend we plan to see that documentary you've been talking about?" Negotiating a more long-lasting change follows the same format. For example, continuing the above scenario regarding the content of dinners, the vegetable-loving partner might say, "I know you're always tired when you get home and the last thing you want to do is extra shopping. So how about if I stop at the produce market on the way home from work a couple of times a week?" It is hard to imagine an other than affirmative response to this validating and collaborative stance.

In many instances a request will involve something more entrenched than what movie to see or what is served for dinner, such as one's long-standing behavior patterns. In such cases, it is helpful to acknowledge one's own role in the problem. For example, in one case in which a wife felt that her husband was withholding about his work life, she offered to communicate a greater respect for his position and make more supportive comments if he would share more with her. In the past when he had spoken with her about work she had often made disparaging comments about his job or his judgment in dealing with co-workers. When she shared responsibility for the problem and offered to change, he began to disclose more about his job.

Editing

In anger or frustration, many distressed spouses will include negative tag-ons in their comments (e.g., "I was upset because you were late *for the millionth time*; what *the hell* happened?"); these tag-ons become the most salient part of their message. Editing involves eliminating unnecessary and unhelpful content (e.g., "I was upset because you were late; what happened?").

Metacommunicating

Metacommunication is *communicating about the communication* occurring between partners, and can serve to repair faulty interactions by pointing out destructive processes as they are occurring and by showing concern for the outcome of the discussion. Examples of constructive metacommunication statements include "We're getting off track," "I can see we're both starting to get upset," "We seem to be getting stuck," "I'm trying to understand but this is difficult," or "It's not my intention to have this turn into a fight."

Stopping the Action

Related to metacommunication, stopping the action consists of suspending all discussion as it begins to escalate out

of control. Either partner can initiate a "stop-action" by identifying the negative escalation process and trying to redirect
the conversation or suggest taking some time to calm down
(e.g., "Look, we're both getting really upset and this isn't going
anywhere. Can we try to figure out what went wrong here?").

Picking the Appropriate Time and Place

Many positive speaker skills, such as being polite, making
requests, giving compliments, and saying what one is willing
to do to help, will enhance communication at any time. However, everyday positive interactions should be distinguished
from more problem-oriented communication. When discussing problems, partners should schedule a mutually convenient
time and place. Often arguments erupt based not on content
per se but because one partner finds the topic intrusive at a
particular moment or setting. For example, when about to
drop her husband off at work in the morning, it is not the
time for a wife to say, "When you wouldn't make love to me
last night I felt rejected."

Instead, when a partner wants to raise a problem, he or she
should arrange with the spouse a setting where they will have
ample time and minimal distractions. This will be especially
important when the couple adds problem solving to their repertoire, which will take additional time (see Chapter 6). Some
couples build regular "communication sessions" into their
weekly schedules (e.g., Mondays and Thursdays after dinner),
to secure time to focus on the relationship. A regularly sched-

uled time to talk also helps to avoid a negative association to the phrase "we need to talk." Using positive speaker skills and avoiding destructive tactics will help keep these sessions on track and productive. To increase the chances of maintaining a positive tone, couples should remember to say what they are willing to do to help, and use these times to express positive sentiments as well. Finally, couples should place a time limit on these sessions, perhaps thirty minutes, and stick to this limit. When possible, couples might even build in a mutually rewarding activity following the discussion (e.g., getting ice cream or going to a movie). This enforced limit will ensure that problems do not fill an entire day or evening, and may thereby reduce the tendency of reluctant mates to avoid such scheduled interactions. Communication efforts will progress more with shorter sessions that are productive than with drawn-out aversive discussions that diminish couples' motivation to interact.

Listener Skills

Listening

Perhaps most obvious is the strategy of truly listening to one's partner while he or she is speaking. Often partners simply pause while the other is speaking and use the time to formulate a response, rather than paying attention to what the partner is saying. Or partners will interrupt and not even offer a semblance of listening.

Table 5-4
Positive Communication Strategies II:
Listener Skills

---

1. *Listen:* Really listen to your partner. Do not interrupt, or simply wait for your turn to speak.

2. *Paraphrase:* Restate or summarize your partner's statements to ensure correct understanding and show that you are listening: "So you'd like it if I helped put the kids to bed?"

3. *Validate:* Show that you accept and see the logic in your partner's feelings. This does not necessarily mean you agree with your partner, but simply indicates that, given your partner's way of seeing things, the feelings are reasonable. "I can understand how you felt hurt if you thought I was ignoring you."

4. *Make Empathic Statements:* Related to validation, empathy refers to the expression of compassion for your partner's experience. "It must have been really frustrating for you when you got stuck in all that traffic."

5. *Show Interest:* Make eye contact, nod, or use other nonverbal behaviors to encourage your partner to keep speaking and to indicate that you are listening. Verbal indications of listening include utterances such as "yeah," "umm-hmm," and "right" interspersed in the speaker's phrases.

6. *Ask Questions:* Ask your partner questions to get more information, to clarify ("You thought I was quiet at the party, or in the car?"), or to show interest ("Wow! So what happened when you told your boss?").

7. *Check In:* Be sure your partner feels heard before moving on: "I want to tell you what I found out about the plane tickets. Do you feel we've settled this, or did you want to discuss it some more?" Also, check on the intent of the speaker's message before assuming the worst: "It sounds like you're criticizing me . . . . Is that your intention?"

8. *Avoid Being Defensive:* Accept what your partner is telling you as a reflection of his or her experience. Try not to counterattack or withdraw; instead, listen, paraphrase, and look for the validity of your partner's feelings. Instead of "How can I call you from work when you're always on the phone?" say "I realize you're upset that I don't call during the day."

Paraphrasing

As discussed in Chapter 4, in order to practice listening, demonstrate listening to one's partner, and ensure matching of impact with intent, spouses should restate in their own words a reflection of what the speaker has just said. So if Lisa says to Keith, "I'd really like it if you could help me put the kids to bed at night. It's really becoming a handful," Keith might paraphrase as follows: "So you'd like it if I helped put the kids to bed because it's becoming a lot for you?"

Validating

As discussed in Chapter 4, validating conveys respect for and acceptance of a partner's feelings. Couples will need to be clear on the fact that validation does not necessarily indicate agreement, but simply lets a partner know that, given his or her perspective, the feelings expressed make sense to the listener. For example, a wife might say to her husband, "I can understand how you felt hurt if you thought I was ignoring you" even if she does not agree with his contention that she had been ignoring him.

Making Empathic Statements

Related to validation is the ability to empathize with the speaker. The expression of empathy involves accurately surmising, or conveying that one can imagine oneself experiencing, the speaker's emotions in a given situation. Empathy is fairly easy to generate when the topic is external to the relationship: "It must have been really frustrating for you to be stuck in all that traffic." However, it is more difficult to convey (and feel) empathy when the speaker is voicing a gripe with the listener. However, because a show of empathy represents the antithesis of a defensive response, the speaker will more likely soften the tone of the complaint and offer support in return, as in the following alternative exchange between Lisa and Keith:

> *Lisa:* I'd really like it if you could help me put the kids to bed at night. It's really becoming a handful.
> *Keith:* So it's getting to be a bit much for you to put the kids to bed, and you'd like some help?
> *Lisa:* Definitely.
> *Keith:* I guess it really must be a handful for you, with three of them! And I'm just sitting down there watching TV, having a grand old time! That must be frustrating.
> *Lisa:* Well, yeah, but that's okay. I know you deserve your time to relax, too. But maybe if you helped me we could get them ready more quickly and then we could watch TV together.

Note how Keith's empathic remarks lead the conversation in a direction where Lisa is able to validate his need to relax, and make a positive suggestion of time they could spend together without needing to intensify her complaint. Even if making these types of statements feels artificial to partners, clients can try them as experiments and see their partner's reactions.

Showing Interest

A listener conveys interest in numerous ways, including verbal statements, facial expression, and body language. Open, nondefensive indication of interest critically affects the course of a conversation by inviting a partner to continue speaking without needing to escalate to command the listener's attention. Verbal indications of listening include utterances such as "yeah," "umm-hmm," "right," or "I see" interspersed in the speaker's phrases. Follow-up questions also signal interest.

Nonverbal indications of interest include facial expressions and other body language. Facial signs of active listening include eye contact, nods of the head, and a neutral, concerned, or sympathetic expression (as opposed to antagonistic facial cues such as rolling one's eyes, scowling, frowning, or smirking). Body language that conveys interest includes maintaining a position in which the head and body face the speaker, with hands and arms relaxed at one's sides (as opposed to folded across chest, throwing arms up in despair, or turning pages of a magazine), and posture straight or leaning slightly forward.

Asking Questions

It is helpful for the listener to interject questions to get more information or to clarify. If the listener finds it difficult to validate a speaker's viewpoint, it is often because the listener has not yet understood enough about the speaker's perspective. In such a case, instead of dismissing the speaker's feelings, as often happens, the listener should ask the speaker to explain it in more detail until he or she understands (e.g., "I still don't think I understand why you think my father was being rude to you. Could you say more about what he did and what you were experiencing?"). As mentioned above, asking questions is also an effective way of conveying interest: "So what happened when you told your boss?"

Checking In

Listeners may move on to another point or even another conversation without checking to see that the speaker is finished and feels heard. Furthermore, listeners often presume the speaker's intent based on the message's impact, rather than checking in about the intent of the message. Partners can check in with each other before either changing the topic or assuming a particular message ("It sounds like you're criticizing me. . . . Is that your intention?").

Avoiding Defensiveness

Of course, it is easier for a spouse to listen nondefensively if the speaker uses constructive communication strategies. However, it is important to point out to couples that this will not always be in their control, and it is in their best interest to avoid being defensive regardless of the speaker's style of communicating. After all, defensive responses will likely intensify the speaker's urgency, leading to increased anger or demands. It can be helpful for listeners to keep in mind that anger often communicates strong feelings, or desperate attempts to elicit a response. A calm, open stance will be most effective in mollifying the speaker's anger and reducing the hostile tenor of the discussion.

Applying Communication Skills to a Selected Problem

Once the therapist has reviewed the communication handouts with the couple, they can try applying the skills to a selected problem in session. One technique involves asking couples to first spend a few minutes communicating as poorly as possible, using tactics from Tables 5–1 and 5–2. This exercise in exaggeration often takes on a humorous tone, as couples attempt to outdo each other's destructive strategies. The therapist can then discuss the exercise with the partners, asking them to note the particular harmful approaches they employed. The therapist can now ask the couple to engage in a discussion of the same problem, trying in earnest to maximize communication skills by referring to Tables 5–3 and 5–4 and incorporating these strategies.

Session Review and Homework Assignment

The therapist should review the concepts from today's session, asking the partners for their reactions to the material and asking them to identify some of the destructive and helpful communication strategies that are particularly characteristic of their relationship.

For homework, the couple should schedule a communication session to last approximately forty minutes during the upcoming week. The assignment will take place in four parts:

1. The clients should first select an ongoing problem to discuss, using their old, familiar modes of communicating. Ideally, they should select a problem of mild to moderate emotional intensity, to allow for focus on the process of their communication, as opposed to being overwhelmed by the content of their dispute. They should discuss the problem in their typical interaction mode and then stop themselves after ten minutes no matter where they are in the discussion. A kitchen timer or stopwatch will help them limit their discussion to ten minutes.

2. At this point, they should review the communication handouts together for about ten minutes. The partners will then take turns identifying any maladaptive or constructive approaches employed, and discuss how those approaches led the conversation astray or facilitated it. To avoid initiating another argument involving accusation and defensiveness, and to reinforce the notion of mutual responsibility for change, it is helpful to ask each partner to identify only his or her *own* destructive methods while identifying only the *partner's* instances of helpful communication methods (e.g., "I realize I interrupted you at that point—it was good you were able to stay calm and listen. I think that helped it from escalating even further").

3. The couple should then resume the discussion for an additional ten minutes, starting from the beginning and making every effort to avoid destructive tactics and to incorporate positive speaker and listener skills. They should again stop themselves after ten minutes regardless of the point in the conversation; the purpose is to evaluate two different approaches to

communication rather than to resolve the particular conflict at this time. (Stopping after ten minutes also increases the likelihood that the couple will sustain the positive interaction throughout. Since they are beginners, a lengthy conversation will likely deteriorate into their habitual ways of interaction.)

4. After stopping the discussion, the partners should spend the final ten minutes reviewing their second conversation and contrasting it with their first, sharing any reactions and observations about how use of different communication strategies was helpful.

In a variation of this exercise, couples audiotape their two conversations and base their comments on the actual recording of their discussion. Although this procedure holds the advantage of not relying on memory, some couples find using tape recordings substantially more emotionally painful. Clinicians should use their own judgment as to the volatility of a particular couple, or discuss the option with the couple, explaining its risks and benefits, and arrive at collaborative decision about whether to use a tape recorder.

6

Session 5:
Problem-Solving

Setting the Agenda

The agenda for Session 5 will consist of positive tracking, review of homework, a brief review of the week, and an introduction to problem-solving skills. The couple will be asked to select a problem to practice the steps in problem solving. Ideally, this problem will be one of the matters on which the couple has been practicing communication skills, so that they can experience from beginning to end the constructive sequence of raising a problem, hearing and validating each other's perspectives, and solving the problem.

Positive Tracking

By now, the couple expects to be asked about positive relationship events from the previous week. Thus, in this and ensuing sessions, it is common for couples to come in prepared with an event to report. This week's comments may concern improved communication, or may relate to the lists of caring gestures. Unless the couple regularly reports that the partner has been engaging in caring gestures, the therapist should, from time to time, query about the lists the partners generated. Are they referring to their lists and engaging in the specified behaviors? Are there factors that are interfering? Difficulty in continuing the ongoing exchange of caring gestures, like any form of noncompliance, merits a brief functional analysis to determine the eliciting and maintaining factors. Even if couples report an improvement in their relationship, they should continue to engage in caring gestures.

Review of Homework

For homework, the partners were asked first to attempt discussing a problem for ten minutes, relying on their usual ways of communicating. They were asked to then review the communication handouts and identify maladaptive approaches jeopardizing their communication along with constructive approaches facilitating it. In the spirit of collaboration, they were specifically asked to focus on *their own* maladaptive methods while pointing out *their partner's* positive approaches. Finally, they were to review the communication handouts and attempt another ten-minute discussion of the same problem using improved communication skills.

The therapist should inquire about each step of this process. Regardless of the outcome, the exercise should provide ample opportunity for learning, as the clients highlight their successes, pinpoint their difficulties, and analyze how their second communication attempt differed from their first. It will also be helpful to ask couples to identify strategies they will want to maintain in their repertoire as well as areas of their communication that still need work.

INTRODUCTION TO PROBLEM-SOLVING

Problem-solving involves a series of steps, beginning with establishing a collaborative set, defining the problem, brainstorming a range of solutions, devising a particular solution, and evaluating and revising the solution. The following sections elaborate upon these steps.

Establishing a Collaborative Set

Establishing a collaborative set moves couples from viewing the problem as a struggle between the husband (Team 1) and the wife (Team 2), to viewing it as a struggle between the husband–wife pair (Team 1) and the problem (Team 2). That is, as described by Jacobson and Margolin (1979), they will need to devote mutual efforts toward addressing a problem for which they come to assign mutual responsibility, rather than adhering to a partner-blaming stance. The better part of this shift will occur as a result of an overall increase in positive relationship behaviors and successful communication about the specific problem. That is, acceptance and understanding gleaned from constructive speaking and listening strategies tend to dissipate anger and blame. Couples who have communicated well about an area of disagreement are often left with the feeling, "Okay, so we're not mad anymore, but we still both want our way, so what do we do now?" This is exactly where we want the partners to be when they begin problem-solving. In fact, if the couple still harbors anger, they probably did not communicate thoroughly enough.

The therapist can enhance the clients' willingness to work conjointly on their problems by pointing out the personal gains in adhering to this approach: they will get further in the problem-solving process if they can, at the very least, agree to behave as if they share responsibility for relationship conflicts. Again, once both spouses have listened to each other's view on the matter, and have refrained from attacks or judgments, they should find it easier to see the problem as a relatively benign difference between them rather than as a reflection of one partner's unreasonable or malicious stance. The therapist can assist with this process by offering helpful cognitions the couple might substitute for noncollaborative thoughts, such as replacing the thought "She's just being pigheaded" with "This issue is really important to her. We're going to have to work extra hard together to tackle this one." It is critical that couples not begin problem solving while they are feeling intensely emotional about a topic; this would signal a need for more time on the expression of feelings, with paraphrasing and validation.[1] Strong negative emotional states will reduce partners' willingness to collaborate and their ability to think rationally about the problem.

Once partners can agree to fight the problem rather than each other, the therapist can provide them with the following rationale for learning problem-solving skills. Disagreement is a normal part of relationships; it would be impossible for two people to live together intimately and not differ in perspectives or needs. What differentiates happy from distressed marriages is *not the presence of problems but the ways couples handle them*. Good communication is the first step toward positive resolution of problems; the second step involves a progression of phases in developing and evaluating solutions. Today's session will outline these phases.

---

1. Of course, intense emotions can impede communication efforts as well; if this occurs, the couple should initiate a "stop-action."

Defining the Problem

Carefully defining the problem is a central aspect of problem-solving. It involves the translation of two differing (and
valid) points of view into a specific problem statement. The
couple must learn to incorporate each partner's viewpoint into
a problem statement free of implied blame or judgment. Note
that in this process clients may decide that solving the problem is not the priority—they simply want to air their feelings
about it. For example, a wife may wish to vent about a difficult interaction she had with a colleague, and may feel dissatisfied by her husband's attempt to problem-solve rather than
simply listen. Therefore, partners will need to clarify whether
they see the problem as one in need of solution or simply validation. In selecting a problem for initial in-session practice, it
is useful to choose one of moderate emotional intensity, as opposed to a hot topic that will elicit strong emotions that may
interfere with the acquisition of skills involved in problem-solving. Ideally, the therapist will help the couple select a topic
about which they have been successfully communicating over
the most recent sessions.

To illustrate the problem definition phase, consider the example of Mike and Jenny, a young couple who have been quar-
reling over Mike's mother since the beginning of their recent
marriage. Jenny had felt incessantly chided by her mother-in-
law, and each visit by Mike's parents was followed by an
argument between Jenny and Mike. Jenny raged at her mother-
in-law's subtly disapproving comments about her housekeep-
ing and cooking and Mike's lack of protectiveness (he never

confronted his mother, held Jenny equally responsible for the interaction, and even went off with his father at times, leaving Jenny alone with his mother). Mike countered that Jenny exacerbated the situation by dwelling on the negatives, failing to consider his mother's perspective, thinly veiling her anger in the presence of his mother, and attacking him as though he were responsible for his mother's behavior. When they entered therapy, their arguments had escalated to the point of Jenny denouncing Mike as "weak-willed," "passive," and "ineffectual," and Mike accusing Jenny of being "difficult," "impossible," and "an instigator."

Through enhanced speaker and listener skills, the couple came to realize that Jenny felt hurt and deserted when Mike did not defend her against his mother's critical comments and when he left her alone with his mother, despite knowing of her extreme discomfort with the relationship. Furthermore, although basically confident about her role, Jenny had developed a budding fear that Mike might begin to echo his mother's sentiments about her apparent inadequacies. This was especially frustrating and disheartening, as she had been making a conscious effort to devote time to the relationship and their home to start the marriage off on the right foot. Finally, she felt angry and alone when Mike blamed *her* for stirring up trouble and failed to acknowledge her efforts to make things go well. Mike, on the other hand, felt powerless and torn, caught in the middle of the conflict between Jenny and his mother. Treating his mother with respect meant neglecting Jenny's feelings, and protecting Jenny meant hurting or distancing his mother. He felt disappointed that things were turning out this way, saddened that they were not experiencing the happy family life he had envisioned, and stuck in not knowing how to improve the situation. He also felt angry and found it hurtful that Jenny was sharply critical of his mother, and was, as he saw it, putting him in the position of having to choose between them.

After Jenny and Mike both felt their positions were heard and validated, they were ready for problem-solving. Expressed in these ways, each perspective made sense to both of them, and their anger and defensiveness diminished. They had both reached the point of empathizing with the other's position, were no longer focused on blaming, and were considerably calmer, yet did not know what to do to address the situation.

In helping a couple define the problem, the therapist needs to remember the importance of keeping the statement neutral vis-à-vis blame or judgment of one partner. In Mike and Jenny's case, the problem was defined in the following way: "We would like to reduce the tension level between Jenny and Mike's mother during her visits, and prevent the arguments between Jenny and Mike after every visit." Second, consistent with all communication in CBMT, *the problem should be worded specifically*. It would be very difficult to work with a vaguely worded problem such as "Things have to get better when it comes to Mike's mother and Jenny." What is meant by "better"? Better in what situations? How would we know if we reached that goal? Here, the partners started with the specified goals of reducing tension during Mike's mother's visits to the house, and on stopping their predictable fights after every visit. Third, the goal should be limited in scope. Rather than attempting to solve all aspects of a problem at once, setting a narrow goal increases the chances of arriving at a workable plan. For Mike and Jenny, after solving the problems of tension over Mike's mother's visits and fighting after each visit, they can take the next step, if it is still needed, of working on other aspects of the problems between Mike's mother and Jenny. Sometimes, however, a narrow solution generalizes to the broader problem. For example, a reduction in tension in Mike's mother's visits may begin to improve Jenny's relationship with her in general and may reduce Mike's feelings of conflicted loyalty.

Once the problem is defined, the couple or therapist should write it down at the top of a sheet of paper. The next step will be to develop a list of possible solutions, which will be written underneath the problem statement.

Brainstorming Solutions

The next stage of problem-solving allows both partners to brainstorm suggestions for handling the defined problem. At this point, they should place virtually no constraints on their proposed solutions, but should be encouraged by the therapist to list any solution that comes to mind.

Several guidelines will increase the effectiveness of the brainstorming phase. First, partners should avoid hostile suggestions such as, "You could try growing up; that might work!" Such negative comments indicate a need for additional communication about the problem. Second, the couple should refrain from critiquing solutions; at this stage anything is fair game. The therapist should *not* allow partners to make inhibiting comments such as "That'll never work" or "Come on—you're not taking this seriously." The idea is to promote flexible and creative problem-solving while breaking the ineffective and often rigid patterns of responding that the couple adhered to previously. Brainstorming can actually provide some comic relief in session, as partners suggest solutions that are absurd or outlandish. Humorous or irreverent comments are allowed and even encouraged, as long as they are, again, not tinged with hostility. Third, both partners should participate in brainstorming solutions. Often one partner plays the role of "naysayer"; partners should both be encouraged to relax, say anything that comes to mind, and even have fun with the task.

If in their initial attempt the couple has difficulty generating many solutions, the therapist might model options. Even if few agreeable solutions emerge, the couple can be urged to think more flexibly about the problem by considering solutions such as one partner relinquishing a position now in return for getting his way next time, or both partners agreeing to appease neither.

Each suggestion should be written down and numbered. The partners should continue until they've written approximately ten to fifteen suggestions. Table 6–1 illustrates the list Mike and Jenny arrived at in brainstorming solutions for preventing fights following Mike's mother's visits.

Table 6–1
Problem-Solving Worksheet: Brainstorming Phase

Couple: Jenny and Mike   Date: August 23

PROBLEM DEFINITION: We would like to reduce the tension level between Jenny and Mike's mother during her visits, and prevent the arguments between Jenny and Mike after every visit.

POSSIBLE SOLUTIONS:

1. Mike and Jenny will cease all contact with Mike's parents.
2. Jenny will leave the house each time Mike's parents come over.
3. Mike will physically separate Jenny from his mother during any brawls.
4. Jenny will pay a compliment to Mike's mother at the beginning of the visit to set a positive tone.
5. Mike will praise Jenny's efforts after a visit rather than faulting her for the problems.
6. Mike will gently change the topic if his mother brings up sensitive issues.
7. Jenny will try to notice positive behaviors of Mike's mother during a visit, and point them out to Mike afterwards.
8. Only Mike's father will be allowed in the home.
9. Mike will help engineer activities so that he does not go off with his father and leave Jenny alone with his mother.
10. Mike will politely but firmly come to Jenny's defense if his mother makes unreasonable accusations or criticisms.
11. Mike will make more eye contact and give more smiles and nods to Jenny during visits to increase her sense of his support.
12. Jenny will not make threats about Mike choosing between her and his mother.
13. Mike will take Jenny to the Caribbean after each visit to reward her.

Devising Solutions

Once a list of possible solutions is generated, the couple will be ready to narrow the list. Together, the partners will go through each solution and cross out any that both agree are impractical for any reason. The therapist should encourage partners to keep an open mind, since critical or judgmental remarks during this process can undermine the couple's positive momentum in working together.

The couple should then go through the list a second time, evaluating any retained solutions. They can now discuss the remaining items in terms of costs and benefits to each partner and relevance to solving the problem. Solutions making it to the "final cut" will be agreeable to both partners. After further discussion and evaluation, the partners should cross out any remaining unworkable solutions. Table 6–2 contains

---

Table 6–2
Problem-Solving Worksheet: Narrowed Solution List

Couple: Jenny and Mike   Date: August 23

PROBLEM DEFINITION: We would like to reduce the tension level between Jenny and Mike's mother during her visits, and prevent the arguments between Jenny and Mike after every visit.

POSSIBLE SOLUTIONS:

4. Jenny will pay a compliment to Mike's mother at the beginning of the visit to set a positive tone.
5. Mike will praise Jenny's efforts after a visit rather than faulting her for the problems.
6. Mike will gently change the topic if his mother brings up sensitive issues.
7. Jenny will try to notice positive behaviors of Mike's mother during a visit, and point them out to Mike afterwards.
9. Mike will help engineer activities so that he does not go off with his father and leave Jenny alone with his mother.
10. Mike will politely but firmly come to Jenny's defense if his mother makes unreasonable accusations or criticisms.
11. Mike will make more eye contact and give more smiles and nods to Jenny during visits to increase her sense of his support.
12. Jenny will not make threats about Mike choosing between her and his mother.

---

the solutions Mike and Jenny retained after narrowing their list.

After this step, the few remaining solutions will be those that neither partner has eliminated, and so will likely be useful in formulating an actual solution to the problem. The proposed solution can consist of either a single solution or a combination of suggestions. The couple must agree on which solutions to incorporate, and then together devise a solution worded to be *specific* and comprised of *relatively equivalent costs and benefits for each partner*. The therapist will of course coach substantially in this first effort. After carefully wording a specific and balanced solution, each partner signs and dates the problem-solving sheet. This formalizes the proposal into a contract.

Table 6–3 illustrates the proposed solution Mike and Jenny derived from their various brainstormed solutions. Note that their solution collapses several individual suggestions into a fairly detailed plan. It is also possible to develop a shorter solution. The nature of the proposed solution will depend on the complexity of the problem and the feasibility of the brainstormed solutions.

Evaluating and Revising the Solution

Despite the effort and teamwork that goes into devising a problem solution, a written solution does not guarantee effectiveness. The therapist asks the couple simply to agree to follow the contracted solution at the next opportunity and suspend judgment until then. Upon implementing the proposed solution, the couple can evaluate it by discussing whether it

---

Table 6–3
Problem-Solving Worksheet: Solution Phase

Couple: Jenny and Mike   Date: August 23

PROBLEM DEFINITION: We would like to reduce the tension level between Jenny and Mike's mother during her visits, and prevent the arguments between Jenny and Mike after every visit.

PROPOSED SOLUTION: Jenny will compliment Mike's mother within the first five minutes of the next visit, to establish a positive tone. During the visit, Mike will avoid leaving Jenny alone with his mother and will change the topic if it involves any criticism of Jenny. Mike will also pay more attention to Jenny during visits, by sitting in close proximity to her, demonstrating physical affection (such as holding hands), and by twice during the evening privately asking her how things are going for her. Afterwards, Mike will praise Jenny's efforts, and Jenny will make the effort to give a balanced evaluation of how the evening went, pointing out positives and not threatening Mike.

Jenny	8/23	Michael	8/23
Signature	Date	Signature	Date

---

helped, or whether parts were helpful and parts were not. Still collaborating, the partners can then repeat the brainstorming process and revise their solution. They should then formalize the revised solution and continue the process of implementing, evaluating, and revising it until they are both satisfied with the outcome.

HANDLING DIFFICULTY IN PROBLEM-SOLVING

Identifying Hidden Agendas

At times the therapist will encounter a situation in which a couple seems to communicate repetitiously about a series of problems but cannot settle on one problem definition. Or a couple effectively generates and implements solutions, solving the apparent problem, yet one or both partners remain vaguely dissatisfied. Or the issue will appear to be settled, but in the ensuing weeks various forms of the problem arise repeatedly. In such instances the couple or a partner may be harboring a hidden agenda or an unspoken (and perhaps not consciously articulated) problem. Hidden agendas often reflect underlying distress-related themes such as questions of love and caring, power differentials, intimacy and autonomy, or respect. These below-the-surface issues, while not directly expressed, may underlie a couple's inability to pinpoint a satisfying solution.

Clients may not be aware of the hidden agendas that subvert their communication and problem-solving efforts. Alternatively, they may recognize these underlying issues, yet feel hesitant to voice them for fear of hurting the partner, damaging the relationship, or appearing vulnerable. The therapist can assess for hidden agendas by pointing out signs of unresolved communication attempts and inquiring about additional, undisclosed sentiments. Partners can then be urged to discuss hidden feelings using constructive communication skills, since continuing to veil them will only lead the couple to a dead end.

The following dialogue illustrates a wife's hidden agenda of feeling unloved, which is stalling the couple's ability to move beyond the apparently solved problem of her husband's business trip:

Therapist: So, let's take a look at your proposed solution for how you will manage with the new baby when Carl is away.

Carl: We've got the whole thing worked out. My mother will come three days to help out, Debbie's sister will come for two, and that will leave Debbie with only two days on her own. I'll keep my beeper so Debbie can page me in an emergency, and I'll call every night to check in.

Therapist: (to Debbie) And this is all agreeable to you?

Debbie: (shrugs) Yes, it's fine. We'll manage fine on our own.

Carl: What do you mean "on your own"? You'll have help almost every day!

Debbie: (slightly annoyed) You know what I mean. Look, I said the plan is fine. It's the only thing that makes sense.

Therapist: Did you two come up with this plan together and limit the proposed solutions to ones you both felt comfortable with?

Carl: Yeah, we did. Debbie had equal say and even came up with the idea of asking her sister to come. And she was fine with it before. So I don't know why she has an attitude now.

Debbie: I also said you could tell your boss you shouldn't be going away with a three-week-old baby. But you rejected that one.

Carl: Oh, here we go back to that again. You know the business world doesn't work that way! Look, how many times have we been over this?

Debbie and Carl might develop several workable solutions to her handling the new baby on her own when he travels on business, but they will ultimately keep spinning their wheels because of Debbie's ambivalence about his going away. On the one hand, she understands the importance of this trip to his career. However, there is also a hidden agenda: Carl's willingness to go away so soon after their baby's birth confirms Debbie's core belief that he does not care enough about her, and, by extension, their child. Since this conclusion feels so overwhelmingly hurtful and frightening to her, it is easier for her to simply push it to the back of her mind and deal with the problem at hand, that of securing help with caring for the child in his absence. She therefore has cooperated with the problem-solving process but maintains her feelings of hurt and abandonment, which will persistently break through the surface as Carl and Debbie discuss the issue. Since the hidden agenda is not likely to simply dissolve, the therapist would be most helpful here by observing the problem-solving impasse, noting the possible presence of a hidden agenda, and encouraging the couple to communicate openly and constructively about it. Speaking to one or both partners alone may facilitate revelation of a hidden agenda when the therapist senses reluctance to examine the issue in the presence of the other partner. In the example of Debbie and Carl, the therapist might note the possibility of a hidden agenda as follows:

Therapist: Let's step back a minute and look at what's happening here. Although the two of you worked out this problem together, Carl, you are picking up that Debbie still has some feelings about it. Debbie, it seems as though you are not fully comfortable with the agreement you two came up with.

Debbie: No, I'm not entirely comfortable with it.

Carl: I don't understand her. I thought we communicated about this, and I thought we were in agreement about the best way to handle the situation.

Debbie: We were, but for some reason it's still not sitting right with me.

Therapist: That's okay, Debbie; sometimes what feels like the right decision at one time feels wrong later on. Or it doesn't feel quite right at the time, but we feel our objections are unjustified and just agree to what we think we should do. What we need to figure out is what feels uncomfortable about it for you now. You were saying that you'd suggested Carl tell his boss that he shouldn't be going on this trip at all with a three-week-old baby.

Debbie: No, no, it's fine. He's right. He can't change his plans.

Therapist: Maybe Carl *can't* change his plans, but that doesn't mean you wouldn't *like* him to be able to change them. The fact that he's going seems to be troubling you, yet you seem hesitant to talk about this; it seems like you bring it up and then back off, but then it comes up again.

Carl: Exactly.

Therapist: I'm wondering if perhaps there are some other feelings you're having about it that may be hard for you to talk about.

Debbie: No, listen, it doesn't matter. I don't want to . . .

Carl: *(gently)* No, Deb, go ahead. It's okay.

Therapist: That was nice, Carl. You changed to a softer tone of voice, and that sounded supportive. Debbie, are you able to share what you're experiencing?

Debbie: Well, all right. I guess it's just that rationally, I understand that he has to go for his job. But emotionally, I can't really understand why he's *willing* to go. If it were my job, I couldn't imagine going and leaving my brand new baby, no matter what the consequences. I mean, what are his priorities?

The therapist, with relative ease, has now begun to uncover the hidden agenda. From this point on, the therapist would continue to pursue the hidden agenda, conveying to Debbie that her feelings are acceptable and encouraging both partners to use their communication skills to discuss them. Note that the therapist normalized Debbie's ambivalence about the problem solution, and reinforced Carl immediately for supporting Debbie. This facilitated Debbie's willingness to bring up the topic she had previously been avoiding.

Contingency Contracts

At times, problem resolution will not be attained easily, and no hidden agenda will emerge. Instead, despite their best efforts at communication, problem definition, and brainstorming solutions, some clients may be too disengaged, mistrustful, or otherwise unmotivated to noncontingently invest in the relationship. This disinclination might become apparent during the generation of solutions or after the proposed solution is implemented (that is, in the next session). "Contingency contracting," initiated by the work of Lederer and Jackson (1968), Rappaport and Harrell (1972), Stuart (1969), and Weiss and colleagues (1974), although an optional component of CBMT (Jacobson and Margolin 1979), is a form of problem-solving that employs contingencies to motivate adherence to a behavior change plan. They are used to provide temporary reinforcers for behavior change efforts until natural environmental contingencies take over to maintain the changes. Unlike contracts developed during the solution phase of the problem-solving procedure outlined above, these contracts build in clauses explicitly stating the contingencies for compliance or noncompliance with the solution. As such, contingency contracts "guarantee" a return on partners' behavioral investments, providing additional motivation and support for collaboration. Thus, when indicated, they can provide a needed jump-start to a cycle of positive reciprocity. The following sections detail the two types of contracts used in CBMT: good-faith contracts and quid pro quo contracts.

Good-Faith Contracts

Good-faith contracts address one partner's requested behavior change at a time, providing contingencies for the person changing the behavior that are not dependent on the partner's behavior. For example, Len would like his wife, Val, to spend more time accompanying him to movies, leisure activities, social events, or family-centered activities on weekends. Val, a freelance writer, likes to use one full weekend day to catch up on work, since her weekdays are often consumed by child-care responsibilities. Val's increased weekend time with Len would be Len's target desired behavior change. Val may, in addition, wish that Len would take a more active role in caretaking activities for the children, rather than spending most of his time at home engaged in playful activities with them. Len's increased responsibility for child care would be Val's target desired behavior change. Good-faith contracts would involve writing parallel agreements in which Val and Len were both rewarded for engaging in their partner's desired behavior change target, but would *not* make each partner's desired change contingent on the other's. Obviously, rewards will nevertheless need to be reinforcing enough to provide incentive for change. Len and Val's parallel contracts might be worded as illustrated in Table 6–4.

Table 6–4
Example of Parallel Good–Faith Contracts

Val agrees to limit her weekend writing to no more than three hours a weekend, on a Saturday or Sunday morning, stopping by noon. In addition, she will spend at least eight hours over the weekend (defined as Saturday waking time to Sunday bedtime) engaged in recreational activities with her husband. The children may be involved in some or all of these activities, as mutually decided by Len and Val. On weekends in which Val follows this plan, Len will in return make child-care arrangements (i.e., calling, scheduling, and handling payment) for a full weekday of Val's choosing, with a caretaker approved by Val.

Signed: _____   _____   _____
                (Val)   (Len)   (Therapist)

Table 6–4, continued:

Len agrees to do at least one activity (other than playing) of his choice with the children each weekday evening, among the following: checking and changing diapers, feeding them, giving them a bath, or putting on their nightclothes and reading a story before bed. In the mornings following evenings when Len has abided by this agreement, Val will wake up with Len and prepare breakfast for him before work.

Signed: _____   _____   _____
                    (Val)   (Len)   (Therapist)

Here, Len provides a reward for Val contingent on her living up to her part of the agreement; Val provides the same for Len. However, each contract focuses only on one partner's target behavior change; the targets are not interdependent. Len's caretaking activities with the children will not buy him Val's time on the weekend, nor will Val's limiting her writing time buy her Len's increased caretaking with the children— hence the term "good faith."

In the above examples, the contracts were worded specifically, to avoid misinterpretation. For example, had Val simply agreed to "decrease her weekend writing time," the couple may have ended up later disputing the amount of time and times of day she worked. The more precise the conditions of a contract, the more likely it will serve its purpose of forging a settlement while averting conflict.

Quid Pro Quo Contracts

The quid pro quo contract differs from the good-faith contract in that the contingencies involve both partners' desired target behavior changes rather than independent rewards. Each partner engages in the agreed-upon behaviors when and only when the other partner lives up to the contract. For example, Len's desire for Val to work less on weekends would be made directly related to Val's desire that Len engage in more child-care activities. Their quid pro quo contract might look like the example in Table 6–5.

Table 6–5
Example of Quid Pro Quo Contract

Val agrees to limit her weekend writing to no more than three hours a weekend, on a Saturday or Sunday morning, stopping by noon. In addition, she will spend at least eight hours over the weekend (defined as Saturday waking time to Sunday bedtime) engaged in recreational activities with her husband. The children may be involved in some or all of these activities, as mutually decided by Len and Val.

On weekends in which Val follows this plan, Len will in return do at least one activity (other than playing) of his choice with the children each weekday evening, among the following: checking and changing diapers, feeding them, giving them a bath, or putting on their nightclothes and reading a story before bed.

If Val does not limit her weekend work as agreed, Len will not engage in child-care activities during the following week's evenings. However, he will resume these activities in the next week following Val's return to the agreement.

If Len does not engage in a caretaking activity with the children each night of the week, Val will spend a full day of the following weekend working. However, she will return to her side of the agreement once Len has resumed a week's worth of child caretaking activities.

Signed: _____ _____ _____
                (Val)   (Len)   (Therapist)

Choosing the Type of Contract

As illustrated in Table 6–5, quid pro quo contracts target

reciprocal agreements for behavior change, so that each partner's efforts directly influence the payback from the other partner. A risk, of course, is the potential breakdown of the chain of reciprocity when one partner does not follow through (unlike good-faith contracts, in which the breakdown of one contract will not necessarily affect the parallel contract). The quid pro quo contract is thus best written to include clear conditions for resuming the agreement as written. When adhered to, however, such agreements can promote a new system of interactions that greatly satisfy both partners and develop a momentum of their own. Although this method of contingency contracting emphasizes positive reciprocity in its focus on mutual rewards, some might regard the interdependent contingencies as loosely veiled threats. Thus, if misconstrued, quid pro quo agreements risk encouraging a mode of aversive control of the type CBMT so strongly attempts to abolish. Good-faith contracts are less susceptible to such interpretation. Still, quid pro quo contracting can help to break the inertia when problem solving reaches a stalemate.

As argued by Jacobson and Margolin (1979), quid pro quo contracts offer the advantage over good-faith contracts that the rewards have affirmed reinforcement value, consisting of behaviors targeted for change by each partner. Furthermore, they are more efficient than good-faith contracts, since reinforcers have already been spelled out and only one contract is made in the place of two.

However, because the quid pro quo contract sets in motion a chain of behavior exchanges, one partner must be willing to begin the chain by being the first to change his or her

behavior. For severely discordant couples, where neither partner agrees to go first, parallel good-faith contracts may be initiated at the same time. Moreover, quid pro quo contracts
require comparable levels of behavior change desired by each
partner to form balanced agreements. If partners do not request equitable changes in behavior, good-faith contracts may
be most appropriate.

Final Comment on Contracts

The use of contracts may seem to some to be overly formal, structured, or artificial. It is helpful to note that, while
not relying on written agreements, nondistressed couples make
similar arrangements routinely, explicitly or implicitly. For example, in many satisfactory marriages, couples have worked
out systems of dividing household chores, rotating child-care
responsibilities to allow one partner time off, alternating
choices of leisure-time activities, compensating a partner for
a sacrifice, and so forth. We would think nothing of hearing
one spouse say to another, "If you drive now, I'll drive the
rest of the trip after we stop for dinner." In conflictual marriages, these understandings have somehow gone awry, with
partners not contributing equitably or in a way that satisfies
both partners. Here, as with other components of CBMT,
contracting provides a structure to encourage functioning in
a way that nondistressed couples do naturally, in this case by
building in mutual reinforcements. Later, as marital satisfaction improves, this type of contracting will become automatic,
and may not even be noticed by the couple.

It should be noted that contingency contracting contrasts with the noncontingent relationship investment stance encouraged throughout much of CBMT. Thus, it is best viewed as a strategy to follow when routine communication and problem-solving procedures fail to produce the desired change and hidden agendas do not seem to be causing the impasse. When hidden agendas do emerge, additional communication with the aim of validation and understanding is needed before redefining the problem and developing solutions. When first-line means of problem resolution prove sufficient, contingency contracts will be unnecessary.

Session Review and Homework Assignment

To review the session, the therapist should ask the clients to recite the steps involved in problem solving, praising them for correct responses and coaching them where needed. It can also be helpful to test the couple's knowledge with questions such as, "What might you do if you find yourselves very angry with each other during the brainstorming phase?" or "What are some important characteristics your solution should have?" Questions are especially helpful if they target material the partners raised in session; the therapist can thus check on mastery of the material before sending them home to practice.

The homework assignment for this session will involve two parts:

1. The couple will implement the proposed solution to the problem addressed in session and evaluate the outcome. This

will provide them with experience executing a collaboratively derived solution and evaluating its effectiveness. They should be prepared to discuss the outcome from the perspective of both partners. Should the proposed solution present difficulties, they should revise the proposal for a solution, including both partners' input, based on troubleshooting difficulties with the attempted solution.

Note that in order to complete this homework, the partners must have addressed a problem they expect to encounter within the next week, such as discussing finances or handling the children. The therapist should guide them in their problem selection with this in mind, encouraging work with an ongoing problem[2] (e.g., if the problem involves Thanksgiving dinner arrangements and the discussion in therapy takes place in the week following Thanksgiving, implementing a new solution will not make a practical homework assignment). If the couple has selected a problem the resolution of which cannot be attempted in the following week, then the assignment should include only Part 2.

2. The second part of the homework assignment will require the couple to set aside a convenient block of time lasting between forty-five minutes and an hour (or two blocks of time lasting approximately one-half hour each). To get addi-

---

2. This focus on present problems will be helpful in all areas of therapy. For acquisition and maintenance of new skills, the partners will benefit more by applying them to real, ongoing conflicts rather than discussing only how they *might* apply them to hypothetical or future scenarios.

tional practice with the process of problem solving, the couple should select another conflict area (again, it is best to select a conflict of moderate severity, balancing the ability to stay focused on the problem-solving process with effective generalization), communicate about the issue to the point of arriving at a clear problem definition, brainstorm solutions, and develop a contract detailing a solution. The problem definition, list of solutions, and contract should all be in writing and brought to the next session. If contingency contracting has been introduced in the session, the couple may elect to develop a good-faith or quid pro quo contract for the solution.

7

Session 6:
Marital Cognitions:
Automatic Thoughts
and
Cognitive Distortions

Setting the Agenda

After positive tracking, problem-solving homework, and a review of the week are completed, the focus will turn to dysfunctional relationship-focused cognitions. The couple will learn to identify automatic thoughts and become familiar with the types of cognitions that drive them. They will also study the cognitive distortions that affect the way people process information relevant to their relationships. Finally, they will be instructed on the use of the Relationship Thought Record (RTR), a modification of Beck and colleagues' Daily Record of Dysfunctional Thoughts ([1979]; cf. Baucom and Epstein [1990] and Dattilio and Padesky [1990]) to record and challenge their thoughts.

Positive Tracking

After the agenda is set, proceed with positive tracking, as described in previous chapters.

Review of Homework

The therapist can now review with the clients (1) their attempt to implement a problem solution derived in the previous session, and (2) their attempt to complete the steps of a problem-solving discussion on their own.

For the first part of the assignment, the partners will have attempted to solve and evaluate the solution for an imminent or ongoing problem (if they were not able to select an imminent or ongoing problem at the end of the last session, the therapist should move to reviewing the second part of the assignment). If the clients had the opportunity to implement their solution, the therapist should evaluate its success with them while remembering to stress that *this evaluation is part of the problem-solving process*. They need not have concluded that problem solving failed if their solution fell short of expectations; instead they should have simply progressed to the next step of determining any helpful aspects of their solution, making adjustments in their proposed solution (repeating the brainstorming phase, if necessary), and then testing their revised plan. If the solution did pose problems for the couple, ask if they worked together to troubleshoot the problems and revise the agreement accordingly. If not, assess the reasons for this. Did they become discouraged? Did their communication break down when they were evaluating the insufficient solution? Did they understand that evaluating and revising the solution are normal parts of the problem-solving process?

For the second part of the assignment, the couple will have selected another conflict area during the week and implemented communication and problem-solving skills to define the problem, brainstorm solutions, and devise a contract. The therapist should review the written material the couple brings to session, asking the couple about any difficulties, and also finding out which parts of the process worked well. If the therapist notices areas in need of improvement in the written assignment, he or she might point these out or ask the clients if they can critique their own work (e.g., "It's great that you were able to empathize with each other and let go of blaming in approaching this problem. But can you think of a potential difficulty with the problem definition as you've written it here?"). Remember that whenever reviewing assignments (or in-session practice material), it is most helpful to provide balanced feedback, pointing out what is done well in addition to what needs improvement. This both reinforces couples for progress and models effective communication.

COGNITIONS AND RELATIONSHIP DISTRESS

From the perspective of CBMT, much of marital distress derives from real, displeasing events and interactions in the relationship. However, the focus on cognitions in CBMT stems from the premise that a substantial portion of marital distress arises from erroneous inferences based on ambiguous or inaccurate information and an absence of proper distinctions between beliefs and reality. Distortions in experience are then supported by a set of information processing errors, leading to a vicious cycle of apparently substantiated distorted beliefs. These distortions can be hard to detect, since individuals normally accept their own sense of reality as factual, and can be hard to change, since the distortions tend to maintain themselves and reflect long-standing patterns of thinking. The next two sessions will help couples to determine those aspects of their relationship distress that result from cognitive distortions and to incorporate alternative ways of viewing marital events.

Detecting the Influence of Cognitions

Because cognitions are covert, the therapist will sometimes have to do some detective work (and teach the couple to do the same) to discover their presence as they contribute to problematic marital interactions and inhabit the mental life of the relationship. On the other hand, couples at times will bare glaringly influential cognitions through their interactions and statements in therapy. Note that while prior sessions have not included any formal didactic presentation on cognitions, the therapist can briefly assess or address cognitions as they emerge throughout therapy. This can be accomplished in subtle ways without losing the major focus of the session agenda. For example, simple therapist probes, such as "Can you think of other possible reasons she may have said that?" can be asked at any time and can set the stage for later actively challenging cognitions. In fact, when the therapist notices a partner discounting a gesture made by the other partner as "due to the therapist" or "done for his own selfish reasons," the therapist is witnessing a distortion in the interpretation of a partner's behavior that helps to maintain a negative relationship climate. In addition, other points of intervention will directly or indirectly target a couple's cognitions. For example, positive tracking helps break the pattern of selective attention to negative events, communication training increases empathic listening and can transform a partner's attributions or assumptions about a problematic spouse behavior, and increased caring gestures or success with problem-solving can alter expectancies for improvement in the relationship. By the time the couple reaches this phase of treatment, the therapist will have already formed hypotheses about the cognitions affecting the couple's interactions, and should find it relatively easy to draw examples from previous session material for illustrative purposes.

Rationale

A rationale for incorporating a focus on cognitions with the work on behavior change may be conveyed to the couple as follows:

1. The marital relationship is affected not only by outward behaviors and events but also by how each partner appraises those behaviors and events.
2. Partners' interpretations of events may not always reflect reality.
3. People tend to hold their interpretations of events as objective truths, rather than subjective impressions subject to distortion. Thus, they rarely check out the evidence behind their interpretations.
4. Cognitions strongly affect emotional and behavioral reactions in the marital relationship. Similarly, negative emotions can lead to distorted cognitions, thus forming a vicious cycle. Detecting inaccurate cognitions can help curb distressing emotional experiences and behaviors harmful to the relationship.
5. Therapy will teach couples to collect evidence for their positions or interpretations, and to help differentiate those that are reasonable from those that are less reasonable.

Thought Monitoring

After the therapist provides the rationale for working with cognitions, he or she can introduce clients to the notion of learning to identify their own stream-of-consciousness cognitions, or *automatic thoughts*. It is through becoming more aware of their automatic thoughts that clients will be able to begin examining them. Automatic thoughts occur spontaneously and in reaction to events that can be either external, such as a spouse's remark, or internal, such as a realization.[1] Although often occurring outside of awareness, automatic thoughts become accessible with practice, and are generally testable and flexible. People can usually begin to gain awareness of their automatic thoughts with promptings such as "What were you just thinking?" or "What were the first couple of thoughts that came into your mind after she said that?" or through coaching to simply notice the thoughts that are going through their minds in a given moment. When initially working with clients to recognize their automatic thoughts, it is helpful for them to report the thoughts that occur after a particularly salient event where they notice a pronounced shift in their mood or behavior (e.g., beginning to raise their voice with a partner). Automatic thoughts typically flood our minds at such times, so they should be particularly accessible. With practice, clients will become increasingly facile at detecting their automatic thoughts. To explain automatic thoughts to

---

1. Automatic thoughts are specific, readily accessible, and relatively malleable, in contrast to *schemas,* which are general, core, rigid beliefs requiring more extended therapeutic intervention to access and modify. The short-term format of this treatment volume prohibits discussion of schemas and couples therapy; however, the reader may consult Appendix II for further reading on the topic.

couples, the therapist might offer the following instructions:

I'm now going to ask you to begin examining your *automatic thoughts*. Automatic thoughts are those thoughts that pass quickly through your mind—you may not even notice them—in reaction to events. Although we may not register them, automatic thoughts actually exert a very strong influence on our emotions and behaviors. So, for example, one of you might correct the other one when describing a situation to me, and the one who got corrected might have the automatic thought, "He's trying to make me look foolish!" and an associated feeling of hurt or anger. If that was your reaction, you might shake your head, sigh, and roll your eyes. On the other hand, you might have the automatic thought, "She's trying to be supportive by helping me explain this." In that case, you'd probably feel pretty good, and simply nod, smile, and say something like, "Oh yeah, that's right," and go on with your story. The difficulty comes when your partner actually *intends* to be supportive yet you *infer* that you were being made to look foolish. These faulty interpretations can be at the root of a great many negative marital interactions. With practice, though, we can become much better at recognizing an automatic thought speeding through our mind, and then take a good, critical look at the validity of the thought.

When clients understand the concept of automatic thoughts, the therapist can introduce the Relationship Thought Record (RTR).[2] The RTR is a device used to help clients track their

---

2. For a comprehensive introduction to cognitive restructuring see J. Beck (1995).

relationship-related automatic thoughts along with the eliciting events and the accompanying emotions and behaviors. As in the sample RTR in Table 7–1, on the top of the page the client records a particular marital event, usually one that led to distress. Then, in the first column, the client lists the automatic thoughts he or she experienced in relation to the event. The therapist should give each partner a blank RTR and ask each to select an event for practice. Partners may consider the same event but do not have to. An advantage of choosing the same event is that this sends partners the message that the negative automatic thoughts of *both* partners contribute to marital conflicts.

Current, in-session events are useful for initial practice attempts because they will be less subject to distortions in recall. For example, if some aspect of positive tracking or reviewing the homework assignment seemed to elicit an emotional reaction in the clients, the therapist might ask them to use that event to record their associated automatic thoughts. Events may be positive or negative. Events resulting in negative emotions risk adverse partner reactions that may distract couples from the process of identifying their thoughts (e.g., "How could you think that is what I meant? You always think the worst!"). If such a reaction does develop, the therapist can point out that this is a good in vivo opportunity to observe automatic thoughts, ask the offended partner, "What is going through your mind right now?" and ask about the associated emotions. In general, however, clients should be urged to refrain from critiquing each other's automatic thoughts and to simply observe their own thoughts.

Table 7-1
Relationship Thought Record

Situation: _____   Date: _____

Automatic Thought(s) Record each and rate belief in each (1–100)	Emotion(s)	Behavior(s)	Alternative Response

Note: The Relationship Thought Record is based on the couple-based modifications of Beck and colleagues' (1979) *Daily Record of Dysfunctional Thoughts* made by Baucom and Epstein (1990), and Dattilio and Padesky (1990).

When identifying automatic thoughts concerning events occurring days or weeks ago, the therapist can help the couple recall thoughts through the use of imagery. Asking the client to describe detailed images of scenes (the way the room was laid out, what sounds and smells were present, etc.) helps enhance memories of situations and the accompanying thoughts. Asking the couple to role-play (i.e., re-create) a particular problematic discussion will also tend to stimulate recall of automatic thoughts.

In session, partners can be asked to identify and log at least two or three thoughts on the RTR pertaining to the selected event. Each partner will record his or her thoughts individually, without input from the other. As clients write their thoughts, the therapist can read them and offer feedback as needed. Clients will at times need coaching to further elaborate on imprecise thoughts to get at the specific underlying cognition. For example, a wife who suddenly crossed her arms and turned away with a sigh of exasperation during a discussion with her partner on household chores might report the automatic thought, "It's just not fair!" Further prompting might reveal the underlying thoughts, "He's not willing to do his share; he only thinks about himself" and "He'll never change." The therapist should be certain clients understand the process (and engage in self-prompting if needed to specify their automatic thoughts) and have become adept at identifying their thoughts before moving on to filling out the next part of the RTR. The therapist might ask the clients to select one or two additional events and identify the related automatic thoughts to ensure that each partner comprehends the technique.

After both clients have, with the therapist's aid, clearly identified the thoughts accompanying a relationship event, they are ready to continue filling out the thought record. Next to each thought, the client indicates the degree to which he or she believes each thought listed, on a scale of 1 to 100 (1 indicating a belief that the thought is entirely untrue and 100 indicating that the belief is entirely true). This rating process helps the client begin to view *cognitions as hypotheses requiring further evaluation, rather than facts*, a critical distinction for the later process of questioning the accuracy of the thought. Rating the believability of the thought also gives the therapist information about which cognitions will prove the most entrenched and resistant to change.

In the next column, clients record the emotions that accompanied their automatic thoughts. Some clients will need prompting here on what constitute emotions, as many clients will record additional *thoughts* when asked to indicate their *feelings* about a situation (e.g., "I felt like things were never going to improve" instead of "I felt sad"). Chapter 4 addresses information on working with spouses to identify emotional states.

In the next column, partners record the behavioral response that accompanied or followed the thoughts and emotion. If no particular behaviors occurred, clients can write down their behavioral *urges*. For example, a partner may have controlled himself in the presence of company but may have wanted to leave the room or yell. Recording behavioral responses allows the therapist and client to ascertain the links connecting thoughts and emotions to specific marital interactions, such as escalations of conflict. For now, clients should disregard the column labeled "Alternative Response."

Types of Marital Cognitions Experienced by Couples

After clients become adept at recognizing their automatic thoughts, the therapist can begin educating them about the various *types of cognitions* couples bring to interactions with their partners. These categories of cognition often feed specific automatic thoughts. Baucom and Epstein (1990) classify cognitions into *perceptions*, or subjective notions of what events occur; *attributions*, or the reasons individuals give for relationship events; *expectancies*, which involve predictions of what events will occur; *assumptions*, which involve views of how events relate to one another and of *how things are*; and *standards*, which are beliefs about *how things should be*.[3] While clients need not spend time memorizing these areas of cognition, familiarity with these categories should facilitate both recognition of automatic thoughts and acceptance of these thoughts as mental classification mechanisms (i.e., cognitive structures) rather than facts. In addition, recognition of these different types of cognition will have implications for how clients evaluate and work with their automatic thoughts.

---

3. See Baucom and Epstein (1990) for an excellent, in-depth discussion of research and clinical applications concerning each of these cognitive phenomena.

The following paragraphs contain descriptions of these five categories of cognitions, with examples as they might be explained to the couple. The therapist can explain that these cognitive structures influence one another and drive our automatic thoughts. For example, one's standard may be "People shouldn't consume alcohol except on occasion." This standard may influence one's perception that a partner who drinks a · glass of wine with dinner several times a week "drinks *all the time*." This perception may then lead to the automatic thought and assumption, "My partner is an alcoholic." As the therapist illustrates each, he or she can use examples, should they be apparent, from the couple's own relationship. The therapist should stop and answer any questions and welcome input from the partners regarding their recognition of these cognitive phenomena in themselves.

Perceptions

Perception refers to the process of noticing events. Basically, people tend to notice particular aspects of their environments but not others. What we notice is influenced by our past learning, our assumptions and standards, and our mood states. Biases in perceptions occur frequently in marital relationships and can lead to problems when spouses see different things in the same situation, leading them to have different responses to it. For example, a wife might feel overloaded with social engagements while her husband sees their social calendar as skimpy. Differing perceptions can also cause distress when partners *selectively attend to the negative aspects* of the relationship. What makes matters worse is that once partners develop negative feelings about the relationship, they develop biases toward noticing those things that *confirm* their views, while missing the events that *disconfirm* their views. An example of this is the wife who has the automatic thought, "My husband does nothing to keep the house in order" after she sees his newspapers spread out on the coffee table, neglecting to notice that he washed and folded all the laundry and took out the garbage.

Attributions

Attributions are the explanations partners assign for events. Couples in distressed relationships make more negative attributions for their partners' behaviors, both in terms of what factors *cause* these behaviors and how *responsible* they see their partners for the behaviors.

Causal attributions may include the belief that a partner's problematic behaviors result from long-standing qualities in the partner that are unlikely to change and that are likely to impact many different situations. This is in contrast to the views that happy couples are more likely to hold—that problematic behaviors by the partner are due to external factors, are temporary aberrations, and are specific to one situation. In terms of responsibility for behavior, distressed couples are also more likely to view undesirable partner behaviors as selfish and intentional, and to feel their partners should be blamed.

Like perceptions, attributions are influenced by past learning, by one's standards and assumptions, and by mood. Inaccurate attributions can hurt the relationship by leading one to believe that a partner's negative behaviors are intentional while positive behaviors are a fluke and unlikely to recur. Even one's best efforts to please one's partner may be discounted by the attribution that the effort is somehow selfishly motivated, or is just a one-time occurrence.

Expectancies

Expectancies are one's current or previous predictions about one's partner or marriage. They are also based on learning, and can be shaped by factors such as personal values, social standards, and cultural background. Expectancies affect one's emotions and behaviors with one's partner. For example, a current expectancy might be, "When I express my feelings to my husband he will put me down." A wife who holds that expectancy might keep her feelings to herself, which is a behavior influenced by the expectancy, and also might feel angry at her partner for "causing" her to hold her feelings in, which is an emotional reaction influenced by the expectancy. An example of a previously held expectancy might be, "When I'm married, we'll live in a big house in the country." Finding oneself living with one's spouse in a cramped apartment in the city may then breed disappointment and resentment. The problem arises when we base our behavior on and react emotionally to inaccurate, unrealistic, or outdated expectancies.

Assumptions

Assumptions are conceptions about characteristics of things

or how things are related to one another. Destructive marital assumptions can develop from learning or from biased perceptions, can affect marital quality, and can lower a couple's motivation to work on the relationship. For example, one spouse may make the assumption, "My partner is not interested in working this out," which may diminish the spouse's *own* investment in the relationship.

Standards

Finally, both partners bring to the relationship standards about *how things should be*. The biggest hint that clients are tapping into standards is when they use the terms *should* or *ought to*. Some standards may actually help preserve the relationship, as in the case of living by one's standard that "Spouses should remain faithful." However, relationship standards can cause problems when partners feel their standards are not being met. This is more likely to happen if the standard is unrealistic, such as the standard, "My partner should anticipate my needs without having to be told."

Even if one's standards are perfectly reasonable, they can lead to distress when they are simply incompatible with those of one's spouse. For example, one partner may think, "Couples should involve their parents in major life decisions," while the other believes, "Major life decisions are personal and should be decided privately by the couple." These two positions simply reflect personal values; neither position is more "right" than the other. However, clashes might develop as a result of these standards as soon as the first major decision arises.

Detecting Cognitions through Assessment and Session Material

To help the partners by suggesting examples of cognitions specifically relevant to their relationship, and by coaching them in their attempts to uncover automatic thoughts, it is useful for the therapist to begin Session 6 after having a look back on other data from the couple pertaining to cognitions. The pretreatment interviews, behavioral observation task (i.e., ten-minute problem-solving discussion), and self-report instruments will provide the clinician with preliminary information regarding the couple's thoughts and beliefs. Moreover, the therapist will have routinely noticed cognitions during the couple's in-session interactions. With regard to perceptions, it will often become clear that partners offer starkly different impressions when discussing marital events. The therapist may observe couples' tendencies to miss positive relationship events or, also potentially destructive, to ignore important negative relationship events, such as indications of an affair. Techniques to facilitate detection of couples' differing perceptions include use of paraphrasing (it becomes apparent whether partners have difficulty with this skill caused by misperceptions of communication content when partners repeatedly feed back distorted messages) or noticing partner discrepancies in reports of weekly events.

Additionally, the couple will often offer unsolicited attributions as they explain or comment on relationship events (e.g., "He did that because . . .," "That's the way she is," or "He does it deliberately . . ."). When the partners do not volunteer their attributions, the therapist might probe for them with questions such as: "What's your explanation for this difficulty?" or "Why do you think that happened?" Attributions commonly emerge during the discussion of caring gestures when some couples minimize a partner's caring behaviors because of their link to a therapeutic assignment. Expectancies also emerge in interactions throughout therapy, and can further maintain marital distress by forestalling implementing solutions. A couple's belief that a particular pattern of interaction cannot change would logically reduce the motivation to attempt new solutions.

A couple's basic assumptions about each other, the world, and the relationship will tend to emerge during partner interactions as well. The goal is to assess for assumptions, usually concerning the relationship or the partner, that seem to play a role in causing or maintaining marital dysfunction. This will often involve clarifying and examining the basis for the assumption. Finally, the clients will reveal their specific relationship standards during sessions; problem discussions frequently contain implicit or explicit identification of standards and indications of how they have been breached.

Throughout therapy, a partner's shifting emotional state in session provides an excellent opportunity to assess the content of his or her thoughts, as the experience of emotions can often bring into sharper focus the associated cognitions. For example, the therapist might ask gently, "Why are you crying now? What thoughts are going through your mind?" The client's reply will likely reveal centrally important cognitions (e.g., the assumption, "He doesn't love me anymore").

Linking Cognition Types to Automatic Thoughts

In session, the therapist can use the automatic thoughts listed by clients to point out examples of the five types of cognitions. For example, one troubling event for Kevin concerned an argument over his wife Andrea's statement that she wanted to go out dancing with her girlfriends over the upcoming weekend. Kevin's automatic thoughts included the following:

1. She's doing that intentionally to upset me because she's mad at me for going to the game last week.
2. She will dance and flirt with other men.
3. She is getting bored with our marriage.
4. Married women shouldn't go out without their husbands; she's being selfish.
5. She always plans something to interfere with our weekend time together.

Kevin's first automatic thought contained attributions concerning both how irresponsible Andrea was for making this upsetting plan ("She's doing that *intentionally* . . .") and the reason behind it ("Because she's mad at me . . ."). His second was an expectancy, that Andrea "*will* dance and flirt . . .," while the third was an assumption that Andrea's behavior reflects the fact that "she is getting bored with our marriage." Kevin's fourth automatic thought exposed his standard that "Married women *shouldn't* go out without their husbands." Finally, his fifth automatic thought revealed his perception that Andrea "*always* plans something" that cuts into their weekend time together. Further probing might uncover a related standard linked to this perception as well, along the lines of "Andrea should want to spend the whole weekend with me."

Again, the therapist may sometimes have to probe for the type of cognition underlying an automatic thought, as it may not be stated completely. For example, if Kevin had recorded as an automatic thought, "I can't believe she's doing this to me," the therapist might ask, "What is it specifically about this that is upsetting you?" or "Can you say what it is exactly that you see her as 'doing to you'?" This type of inquiry should reveal more detailed thoughts (e.g., the assumption that "she's trying to hurt me") that lend themselves to systematic examination. Automatic thoughts in question form might similarly veil the type of cognition driving the thought, as in Kevin's potential thought, "What am I going to do now?" Further query might reveal the underlying assumption, "My marriage is falling apart."

The focus may now switch to the automatic thoughts of the other partner. In the case of Kevin and Andrea, Andrea's thoughts included the perception that "Kevin always puts a damper on any fun I try to have," and the standard, "Husbands and wives should be independent."

The Role of Cognitive Distortions

The various types of cognitions outlined above serve useful functions, as they facilitate our reading of social cues and allow for the organization and efficient processing of information. For example, our expectation about a spouse's sensitivities allows us to temper our communication; our assumption that a partner's behavior reflects a particular mood allows us to respond appropriately. However, as Beck (1988) and others (Baucom and Epstein 1990, Fincham and O'Leary 1983) have contended, errors in information processing can lead to distortions in automatic thoughts, with dysfunctional marital interaction as a consequence. For example, consider the following scenario: Jack, determined to improve his troubled relationship, goes out of his way to please Barbara with loving gestures. Yet Barbara may not be pleased by these gestures and she minimizes them due to exceedingly high standards, attributes them to selfish motives, assumes he doesn't really care about the relationship, expects the loving gestures to cease, or fails to notice them altogether. A set of information-processing errors, described below, causes Barbara to negatively distort her appraisals of Jack's behavior. While plausible to Barbara, her cognitions may be at odds with reality. Moreover, negative marital cognitions can become *self-fulfilling*, as cognition-driven destructive behavior results in reciprocal negative behavior from the spouse. Barbara's inaccurate processing of Jack's loving gestures may result in unresponsiveness to his efforts; this might reduce Jack's motivation to invest in the relationship. His reduced efforts would then confirm Barbara's beliefs (e.g., "I knew this couldn't last; he never really cared!").

Distorted cognitions can thereby promote negative interpretations of even positive partner behaviors, and risk undermining the couple's ability to fully benefit from treatment components covered thus far. In fact, from a cognitive therapy perspective, much of what has traditionally been labeled "treatment resistance" can be accounted for by thoughts that are impeding the change process. The therapist might illustrate this idea using frustrations expressed by the couple, such as, "More communication won't help—we just go around in circles and never get anywhere," or "I tried to make an effort and my partner dismissed it, so what's the use?" The therapist can then point to the possibly distorted role cognitions played in their conclusions as an example of these cognitions' strong influence.

Once the therapist has explained the notion of cognitive distortions, he or she can introduce Beck's (1988) list of common cognitive distortions in relationships (Table 7–2). The

Table 7-2	
Cognitive Distortions of Couples	
Tunnel Vision	Focusing on one detail (which fits one's current state of mind) and ignoring the larger picture. *Example*: Focusing only on a particular argument that took place a week ago and failing to notice the pleasant interactions that have taken place since.
Selective Abstraction	Similar to tunnel vision, selective abstraction involves misinterpreting a statement or event by taking it out of context and missing other important information. *Example*: When his wife announces she has called a plumber to fix a leak, a husband angrily concludes that she believes he is too unskilled to fix it himself. He fails to take into account that she was responding to his complaints about how busy he is and how he feels overburdened by one household project after another.
Arbitrary Inference	More extreme than selective abstraction, arbitrary inference involves coming to a negative conclusion in the absence of any evidence for it. *Example*: In a phone call from the office, a husband unwit-

	Table 7-2, continued:
	tingly gives his son permission to do something that his wife has forbidden. His wife concludes that "he's deliberately trying to undermine me because he's envious of me for being home with the kids."
Overgeneralization	Overgeneralization involves thinking in absolutes (often using the terms "always" or "never"), by concluding that a pattern of behavior is typical based on just one or a few instances. This type of thinking can fuel feelings of hopelessness and create vicious cycles. *Example:* A wife who had been working hard in therapy to improve her marriage got delayed at work and showed up twenty minutes late for a session. Her husband angrily berated her, accusing, "You always put your work before this relationship! You'll never change!" The wife then thinks, "He's always attacking me. This marriage can never be saved."
All-or-Nothing Thinking	All-or-nothing thinking involves seeing only the extremes and failing to see any middle ground. People's thinking under stress tends to become polarized, leaving them with rigid choices such as good or bad, black or white, worthwhile or worthless, competent or incompetent, perfect or totally flawed. *Example:* A husband makes an error balancing the checkbook and his wife concludes, "You can't do anything right."
Magnification/ Minimization	Magnification involves exaggerating a person's negative qualities or catastrophizing the likely consequences of an event. The flip side of this is minimization, or downplaying the significance of an event. *Example of magnification:* A woman has a minor disagreement with her fiancé and thinks, "Now he'll want to call off the wedding." *Example of minimization:* A woman tells her partner that a particular issue is a significant problem for her; her partner ignores the seriousness of the message, thinking, "She'll get over it."

Table 7–2, continued:	
Biased Explanations	Making overly negative attributions for a partner's behavior, or pinpointing ulterior motives or flawed personality characteristics. *Examples:* "It's no accident that he forgot our anniversary; he just doesn't care" or "She keeps asking me if I've done this or if I've done that; she's incapable of trust."
Negative Labeling	Attaching a critical label to a partner's actions or character (as opposed to specifying the specific troubling behavior). The partner ascribing the label then really comes to see the partner as fulfilling the characteristics of the label. *Examples:* A partner's failure to call during the day is seen as "inconsiderate"; a partner expressing emotion is deemed "irrational."
Personalization	Erroneously concluding that events revolve around oneself. *Example:* "He deliberately drives that way because he knows it makes me crazy!"
Mind Reading	Assuming one knows what a partner thinks and feels without checking it out, or expecting one's partner to know what one thinks and feels without expressing it directly. *Examples:* "My partner is no longer attracted to me" or "My partner should have known that was going to upset me."
Subjective/Emotional Reasoning	Believing that one's emotions reflect the way things are; living by the notion that "If I feel it, it must be justified." *Examples:* A wife holds that since she feels jealous, her spouse must be interested in another woman; a husband believes that because he is angry, his wife's behavior was wrong.

Note: Cognitive distortions, definitions, and examples presented are adapted from Beck (1988).

therapist should give the clients a copy of this handout and read through it with them, discussing each item and helping to clarify with additional examples from their relationship.

Couples may immediately recognize some of these cognitions as characteristic of their own styles of thinking and may offer their own examples. It is not necessary for couples to become proficient at identifying each type of cognitive distortion; rather, the list can provide them with a general sense of the various thinking errors that lead to thought distortions.

To help couples see how cognitive distortions influence their thinking, the therapist should ask both partners to take another look at the automatic thoughts they recorded. Ask them to consider whether any thoughts are characterized by the distortions described in Table 7–2. Although clients will gain more experience with challenging their thoughts in the following session, they can begin to evaluate the logic in their thoughts at this time. For instance, in the example of Kevin and Andrea above, Kevin identified the following potential cognitive distortions in his automatic thoughts:

Thought	Distortion
1. She's doing that *intentionally to upset me* because she's mad at me for going to the game without her last week.	Personalization
2. She will dance and flirt with other men	Arbitrary Inference; Emotional Reasoning
3. *She is getting bored* with our marriage.	Mind Reading
4. Married women shouldn't go out without their husbands; *she's being selfish*.	Negative Labeling

5. She *always* plans something to   Overgeneralization
   interfere with our weekend
   time together.

Learning about various cognitive distortions takes clients a step closer to examining the validity of their own thoughts. Couples should by now accept that *thoughts are not necessarily synonymous with truths*, and feel prepared to gather evidence to support their beliefs in the next session.

Nondistorted and Reasonable Negative Cognitions

Note that while the negative cognitions of distressed couples may be distorted or unrealistic, they will at times be accurate or reasonable. Thus, it will be important for the therapist to help the partners evaluate the degree to which their cognitions are accurate or reasonable for them, rather than presuming distortion or extremes. Cognitions that are not colored by distortion, yet contribute to relationship distress, generally call for interventions at the level of behavior change, negotiation, or acceptance, rather than restructuring the cognitions themselves. This subject will be addressed further in Chapter 8.

Session Review and Homework

Today's session introduced many new and potentially confusing concepts (e.g., one can identify both a *type* of cognition and a type of *distortion* in the same automatic thought).

While reviewing the session, encourage clients to ask questions about the material. In a brief therapy format, the therapist does not have the luxury of drilling the same concepts week after week; thus, reviewing material and ensuring understanding before moving on becomes particularly important. Homework will also ensure additional practice with the opportunity for therapist feedback. We recommend that the review focus mainly on identifying automatic thoughts with associated emotions and behaviors, and the notion that thoughts may be (1) products of information-processing errors and (2) of questionable validity.

Once couples understand the steps involved in recognizing their automatic thoughts and their impact on emotions and behavior, they are ready to attempt this process on their own. The homework assignment has two parts:

1. Each partner should complete a Relationship Thought Record for two different situations that occur during the week. Partners may choose separate events and need not consult each other. They should complete the assignment as soon as possible following the selected situations (or during the situations, if possible, such as while waiting for a late partner or during a stop-action) to facilitate accurate recall of thoughts, emotions, and behaviors. The partners will practice tracking thoughts, rating their belief in the thoughts, and recording related emotions and behaviors. For now they should leave blank the "Alternative Response" column of the RTR. They should bring in their records the following week to review their efforts with the therapist and to prepare for the next step: challenging their thoughts.

2. Partners should review the list of cognitive distortions. This handout will be incorporated into the next session as clients learn to critically evaluate their thoughts.

8

Session 7:
Marital Cognitions:
Testing
and Challenging
Thoughts and Beliefs

Setting the Agenda

In today's session, the couple will continue to work with cognitions by learning to (1) test and challenge invalid, unrealistic, or extreme cognitions; and (2) negotiate to solve problems related to valid or reasonable cognitions that nevertheless contribute to relationship dysfunction. These will of course follow positive tracking, homework review, and a brief review of the week.

Positive Tracking

Begin by asking partners to report on what went well during the previous week, giving feedback and praise as warranted.

Homework Review

As each partner will have completed all but the final column of a Relationship Thought Record for homework, the therapist can review these with the partners, asking about any difficulties they encountered while tracking their thoughts or completing the thought record. The therapist can also read the clients' RTRs and provide feedback on parts correctly done while helping to modify portions in need of improvement, such as incomplete or vague thoughts, or thoughts recorded in place of emotions. The therapist can also elicit from clients their general impressions of the exercise, ensuring their comprehension that cognitions serve as a liaison between marital events, emotions, and behaviors toward a partner. Regarding the second part of the assignment, the therapist can inquire whether the partners have questions or comments concerning the handout on cognitive distortions that they reviewed.

CHALLENGING COGNITIONS

In the previous session clients were introduced to tracking automatic thoughts; recognizing the links between thoughts, emotions, and behaviors; and noting the many types of information-processing errors (i.e., cognitive distortions) that can permeate one's thinking. The therapist might provide the following rationale for beginning the work of examining and revising cognitions:

> While automatic thoughts can provide us with an immediate "read" of a situation, which is necessary for an appropriate response, you now have seen that they can nevertheless lead us astray in our responses toward a partner when distorted or based on unrealistic standards. It'll be helpful for you to learn not only to *recognize* your automatic appraisals of troublesome events in the relationship, but also to *subject these to logical analysis and revise* those found to be somehow inappropriate. We can start now by looking at the automatic thoughts you recorded at home, or we can use the thought records you completed in the last session. Which do you prefer?

The therapist can then begin to teach the partners methods of evaluating the degree to which their perceptions, assumptions, attributions, and expectancies are accurate, and the degree to which their standards are, in the context of the current relationship, reasonable or realistic. The metaphor of a scientist in search of objective data to support or disprove a hypothesis is instructive in this "empirical" approach to examining thoughts. That is, the identification of automatic thoughts provides an opportunity for an individual to examine the accuracy of his or her beliefs. In what has been termed *collaborative empiricism* (Beck et al. 1979), the *therapist and client work in tandem* to discover the validity of automatic thoughts. This approach should be distinguished from a strategy of trying to alter a client's beliefs through logical argument or high-intensity challenges on the part of the therapist. Instead, restructuring beliefs is accomplished through the client's weighing of the evidence for or against his or her beliefs and considering alternatives.

The Challenging Cognitions Worksheet (Table 8–1) may be used to guide clients through the process of testing the validity of perceptions, attributions, assumptions, and expectancies. Standards will require a somewhat different process of scrutiny; because they reflect personal values and preferences, it would not make sense to view them as hypotheses and subject them to the same weighing-of-evidence procedure. Thus, when an automatic thought is based on a standard, the therapist will not use the Challenging Cognitions Worksheet but will instead follow the strategy detailed in the latter part of this chapter. Standards often underlie automatic thoughts, whether they are additional standards or other types of cognitions. For example, the assumption that a partner would want company on a business trip, the perception that a partner travels "all the time," and the standard, "He should want to take me with him on his business trip," might all be fueled by the broader standard, "Partners should spend their weekends together." When a problematic pattern of cognitions reveals an underlying standard, the therapist will move from weighing evidence for the thoughts to examining the impact and function of the standard.

Table 8-1
Challenging Cognitions Worksheet

Initial Thought (belief rating 1—100):

Associated Feelings:

Associated Behavior (or behavioral urge):

Cognitive Distortion:

Weigh the Evidence:

Challenge: (What are other possible ways of looking at this?)

The therapist should give each client copies of the Challenging Cognitions Worksheet and begin completing it, step by step, with one partner at a time. The therapist might initiate this process with comments such as:

I see you've both recorded your automatic thoughts about the argument you had last weekend. Now, as I mentioned before, although the thoughts may *feel* correct to you, and some indeed may be, some of the thoughts you put down may be biased by information-processing errors. So they may not be fully accurate reflections of what was going on in this situation. Let's, then, consider them to be hypotheses rather than facts. Why don't we take a look at them together and see what we can come up with in the way of evidence supporting or disputing them? Then we can write the evidence out on this worksheet. Who would like to start?

The therapist can then ask the first client to write his or her first automatic thought for the chosen situation on the top, taken directly from the Relationship Thought Record. The client should also transpose the thoughts and behaviors from the RTR onto this worksheet. Next, the client can look over Table 7–2 and identify the cognitive distortions that may be operating in conjunction with the thought. If the automatic thought does not appear to reflect a standard, the therapist can then ask the client to weigh the evidence supporting or opposing the thought. The therapist might first ask, "What evidence supports this thought? On what is this thought based?" The therapist can then ask the client to consider evidence that contradicts the thought.

Once the client has examined supporting and opposing factors, the therapist can now direct the client to consider the evidence and write out a challenge to the thought in question in the next section of the worksheet (as the therapist will work with partners in turn, the observing partner should refrain from challenging the other partner's thoughts). Challenges typically take the form of questions, which will lead to developing alternative hypotheses. Depending on the type of cognition, the therapist can use a variety of probes, such as those listed in Table 8–2, to coach the client in looking for oppos-

---

Table 8–2
Sample Probes for Challenging Cognitions

For Perceptions:

"Can you think of a counterexample . . ."

"Can you think of a time when this wasn't true . . . ?"

"How do you think [spouse's name] would see it?"

"Does what you're saying apply in every case?"

"Is it this way all the time?"

"Are you able to come up with any exceptions to what you're saying?"

"Are there other aspects of your interactions on which you can focus?"

For Attributions and Assumptions:

"Is there any other plausible explanation for . . . ?"

"Could there be more than one reason for . . . ?"

"What is the likelihood there were other factors involved in . . . ?"

"Can you think of another reason that . . . ?"

"Can you imagine a different way of looking at this?"

"How accurate is this explanation . . . ?"

"Is this the most reasonable explanation for . . . ?"

"How else might one interpret that?"

ing evidence, challenging initial thoughts, and considering alternatives. Systematically questioning each thought with the client models the types of challenges clients will need to ask themselves when revising thoughts on their own.

Once the client has come up with a challenge to the thought, the therapist may now ask the client to attempt one or two alternatives to the original hypothesis. After writing out these alternatives, the client should rate the level of belief in the new hypotheses from 1 to 100, and indicate the associated emotions and behavioral urges. Table 8–3 contains a sample of a completed worksheet.

Table 8–3
Challenging Cognitions Worksheet

Initial Thought (Belief rating 1—100): "She isn't talking much; she must be angry at me again." (80)

Associated Feelings: Hurt, frustration

Associated Behavior (or behavioral urge): Withdrawal, accusation

Cognitive Distortion: Personalization, mind reading

Weigh the Evidence:

Supporting: In the past, many times she has stopped communicating with me when she's been angry. I ask her what's wrong and she tells me, in an icy voice, she's angry at me. These days, she gets angry at me a lot.

Opposing: She also gets quiet when something else is bothering her. Sometimes she's troubled by work or by a problem in her family. We had a good couple of days; I don't think I did anything that could have upset her.

Challenge: (What are other possible ways of looking at this?) "Might I be jumping to conclusions here? Could there be other likely reasons she's not talking?"

Once clients have weighed evidence, considered challenges, and generated alternatives to the faulty cognitions, they can record their revised thoughts in the final column of the RTR. In continuing to practice these steps, clients should soon be able to circumvent the worksheet and fill out only the RTR; the worksheet provides additional structure when the thinking steps are new and potentially cumbersome. Table 8–4 contains the completed RTR for the above example.

The therapist can at this point have clients focus on the impact of their thinking on their emotions and behavioral urges, and note the changes in these areas following the process of developing alternative thoughts. Couples will ideally find this exercise reinforcing, through mitigation of negative emotional states combined with increased hope that relationship events may not always be as bad as they first seem.

When an individual's cognitions are found to be distorted or unreasonable, the therapist guides the client in accommodating the newly acquired information about them to generate alternative, more valid cognitions. The therapist may note themes that emerge routinely and that reflect overarching assumptions or standards about relationships. If a client's cognitions repeatedly emerge as much more negative than would be expected from the spouse's behavior (e.g., repeated attributions that the spouse's mood shifts are the result of interest in other potential partners, or relentless expectancy that the spouse will leave for a more desirable partner despite consistently loyal and devoted behavior from the spouse), the therapist may want to recommend individual therapy for this part-

Table 8-4

Relationship Thought Record

Situation: Come home from work, wife mumbles greeting and goes about her business, disregarding me.   Date: 2/11

Automatic Thought(s) Record each and rate belief in each (1—100)	Emotion(s)	Behavior(s) (or behavioral urge)	Alternative Response
She isn't talking much; she must be angry at me again. (80)	Hurt, frustration	Withdrawal (behavior), accusation (urge)	1. She did have that important meeting today—perhaps it didn't go well and she's upset about that. 2. Also, she stayed up later than usual preparing for it—maybe she is just exhausted.

ner. Such entrenched cognitions will be unlikely to change in response to the spouse's behavior.

Additional Methods of Gathering Evidence

At times clients will not have immediate access to evidence contrary to their automatic thoughts. The academic practice of considering alternative explanations may not always suffice in the absence of more objective evidence. In such cases, the therapist can suggest the client gather additional evidence through behavioral experiments, direct communication, or examination of objective data. The client would then record this evidence on the Challenging Cognitions Worksheet.

Behavioral experiments involve actually entering or even concocting situations to test one's hypotheses. One would then agree to withhold judgment until encountering the situation and observing whether one's thoughts are accurate. For example, a husband may voice the expectation, "If I apologized to Lois's mother, it wouldn't make the situation any better. She'd probably just start listing all of her other grievances against me, and she'd have me just where she wanted me." The therapist might then ask the husband to try apologizing to his mother-in-law and observe the outcome.[1]

---

1. Note that while behavioral experiments may provide helpful information, discordant couples should be cautioned against "testing" each other in situations where only a perfect response would pass the test. Even if results from behavioral experiments support an initial negative hypothesis, these results do not imply that one should

Direct communication can be encouraged when it is apparent that valuable evidence may be attained from speaking with the other party involved in one's automatic thought. Examples include inquiring about the truth of an assumption ("It seems like you get angry any time I bring up a complaint in therapy; am I reading you correctly?") and verifying one's attribution for a particular behavior ("I thought you took the baby from me because you didn't like the way I was handling him; is that right?"). When the troubling cognition concerns the partner, the therapist can ask clients to check out the evidence during the session.

Examination of objective data may be appropriate when such information exists but has not been taken into account in an individual's appraisal of a situation. An example would be examining the past year's credit card bills when one partner disputes the other's perception that "the bills have been getting higher and higher each month."

When Automatic Thoughts Are Accurate

Sometimes, evidence will support the accuracy of an automatic thought. Obviously, the thought, "She isn't talking much; she must be angry at me again," can be a correct interpretation of the situation. When a careful evaluation estab-

---

have refrained from engaging in a constructive behavior (e.g., an apology); this behavior may still result in a favorable outcome under some circumstances (see section above on addressing accurate automatic thoughts).

lishes the validity of a spouse's cognitions, and yet the cognitions continue to evoke distress, the therapist will need to work with the couple to formulate the difficulties as tasks for communication and problem-solving. One must consider behavior change, or discussing the possibility of accepting a difficult situation as it is, *in addition to* cognitive restructuring. It would obviously feel invalidating to a client for a therapist to encourage altering cognitions that are realistic. Note, however, that the very process of examining our thoughts reduces the chances of jumping to conclusions and acting impulsively and negatively toward a partner, so a balanced evaluation pays off regardless of the outcome of that evaluation.

Furthermore, even when automatic thoughts prove accurate, distressed relationships often produce additional automatic thoughts that contain distortions. For example, the *accurate* thought, "She isn't talking much; she must be angry at me again," may be followed by the magnification, "I can't take this anymore." Although one's partner may indeed be angry, feeling one "can't take it anymore" is likely to produce reactions such as hopelessness, despair, and withdrawal. Weighing evidence, such as remembering times when the relationship felt hopeless but then improved, might produce an alternative response such as, "This is difficult but I can handle it. Withdrawing will only make the situation worse. Maybe telling her how I am feeling would help." Such a revised response might result in feeling calmer and approaching one's partner to talk.

Sometimes automatic thoughts will contain partial truths. For example, a wife may be reluctant to bring up a troubling behavior of her husband's because of the expectancy that he will withdraw, which would only make matters worse. Challenging her thoughts may have uncovered the distortion of overgeneralizing, in which she thinks, "He always withdraws when I bring up these types of issues." Checking out the evidence may reveal that in the past he withdrew in response to her raising similar topics many times, but engaged in helpful discussions on occasion. The wife remains perfectly reasonable in her expectancy because, based on his past behavior, the chances appear to favor his withdrawal. However, the therapist can now prompt the wife and husband to discuss under what circumstances the husband has been likely to withdraw in the past. He may have withdrawn when she raised the problems in hurtful and attacking ways. She may then come to realize that her expectancy, while reasonable, is more accurate under certain circumstances than others, and that these circumstances are in fact under her control (i.e., she can bring up the problem gently using the XYZ formula and avoid destructive communication). Thus, challenging even a partially accurate cognition may be helpful in providing information to the couple about the circumstances under which the cognitions are most accurate. Couples can then adjust their behavior to maximize positive outcomes.

Finally, cognitions may be accurate but may have a detrimental impact on the relationship when they are communicated in hurtful, threatening, or accusatory ways. In such cases, the therapist will want to point out the destructive enactment of the cognition and encourage communication and the use of problem-solving skills to address the situation.

Addressing Standards

As Baucom and Epstein (1990) have pointed out, an individual's standards cannot be subjected to the same evaluation of accuracy as can other types of cognitions. Standards tap idiosyncratic values and ideals, and are therefore neither true nor false, but rather appropriate for some people and not for others, in some situations and not in others. When a partner's standards pose problems for the relationship, the most helpful approach may be for the individual to consider adjusting either the standard or the behavior that follows from it.

For an example of adjusting a standard itself, consider the example of Mimi, who may believe that her husband Roger should react nondefensively to any feedback, regardless of its critical or hurtful nature. The positive consequences of living by this standard may include Mimi's ability to express anything on her mind and to handle small problems before they become worse. Also, with Mimi's low threshold for critiquing Roger's behavior, Roger will always know when something is bothering Mimi and will not have to wonder. However, the negative consequences of living by this standard include Roger's diminishing affection for Mimi because of her frequent derogatory comments, his eroding self-respect, and Mimi's own increased antipathy for Roger because of her focus on his negative behavior. In this case, evaluating the positive and negative consequences of Mimi's standard may lead Mimi to adjust her standard, since it appears unhelpful and a bit extreme. A revised standard, taking into account the positive and negative consequences of the original one, might be: "Maybe Roger shouldn't embrace critical feedback after all. Instead, for the sake of the marriage, Roger should try to listen to feedback when it is given in a noncritical manner." Helping a partner to recognize that a standard is operating, and to consider the ways that it might affect the relationship, can help an individual to alter it. Table 8–5 contains probes the therapist can use to help a client evaluate whether a standard is realistic or excessive in the context of the relationship.

Table 8–5
Sample Probes for Evaluating Standards

"How realistic is it that your partner could meet this standard?"

"What are the advantages and disadvantages (for you/for the relationship) of holding to this position?"

"How has holding to this standard been helpful to you in the past? Do those factors still apply?"

"Let's look at the positive and negative consequences of holding this view of how things should be."

"How does having these clashing positions on the matter contribute to your relationship distress?

"Is maintaining this standard interfering with the relationship?"

"Could other positions on this matter be acceptable?"

"Is it possible for another point of view to be valid?"

"Is the way this standard is getting expressed posing a problem?"

Note: Probes in this table are based on the discussion of standards by Baucom and Epstein (1990).

The clinician must exercise caution in deeming a standard unrealistic, since what seems ludicrous to one partner (or to the therapist) can often seem perfectly logical to the other. Even when both partners' standards seem perfectly reasonable, they may create problems for the relationship simply because they clash. For example, Mimi might be applying the general standard that partners should air their gripes with each other to prevent an accumulation of resentments. Roger, on the other hand, may hold the standard that most complaints are best kept to oneself and accepted, to avoid an atmosphere of conflict. Mimi and Roger may have developed these standards from past relationship experiences, their families, or cultural differences. They may be following an unspoken rule they saw work well, or rejecting a style of relating that worked poorly. In any case, each partner's standard is valid for him- or herself. When partners have differing standards, the clinician, rather than judging either as extreme, can help the couple identify the diverging standards, recognize the ways in which they are exacerbating marital difficulties, examine advantages and disadvantages of maintaining each standard, and help the couple arrive at a revised standard or negotiate a way to accommodate both partners.

At times, it will not be the standard itself that causes a problem but how the standard gets translated into behavior. Mimi, who applies the standard that partners should air their gripes with each other to prevent an accumulation of resentments, may be violating effective communication strategies. If she brings up her complaints without regard to her level of criticism, her tone of voice, the appropriateness of the time, and so forth, this standard may aggravate marital difficulties. On the other hand, if she adjusts her behavior to engage in constructive communication strategies and limits the frequency of her complaints, her standard may have a neutral impact or even alleviate marital difficulties, despite Roger's opposing standard.

Similarly, it is critical that each partner communicate standards as reflections of preferences to prevent a defensive response in the other (e.g., "I would really like it if we could talk openly about our problems" will be much more effective than saying, "*It is better* if we tell each other everything we are upset about"). If a partner feels unable to compromise on a particular standard, the therapist can help the couple problem-solve regarding the specific issue of disagreement. At the very least, this process can provide relief for couples, because they can reattribute each partner's rigidity about an issue to different standards (developed historically and with influences outside of the relationship) rather than to character flaws such as stubbornness.

As mentioned earlier in this chapter, standards may drive other types of cognitions. For example, Mimi, who favors airing gripes, might voice a complaint four times a week; Roger, who feels the majority of complaints are best kept to oneself, may then develop the subjective perception, "Mimi brings up complaints all the time." Roger may be able to generate contradictory evidence to his perception, such as noting that on Wednesday, Thursday, and Saturday of the previous week Mimi raised no complaints. But he may insist that it still *feels* to him that problems come up "all the time." It may thus become apparent that his standards are swaying his perceptions. In this situation, the focus can again return to the couple's differing standards.

After evaluating the advantages and disadvantages of a standard and considering reasonable alternatives to the standard, the therapist can ask the client to fill out the "Alternative Response" column on the RTR. In Mimi's case, whereas her automatic thought might have been, "Couples should air all of their gripes," her revised thought might be, "It would be nice if Roger was willing to discuss problems more often, but he's not comfortable with that. Maybe we can come up with a compromise."

Similarly, when different standards are driving other types of cognitions, one can return to the Challenging Cognitions Worksheet after addressing the underlying standards. So, Roger's perception that Mimi brings up problems all the time, which may have left him feeling exasperated and wanting to scream, *"Just leave me alone already!"* might now be followed by the revised thought: "Mimi has just been following her own standard of what is helpful in a relationship. Maybe she has a point, but we'll have to talk about how often we can discuss problems because it's uncomfortable for me." Along with this new thought, Roger may feel soothed and may react with the calmly delivered suggestion that they schedule a problem-solving session to discuss their different levels of comfort with voicing complaints. Perhaps a problem-solving session would then yield a mutually satisfactory contract to schedule "gripe sessions" on Monday and Thursday evenings from 8:00 to 8:45. In this way, Mimi could rely on scheduled times to address problems, while Roger would experience such discussions as bounded in measured doses.

Using Self-Talk

Once clients have completed the process of recording the steps of cognitive restructuring on the thought record, the therapist can instruct them to try using "self-talk" or "self-statements" to guide themselves through this process. Self-statements are essentially self-directed thoughts that can be used to help one navigate toward a different path of reasoning and behavior, like having the voice of the therapist as a coach in one's mind. For example, with practice, the process explicated in Table 8–1 might be carried out completely through this self-instructional procedure, rather than by logging automatic thoughts, challenges, and revised alternatives on the Relationship Thought Record. This will be important, since couples will not have their RTRs handy during every marital interaction and will need to make on-the-spot interpretations. The therapist can teach clients to use self-talk by asking them first to relate a statement (such as a challenge to a thought) aloud, and next simply think the statement without vocalizing it. The therapist can then extend this exercise to include an entire logical chain of thoughts and conclusions. For example, a self-talk thought chain of one partner might consist of the following: "What's the matter with him? He gets so little time with the baby, and then he just plops him down in front of the TV instead of playing with him! I'm really upset about this! He doesn't seem to care about him! Well, actually, maybe I'm jumping to conclusions here . . . he was reading to him this morning and then carrying him around for a while. Maybe he just needs some time to relax. Besides, I also heard him narrating to him about what was happening in the basketball game. I guess that's just one of his ways of interacting with his son—and I guess I can let him have his own style with him. It's actually kind of cute!" With its close approximation to the natural process of thinking, this technique should enhance generalization in restructuring one's cognitions. The idea, after all, is not for couples to depend on thought records in their daily interactions, but to begin to automatically recognize and challenge distorted or extreme thinking patterns.

When Cognitions Appear Resistant to Modification

For a subset of clients, the process of objectively evaluating thoughts as hypotheses will consistently confirm their original conclusions, even when the therapist sees clear signs of distortion. It is important to keep in mind that, in the spirit of collaborative empiricism, the therapist's role is to guide the client through a questioning process toward a *possible* alternative conclusion (or suggest that the client elicit information to potentially challenge a particular view) rather than attempting to *convince* the client of the "right" perspective. Even when therapist and client draw different conclusions from the evidence, it is advisable for the moment to accept the client's stance. Some clients need more time to adjust to the idea of critically evaluating their thoughts and will profit from attending to the partner's hypothesis-testing process and more of their own opportunities for practice. Cognitive change will be more robust and less subject to defensiveness when clients reach an altered understanding through their own systematic weighing of evidence or pros and cons.

Still other clients may altogether reject the notion that their thoughts represent anything other than reality. If the therapist observes that persistently rigid thinking is hindering therapeutic progress, the therapist might assess the automatic thoughts *associated with* challenging one's cognitions and encourage the client to subject *these* cognitions to objective evaluation. Individual therapy may also be appropriate in such cases.

Addressing the Functions of Cognitions

Some clients may complete the steps of challenging their cognitions, arrive at new conclusions, and yet continue to think, feel, and behave the same way. When this occurs, it will be critical for the therapist to assess the purpose or function a particular cognition (or pattern of cognitions) serves. Individuals may be reluctant to modify certain cognitions because they operate in a protective capacity. For instance, for a partner in a distressed relationship, maintaining a vigilantly pessimistic or even suspicious outlook may mean that the partner is protecting him- or herself from being taken by surprise with a painful disappointment, abandonment, or betrayal from the other. A client may feel that he or she would rather "be prepared" than relinquish this approach to viewing the partner. Clients may lack awareness of the cause of their reluctance to restructure their cognitions. To help understand the purpose served by a pattern of cognitions, the therapist can ask a client with apparently intransigent cognitions questions such as, "What might happen if you let go of this position?" "Can you imagine any consequences of no longer seeing it this way?" With such partners, it will be important not only to validate the protective function served by this negative cognitive bias, but also to encourage the clients to evaluate both the pros and the cons to the relationship of maintaining this stance. By examining with the client the advantages of maintaining a particular pattern of cognitions, the therapist might discover that it shields the client from some threatening situation.

For example, one client with whom one of us worked clearly held the standard, "My spouse should earn a very large income, have guaranteed job security, and always take care of me." With such a perspective, she felt chronically dissatisfied, had become increasingly critical, and feared her husband's potential job loss so strongly that she became insistent that he scan the want ads and send out résumés any time his job seemed to be going less than optimally. Her husband got the message that he was unsuccessful and a poor provider, despite his managerial position in a large company and their upper-middle-class lifestyle.

At first glance, this wife's standard might appear unreasonable and seem to come from a spoiled sense of entitlement. A therapist might even develop his or her own standard in reaction to this client, such as, "This woman *should* appreciate her husband more, *should* relax her endless demands, or *should* get her own job if she's so concerned." However, in examining the purpose this standard served for this client, it was revealed that she had grown up in poverty, with an erratically employed, alcoholic father, had actually gone hungry for years, and was emotionally deprived as well. She had come to associate financial adversity with both physical and emotional starvation, and had thus appeared to develop a self-protective standard of requiring a financially secure and nurturing partner to ward off any possibility of reexperiencing the extremely painful emotions associated with her past neglect. A problem, however, was that her standard was so extreme as to be nearly unmeetable; she maintained a chronic sense of deprivation. To ask this client to subject this standard to a logical analysis assessing the degree to which it was reasonable would have failed; this standard was not only reasonable for this client but felt emotionally vital. However, in understanding the context from which the standard evolved, both the therapist and spouse developed greater compassion for the client's position. Further, the client's greater understanding of the standard's protective function allowed her to step outside it and recognize its detrimental impact on her marriage. She also developed greater empathy for the ongoing pressure and sense of failure her husband experienced. By addressing the purpose the standard was serving, she became able to formulate less destructive ways of handling her need to guard against returning to a lifestyle resembling that of her childhood.[2]

---

2. This included a willingness to test the accuracy of her perceptions regarding the actual financial state they were in, and to examine the likelihood of realizing her expectations that her husband would lose

Revising Cognitions through Building Acceptance

Identifying elements of marital distress stemming from a partner's differing relationship expectations or standards, as well as coming to understand more about the etiology and purpose of these views, can contribute to an increased acceptance of a partner. In the above example of the client who grew up in a physically and emotionally depriving home, her husband grew more accepting of her insatiable need for financial security, while she became more able to accept her husband for what he was able to provide. With this greater degree of acceptance, a partner appears less deficient and the conflictual situation more bearable, leading to a revised appraisal of the problem and an accompanying lesser need for behavior change.[3] Such a dynamic supports the often-noted paradox that

---

his job and fall into poverty. While this led to her lessening her demands on her husband and acknowledging to a greater extent what he *had* provided, she was unable to entirely let go of her somewhat obsessive fears of declining financial status. Thus, she also decided to finish a partially completed master's degree and develop a career of her own, which gave her a sense of greater control over meeting her own needs and removed some of the focus and pressure from her husband's work status. This client's insight into the protective purpose of her standard led her to actually develop the ability to laugh about it with her husband, and greatly reduced her rigidity about it.

3. See Christensen et al. (1995) for a discussion of integrating acceptance strategies with CBMT.

"acceptance is actually, in itself, a form of change" (Christensen et al. 1995, p. 40).

An additional way to enhance acceptance involves working with clients to find the positive side of problematic partner behaviors. The therapist can point out to clients the tendency to "negatively frame" qualities in the partner that were initially attractive. For example, a partner once regarded as levelheaded and responsible might now be seen as boring and rigid; a partner first seen as spontaneous and happy-go-lucky might now be viewed as impulsive and flighty. The therapist can then prompt both partners to think of one aspect of their mates that they have identified as troublesome, and to then think back to the courtship phase of the relationship and recall an earlier, positive appraisal of the same characteristic or behavior pattern. Partners can be urged to fondly share these earlier outlooks on the now problematic behaviors and to dwell a bit on memories and images of these past positive feelings about the behaviors. For one married couple, the husband complained that his wife routinely turned the house upside down in frenzied preparation for his parents' visits. He wished that she could "mellow out" and refrain from making their visits such a tense and disruptive ordeal. In prompting the husband to consider the flip side of his wife's behaviors, he realized that behind his wife's whirlwind of anxiety lay a desire to please his parents, and a connected investment in her relationship with him. This had been reflected in the attention to detail she had paid from the beginning of their dating relationship. This recollection eased his exasperation, as he was able to recapture the positive light in which he once saw her behavior. The therapist can thus encourage clients to positively reframe bothersome qualities in the partner, accepting that particular characteristics may have both bothersome and appealing aspects.

Session Review and Homework

The therapist should at this point reinforce the points that (1) cognitions influence emotions and behavior, (2) modifying dysfunctional cognitions can reduce distressing emotional states and potentially destructive marital interactions, and (3) clients must repeatedly practice arriving at alternative explanations. The eventual goal is for clients to readily identify thoughts contributing to their distress and routinely test the degree to which they are accurate or reasonable. In this way, they should gradually develop more constructive ways of viewing marital interactions, incorporating restructured beliefs in an increasingly automatic fashion.

The homework assignment will be to review the practice of systematically testing thoughts by having each partner identify a recent distressing marital event and independently complete the RTR in relation to the event. If needed, clients may use the Challenging Cognitions Worksheet to help them walk through the steps, but they should first attempt the process from memory. Again, since the aim is for couples to be able to think in this manner on their own, they should rely on as few prompts as possible. If standards are recorded on a client's RTR, he or she should evaluate the degree to which the standard is reasonable, realistic, or helpful. For automatic thoughts found to be accurate or reasonable but still distress-causing, the couple should attempt communication and problem-solving regarding the difficulty.

For couples who readily master the ability to challenge and revise their thoughts, the therapist can suggest that they conduct this assignment first entirely through self-talk; that is, they should first go through the process mentally without writing down each step. When finished, they should then fill out the RTR as a record of the process to review in the next therapy session.

9

Session 8: Addressing Marital Anger

Setting the Agenda

Today's session will cover anger management, with time reserved at the end of the session for reviewing the treatment as a whole. The therapist should arrange with clients a stopping time for material on anger, and reserve the last portion of the session to discuss treatment progress and feelings about termination.

In covering anger management, the therapist will need to decide, based on the particular couple, which aspects of the session material to emphasize. Some couples will report excessive displays of anger, others will report inhibited anger expression and deficits in emotional expressiveness, and still others will report a combination (e.g., limited emotional expressiveness with periodic angry outbursts). Furthermore, anger serves numerous purposes, and the therapist will want to stress interventions that address the functions of anger at a given time in a given relationship.

In forming the agenda, the therapist provides a tailored description of how today's session material will be relevant to the couple's specific difficulties with anger. Introduction of the new material will follow positive tracking, review of the homework, and a brief review of the week, and will precede the discussion of overall treatment gains.

Positive Tracking

Proceed with positive tracking as always.

Homework Review

Homework from the previous session consisted of asking the partners to each record and systematically test their automatic thoughts concerning a problematic marital situation. In doing so, both partners were asked to weigh the evidence for their thoughts or to examine the extent to which their standards were realistic. They were also asked to develop alternative responses, and, in the case of appropriate cognitions, to use communication and problem-solving skills to attempt to reconcile the problematic situation. The therapist should review this process in detail with each partner, asking them whether they relied on written prompts or completed the assignment through progressive self-statements, and allow them to walk the therapist through the series of questions they asked themselves in evaluating the logic in their thoughts. Finally, the therapist can review revised thoughts or results of problem-solving attempts. This process will allow the therapist to troubleshoot and coach. As always, it is helpful for the therapist to furnish abundant praise for the couple's efforts in attempting the homework.

ANGER CONTROL

Rationale

It is the rare couple in therapy who will not benefit from work on anger control. Even couples for whom anger is not a central problem encounter anger in their relationships, whether expressed outwardly or experienced inwardly. Of course, anger in relationships is normal and at times functional, yet distressed couples have often experienced excessive anger and developed dysfunctional patterns of managing it. Such dysfunctional patterns can be characterized as overly expressive approaches or overly passive approaches. Today's session will address both.

The application of CBMT treatment components up to this point may have already substantially reduced the intensity of anger in the relationship, as couples exchange more positive behaviors, increase emotional expressiveness, increase empathy, reduce verbal attacks and defensive responding, negotiate problems, and revise negative relationship cognitions. However, some degree of problematic anger may linger and may call for direct intervention. In fact, persistent anger might hamper progress in the other areas of treatment by forestalling communication and behavior change efforts and impeding amenability to cognitive change.[1]

The rationale for this component of treatment is that anger often constitutes a destructive force in the marital relationship, whether the anger concerns past resentments or current

---

1. In cases where the anger of one or both spouses makes it impossible to follow the treatment structure, the therapist may opt to employ some or all of this chapter's techniques earlier in treatment. Depending on the nature of the partners' anger and their response to these partners' interventions, the therapist may recommend individual therapy or a longer-term course of CBMT.

difficulties. Although nondistressed couples experience anger, the emotion can exacerbate marital difficulties when couples experience it excessively or express it in harmful ways. Although anger normally occurs *in response to* troublesome aspects of the relationship, it can take on a life of its own, setting in motion conflictual, painful marital interactions. The dysfunctional expression of anger can devastate a relationship, as complaints turn contemptuous and partners reciprocate or withdraw. Even the unexpressed, inner experience of anger toward a spouse can be detrimental, as it erodes feelings of affection, reduces motivation to invest in the relationship, and often gets expressed indirectly. In explaining this rationale, it will be helpful to ask each partner to speak of ways in which his or her anger has been detrimental to the relationship.

The goals of anger-management strategies in couples therapy include reducing the destructive expression (or inhibition) of anger, rather than eliminating anger altogether. Partners will be taught strategies based on the work of Novaco (1975, 1976) and adapted for couples by Deschner (1984) and Neidig and Friedman (1984), including recognizing the advantages and disadvantages of expressing anger, identifying anger-eliciting cues, and employing a variety of coping skills. Further, while learning to control the destructive expression of anger, couples will learn to use the emotion as a signal to attend to a problem. Rather than squelching the communicative role of anger, couples will be encouraged to make use of their communication skills to enhance this function. As proponents of experiential therapies (e.g., Greenberg and Johnson 1988) argue, therapists might best serve clients by handling impassioned emotional states as mechanisms for exploring central beliefs and values rather than as bothersome conditions to be eliminated. Embedded in the intervention for mitigating one's experience and expression of anger will be emphasis on identifying, labeling, and constructively expressing a wide range of emotional experiences and distinguishing the "softer" emotions that often underlie angry states.

ANGER MANAGEMENT: EXCESSIVE EXPRESSION OF ANGER

For clients who express anger excessively, the therapist will want to teach self-calming strategies and constructive means of emotional expression. If partners share this problem, the following strategies can be applied to both. If only one partner expresses excessive anger, the other partner has likely been walking on eggshells and will probably feel relief in devoting time to this problem. In this case, the less angry partner is still part of the context of the other partner's anger and will thus play an important role in the interventions (e.g., understanding a partner's signal for a time-out).

Examining Pros and Cons of Anger Expression

A helpful way to initiate the modification of problematic anger is to ask partners to consider both the positive and negative effects of strong expressions of anger (Neidig and Friedman 1984, Novaco 1976). Individuals seldom take stock of the ways in which anger can be harmful or counterproductive in obtaining goals. Since people generally believe their anger is justified, they may feel hesitant to work on reducing it. Weighing the pros and cons can provide motivation for clients reluctant to relinquish their rage.

The therapist can ask partners about what the positive aspects are for them in getting angry, either in turn or as a conjoint brainstorming exercise. The therapist can then ask the couple to consider potential negative effects of anger, both short-term and long-term. Examples of positive and negative aspects of overt anger expression appear in Table 9-1.

Table 9-1
Potential Positive and Negative Aspects of Anger Expression

Positive Aspects of Anger Expression

- ▸ Signaling to oneself that a right or standard has been violated
- ▸ Motivating oneself for action toward protecting rights or values
- ▸ Maintaining self-respect
- ▸ Obtaining one's way
- ▸ Gaining a partner's attention
- ▸ Punishing a partner
- ▸ Quieting a partner or avoiding an uncomfortable topic
- ▸ Communicating strong feelings
- ▸ Providing a sense of empowerment
- ▸ Releasing tension

Negative Aspects of Anger Expression (short-term)

- ▸ Hurting a partner's feelings
- ▸ Frightening a partner
- ▸ Saying something one later regrets
- ▸ Provoking an escalation of conflict

Table 9–1, continued:

- ▸ Driving a partner to withdraw
- ▸ Failing to resolve a problem
- ▸ Causing an embarrassing situation (e.g., if in public)
- ▸ Sabotaging pleasant occasions or important events
- ▸ Feeling *dis*empowered or out of control
- ▸ Exacerbating one's own negative mood state

Negative Aspects of Anger Expression (long-term)

- ▸ Being a partner who is viewed as unapproachable, or who causes others to "walk on eggshells"
- ▸ Creating distance in the relationship
- ▸ Emotionally scarring one's partner
- ▸ Accumulating a roster of unresolved marital conflicts
- ▸ Creating a poor environment for children
- ▸ Frightening the children
- ▸ Causing difficulty at work
- ▸ Alienating outside relationships
- ▸ Increasing stress
- ▸ Creating health problems

Determining Functions of Anger Expression

Although anger can be harmful to a relationship, it may serve a variety of purposes for the angry partner. It will be important to determine the functions served by anger, since doing so will allow partners to consider alternative methods of obtaining the same benefits. Listing pros and cons is a first step in uncovering these purposes, as clients will reveal many of the ways in which anger has become functional for them. The therapist should take note of the subjective importance of anger expression to each client, since the goal will be for clients to retain many of these advantages while eliminating the harmful aspects of anger expression. To obtain more information on the ways anger is functional for clients, the therapist can ask them to discuss a typical anger episode, indicating what typically happens before, during, and after anger is expressed. This functional analysis may reveal that anger reliably occurs in response to particular antecedent events, or that it is predictably reinforced by particular consequences.

For example, one couple, Sophia and Spence, noticed that Sophia's anger became triggered more easily on days following nights when she was up with a crying baby, leaving her drained and with a short fuse. Her anger on these days typically consisted of her screaming at Spence for not doing his share of child care. Following these arguments, Spence usually participated in more child-care responsibilities for several days, yet also behaved more distantly toward Sophia. In recounting this pattern, they were able to recognize that Sophia's anger often functioned to relieve stress, communicate her feelings of being overwhelmed, and temporarily increase Spence's role in taking care of their child. They also saw that since these benefits offered only short-term gains while costing Sophia emotional intimacy with Spence, it was worth considering other ways of serving these functions.

Although this module of therapy teaches clients ways to reduce the destructive experience and expression of anger, it is not intended to eradicate the emotion altogether. When anger (or any negative emotion) is experienced, individuals should neither ignore it nor focus solely on eliminating it, but use it as a signal to attend to a problem. In fact, anger can be adaptive in that it highlights cues of important relationship distress-controlling variables, which may have serious ramifications if left unattended. Getting angry provides a fortuitous opportunity to examine automatic thoughts, which run abundantly and prominently during strong affective experiences. So, rather than squelching the communicative function of anger, the therapist can encourage couples to take advantage of the chance to gain insight and translate this knowledge into constructive action. By attending to the problems signaled by her anger, Sophia might have realized: "I am feeling overburdened and like I cannot handle this on my own. I need some time to relax, and I need Spence to show some understanding of what I'm going through. I also feel there has been a breach in our agreement about our parenting roles; I feel let down and I need to speak to him about taking more responsibility for our child." With this insight, Sophia's goals would become clearly defined, leaving her more likely to satisfy her needs while incurring few, if any, costs.

Once the functions of anger for a couple have been considered, the therapist can proceed with intervention strategies. These strategies may include recognizing warning cues and applying a variety of calming strategies.

Recognizing Warning Cues

People who excessively express anger typically report that anger overtakes them suddenly and intensely, with little or no warning. They may make statements such as, "It happens all at once. I'm okay one moment and the next moment, boom! I'm furious." By the time these clients recognize their anger, their affect is so intense that it is difficult to control. The therapist can point out to clients that, in fact, there are often many warning signs of anger that we can detect with practice. The goal will be for them to learn to become astute observers of them. By detecting the onset of anger before it reaches full intensity, they will have a better chance of coping with it before it becomes destructive. These cues fall into four categories: physiological, cognitive, behavioral, and environmental.

Physiological Cues

Physiological cues are the bodily sensations that occur as the level of anger rises. A helpful way to facilitate clients' recognition of physiological anger signs is to guide them through a "tour of the body," in which they recall their typical angry state and systematically describe the physical effects of their anger on their bodies, from head to toe. The therapist might provide several examples, such as a tension in the forehead and jaw, a racing heart, or a knot in the stomach, while walking each partner through a progression of body areas and asking them to think about sensations they experience in these areas when angry. The therapist can then direct couples to observe the occurrence of these sensations during future episodes of anger. They will often signal the onset of anger and allow for coping before the emotion has reached peak intensity. Table 9–2 provides a list of common physiological signs of anger.

| Table 9-2 |
| Examples of Physical Signs of Anger for "Tour of the Body" Exercise |

Head and neck:	Head throbbing, forehead sweating, brows furrowed, eyes narrowed, nostrils flared, cheeks flushed, mouth frowning, jaws clenched, teeth grinding
Shoulders and arms:	Shoulders tense, palms sweating, hands clenched in fists
Chest, back, stomach:	Chest tightened, heart rate increased, sensation of increased blood pressure, sensation of increased body temperature, breathing more rapid and shallow, tension or stiffness in back muscles, "knot" in stomach
Legs, feet:	Tension in leg muscles, rapid foot tapping, toes curled

Cognitive Cues

Cognitive cues are the automatic thoughts that race through a client's head as he or she becomes angry. Previous sessions taught clients to detect their automatic thoughts, test their validity, and challenge them. Here, they need to build on these skills in order to recognize their thoughts rapidly. The therapist can instruct clients to notice when their automatic thoughts are inciting anger, or are "hot" cognitions. (Greenberg and Safran 1987, Neidig and Friedman 1984). Hot cognitions may occur in the form of any type of cognition (e.g., perceptions, assumptions), or in the form of short exclamations, and are frequently bursting with cognitive distortions. Examples include thoughts such as, "I can't take this anymore!" or "That jerk!" or "She's impossible!" or "He's doing this just to get to me!" or "She's not going to get away with this!" In session, clients may be able to recall the hot cognitions that typically run through their minds when angry. It may be helpful to ask them to take a minute to remember a recent anger episode, use imagery to sharpen the memory, and notice the anger-provoking thoughts that come to mind. Since automatic thoughts tend to occur rapidly in an angry emotional state, clients may also observe the very experience of "racing thoughts" in addition to noting the content of these thoughts.

Behavioral Cues

Behavioral cues are actions taken while becoming angry. Pointing, gesturing dramatically, raising one's voice, pounding a fist, interrupting, not listening, and speaking rapidly or deliberately are common behavioral indications of anger. The therapist should ask each partner to recall his or her range of angry behaviors.

Environmental Cues

Environmental or contextual cues include the situations that clients know from prior experience are likely to set the stage for the escalation of anger toward a partner. These might include situations related or unrelated to the relationship, such as a partner arriving late, a messy house, a critical remark, a demanding child, a stressful day at work, or an unresolved relationship conflict. Recognizing provocative situations makes it possible to engage in preventive coping to avoid angry outbursts. In session, clients can be asked to discuss typical situations that set the stage for anger.

Coping with Escalating Anger

Various strategies aid clients in coping with each of the four types of anger warning cues. These include physical calming strategies, cognitive calming strategies, behavioral calming strategies, and environment-focused calming strategies.

Physical Calming Strategies

By addressing physiological arousal states associated with anger escalation, physical calming strategies help prevent full-blown anger episodes, and also can provide the desired release of tension that the cathartic property of anger expression can provide. The therapist can teach clients a variety of approaches to calm themselves. One such method is inducing relaxation with diaphragmatic breathing. Clients can be instructed to practice taking slow, deep, breaths (about eight to ten per minute), while placing their hands on the abdomen. The hand should move back and forth in pace with the breaths, while the chest area remains relatively still. This ensures deep breaths, which will begin to quiet the arousal. The therapist should caution clients that large chest movements during inhalations and exhalations indicates shallow breathing, which can lead to hyperventilation and *increased* arousal. Clients may practice in session as the therapist directs them in the proper form of breathing.

Another method of coping with physical anger arousal is to instruct clients to count to sixty before speaking when they notice an increase in anger (of course this time should be used to calm oneself down, and to gather one's thoughts to plan a nonattacking statement; the delay in responding will backfire if the time is filled with anger-inducing thoughts). As a supplementary method, clients can count to ten before each utterance, to prevent the impulsive, often hurtful responses associated with anger. This practice can help keep the discussion from escalating.

In addition, clients can call a time-out when they recognize the physical warning signs of anger arousal. A time-out involves one partner leaving the situation for a specified period of time, with the understanding that the partner will return when calmer. Several guidelines make the time-out procedure especially effective:

1. The range of time for leaving a situation should be specified in advance by the couple in session. It should be long enough to calm down but short enough to avoid punishing or abandoning the spouse (e.g., it would be counterproductive to stay out all night). Somewhere between thirty and ninety minutes should suffice. Importantly, partners will want to be certain that they are physically calm before returning to the interaction; resuming the discussion while still aroused will almost certainly lead to a rapid escalation. If the time-out period is over and a partner notices continued arousal, he or she should explain this to the other in a neutral manner and the time-out should be extended for thirty minutes.

2. Couples should use a preordained signal to call a time-out so that it will not be confused with storming out.

Calling a time-out indicates a constructive effort to prevent a volatile interaction, while storming out suggests an impulsive and usually destructive response to a conflict. This signal can be the hand gesture for time-out (i.e., a *T* sign), or a simple statement such as "I need to take a time-out." Again, partners can develop their signal in the therapy session to avoid ambiguity in a stressful situation.

3. A partner should not try to prevent the one who has signaled the time-out from leaving. Built into the time-out procedure is the understanding that the partner will return once he or she can interact in a more composed manner.

4. Couples should agree in advance on what behaviors they consider acceptable during a time-out. Such behavior might include going into another room and shutting the door, going for a walk or jog, going for a bike ride, or doing yardwork. It defeats the purpose of a time-out to use the time vindictively (such as driving recklessly, downing shots of liquor, or smashing dishes), or to engage in activities that maintain anger (such as hitting a pillow imagined to be one's partner, or ruminating over anger-inducing thoughts or images).

5. During the time-out, it can be especially helpful for the client to engage in calming behaviors. Depending on personal preference, these might include exercising, drinking a cup of herbal tea, taking a shower, doing something athletic, calling a friend, reading the paper,

listening to soft music, watching TV, visualizing pleasant scenes, writing in a journal, lying down, or engaging in yoga or relaxation techniques. In session, the therapist can elicit from each partner several favored calming activities; clients should verbally commit to engage in one of these during the next time-out. This will be more successful than waiting for an angry emotional state to think of an activity.

Cognitive Calming Strategies

To cope with the cognitive cues of escalating anger (i.e., hot cognitions), clients will need to rapidly recognize their hot thoughts and spontaneously rebut them with alternative, "cool" self-statements. Because rapid anger escalation prohibits a leisurely expenditure of time, rather than subject thoughts to logical analysis, the task instead will be to circumvent these steps and quickly substitute "cooler" thoughts. If thoughts are fueling destructive anger, the question of whether they are reasonable becomes irrelevant. Cool thoughts are soothing self-statements that challenge hot thoughts in order to decrease anger. Table 9–3 shows the hot cognitions listed above with countering, cool cognitions. In session, clients can practice generating cool thoughts in response to the angering thoughts they identified earlier. Note that it might be helpful during an argument for clients to take a time-out, or to punctuate their interactions with long counting pauses, to create time to replace anger-evoking thoughts.

Table 9–3	
Hot and Cool Cognitions	
Hot Cognitions	*Cool Cognitions*
"I can't take this anymore!"	"This feels hard but we'll get through it."
"That jerk!"	"He's just saying those things because he's angry."
"She's impossible!"	"She's difficult at times but reasonable at others."
"He's doing this just to get to me!"	"I can't be sure why he's doing this."
"She won't get away with this."	"Punishing her won't help."
"How dare he!"	"He's probably not thinking clearly now, either."

To help clients generate cool responses to hot cognitions, it is instructive to point out the *hostility bias* that research has shown characterizes aggressive behavior. That is, individuals who have problems with anger control tend to make more hostile attributions about the behavior of others. In marriage, this bias may translate into reading more negative intent into a partner's ambiguous behavior, such as assuming that a forgotten phone call home is a deliberate provocation or that an innocent question implies an accusation. Reacting to such assumptions, partners with a hostility bias will respond more frequently and apparently arbitrarily with anger. Couples with anger problems will usually recognize such tendencies in their relationship. If they know to look for it, partners may more easily be able to identify this bias in their automatic thoughts while angry, and rebut with a self-statement such as, "I'm assuming he means that as an attack but I don't know for sure."

Sometimes clients will have difficulty generating a cool response to a hot thought because they are convinced of the thought's accuracy, or simply because they are too angry to think rationally. In addition to taking a time-out, another method of coping with the cognitive aspects of escalating anger in this case involves the use of calming self-statements directed at *replacing, although not directly countering*, the angering thoughts and impulses to attack. Like restructured cognitions and cool cognitions, calming self-statements occur in the form of consciously directed thought, as though one were carrying around a personal, internalized, relationship coach. These self-statements do not rely on being able to generate a cool replacement to an angering thought, but can be used for any angry experience. Such calming pronouncements include statements such as, "Let it go," "It's not worth it," "Calm down," "Raising my voice isn't going to help," "Cool off," "Chill out," "Take it easy," or "Stay in control." Clients should be encouraged to use any calming statements that have worked for them in the past or that feel natural. The therapist can show clients how to adapt these self-statements by using covert modeling, in which (1) the therapist says the statement aloud; (2) the client repeats the statement aloud; (3) the therapist says the statement again, and coaches the client to repeat the statement covertly (i.e., as a thought only); (4) the client repeats the statement covertly. As additional motivation to abide by self-statements such as "it's not worth it" and "let it go," the therapist might advise clients to simultaneously evoke thoughts of one or two meaningful disadvantages of expressing anger that they generated earlier in the session. This strategy, if implemented effectively by the couple, has the advantage over taking a time-out of allowing the interaction to continue immediately.

Behavioral Calming Strategies

The above strategies of diaphragmatic breathing, counting prior to speaking, time-out, and use of cool thoughts or calming self-talk will all contribute to thwarting the menacing behaviors that accompany anger escalation.

Environment-Focused Calming Strategies

In coping with environmentally based anger triggers, time-outs offer temporary refuge from stressful environmental triggers, while cognitive calming strategies may change one's appraisal of an environmental provocation. In addition, making use of assertive communication and problem solving can address problematic situations without impulsive anger outbursts. Clear and nonattacking communication may help avert an angry exchange, whether addressing the problem in the moment (e.g., "I would appreciate your help with the kids now") or allowing for some temporary repose ("I had a very stressful day; I just need to sit and read for twenty minutes to unwind, if that's okay"). If by this session clients are still using angry methods of making demands or avoiding interaction, they may need continued practice with identifying feelings, assertive communication skills, and problem solving. Brief problem solving may work in the moment to forestall conflict escalation as well. However, this may be best scheduled soon at a mutually convenient time, since the heat of anger will likely interfere with constructive problem-solving efforts. Problem solving about a repeatedly troublesome situation will address not only a present conflict but will help prevent future angry episodes as well.

Identifying a Range of Emotions

Additional work on affect identification may benefit partners who (1) seem to filter the majority of their negative emotional states through the label of "anger," or (2) seem unable to recognize subtle emotional cues, and are therefore unable to assert associated needs until they become infuriated at a gross violation by their partner. Components of enhanced affect identification will include increased awareness of emotions, expression of emotions other than anger, and the use of emotions to better determine needs and problems in the marriage.

The therapist can explain to the couple that becoming more familiar with the variety of emotional states we experience will be important for managing anger and communicating effectively with a partner. For example, the XYZ model of communication includes the section "I *feel* Z." Without knowing how we feel, it will be difficult to convey the impact of a partner's behaviors. Moreover, some individuals are less able to distinguish the full spectrum of negative emotions, and label all of their troublesome emotions as anger, a phenomenon that has been called the "emotional funnel system" (Gondolf 1985). The trouble with this proclivity is that the repeated expression of anger, even if it is communicated politely, may leave a partner feeling perpetually censured. In contrast, expressing the "softer" emotions (e.g., hurt, jealousy, sadness, or fear) that often underlie angry states will feel less attacking, as discussed in Chapter 4. Furthermore, accurate perception of emotions steers a couple toward more direct empathy, validation, and problem solving.

Additionally, individuals who are not aware of their feelings may have trouble identifying and asserting their needs. Therefore, they may be prone to intense, uncontrolled expressions of anger when a threshold has been crossed, rather than communicating regularly and before negative emotions have built up. Awareness of a range of emotions allows one to reappraise a portion of emotional experiences categorized as "angry," a shift that might reduce one's sense of blame or distress.

The therapist can convey to the couple that identifying one's fine-grained emotional states can be challenging and takes practice. Additional session time might then be devoted to studying descriptive terms for the range of emotional states (Chapter 4), considering various scenarios and selecting the most fitting emotional labels, and identifying the physiological sensations that normally accompany the different feeling states (a process similar to the "tour of the body" exercise).

ANGER MANAGEMENT: OVERLY INHIBITED ANGER

Perpetually unexpressed anger can cause an insidious deterioration in relationship functioning as resentments accumulate, amorous feelings fade, and distance grows. Angry feelings may be expressed indirectly through moodiness, sulking, withdrawal, or episodic "irrational" expressions of hostility. For couples in which one or both partners overly inhibit anger, the therapist will want to incorporate strategies described in this section.

Beginning with an examination of the *pros and cons of inhibiting anger* will be a useful exercise for clients. In listing the advantages of continually keeping angry feelings to themselves, clients may reveal telling automatic thoughts about expressing anger, including a fear of retribution, a sense of futility regarding attaining desired goals, or a lack of entitlement to feelings. Such beliefs may warrant additional work on challenging and revising cognitions. Examining the disadvantages of inhibiting anger may also counterbalance the stated advantages, and leave clients more open to attempt new anger-management strategies.

Exploring the functions of anger inhibition should also prove fruitful (e.g., keeping anger to oneself may reflect a communication skill deficit or serve to avoid confrontation). At times, unexpressed anger will concern pent-up resentments from past injustices, hurts, or violations of trust. For example, a spouse whose partner terminated an affair may have residual anger about the infidelity but may feel reluctant to raise the subject for fear of reopening painful wounds or needlessly perpetuating a "resolved" problem. When continued feelings about such matters result in ongoing relationship tension, clients may be better off broaching the issue. The therapist can guide clients in initiating a sensitive and empathic discussion about the subject of resentment; in such cases the suffering partner may benefit from nondefensive listening and validation from the spouse rather than problem solving.

Individuals who keep anger to themselves may have a difficult time recognizing when they are angry. Thus, such individuals will also benefit from familiarizing themselves with anger warning signs. Many of the physiological, cognitive, and environmental signals will overlap with those experienced by people with overly expressed anger. However, behavioral cues will vastly differ (e.g., speaking curtly would be more likely than shouting). In addition, practice with feeling identification and assertive communication skills will be useful for clients whose anger inhibition reflects capability deficits rather than negative cognitions about anger expression.

Session Review and Homework

Unlike previous sessions, the session review and homework today will occur before the end of the session, leaving time for discussion of the overall treatment and termination.

Homework will tie in directly with the review of the session. The therapist can hand each partner a copy of the Anger Worksheet (Table 9–4), which they will complete for homework. Before assigning homework, however, the therapist will walk clients through the steps on the sheet in a review of points covered in session. In doing so, the therapist might provide the following explanation while pointing to the relevant sections on the handout:

Let's take a few moments to review what we covered today. This worksheet consolidates the various steps of anger management, so why don't we walk through it together. Starting at the top, let's say we encounter an angering situation, such as . . . (example relevant to couple). Now the first thing we'd do is try to focus in on physiological, cognitive, behavioral, and environmental warning signs, to catch ourselves before the anger gets more intense. Next, we would try to note what behavioral urge we were experiencing, such as storming out of a room, and ask what purpose would it have served. Would it have helped? Made things worse?

Now, we would ask what the emotion is signaling, asking ourselves what problem is in need of attention. This could be many different things. We may realize a right or standard has been threatened or violated, or that our self-respect has been threatened. In such a case the anger may be helping us to feel more empowered as we get ready to stand up for ourselves. We may feel a strong need to get our way—to get our partner to do what we want. Similarly, we may be trying to communicate strong feelings or let our partner know we need attention or some kind of help. We may want to express our anger to punish our partner, or we may be trying to find a way to avoid something. It's also possible that any of these problems may have left us reaching the boiling point on the inside, and the main objective now is to release tension, to reduce the aversive arousal we're feeling.

We'll also want to look for any other emotions that might be underlying the anger, such as hurt, sadness, or shame. Remember that it might be helpful to focus on expressing these more vulnerable emotions and also to ask ourselves what these other emotions may be signaling.

Next, we can look at our coping options. Immediate, "crisis-coping" efforts might include time-out, calming self-statements, or assertive communication. We can also ask what other ways there are of coping to address the problems the anger was signaling? Are there longer-term issues to address? Such attempts will usually be based on skillful use of communication and behavioral negotiation strategies, or cognitive restructuring.

Finally, we should consider the results of our coping attempts. When we go through these steps, we may not yet have gotten to longer-term coping efforts, but we can at least look at our short-term efforts and see which strategies were helpful.

While walking the couple through the handout, the therapist should pause to answer questions and encourage clients to supply examples.

This assignment will be based on an experience of anger in the upcoming week (if clients do not experience anger over the next week, they should select their most recent anger episode). Clients will complete the worksheet at home, ideally *as they observe their anger increasing*, before it reaches a peak level of intensity and before they engage in destructive interactions. If they are not able to do this, then they should complete the worksheet following an episode of anger, filling out the sections retrospectively.

TREATMENT REVIEW

As this is the last regular therapy session (the next scheduled appointment consists of homework review, outcome as-

---

Table 9–4
Anger Worksheet

Situation: Date:

Warning Signs of Increasing Anger:

Physical:

Cognitive:

Behavioral:

Environmental:

Behavior (or behavioral urge):

---

sessment, and relapse-prevention strategies), the therapist can now turn to reviewing the treatment gains. The therapist can do this both by eliciting the couple's perspectives and by sharing his or her own. The therapist can ask the partners what areas they felt were especially helpful to them, in what domains they made the most progress, and in what areas they feel they still need to work. The therapist can also begin to elicit clients' feelings about treatment termination. We will say more about this in Chapter 10.

10

Post-Treatment Session: Continuing Treatment after Termination: Relapse Prevention

Setting the Agenda

Although this session technically constitutes a post-treatment encounter with couples (and should occur in the week following the eighth session), the very point of this chapter is that treatment, that is, the skills and strategies learned, can and should continue past the official end of weekly sessions with the therapist. This post-treatment session will run *an additional hour* in length to allow for assessing treatment outcome. The therapist should inform the clients that the session will begin with post-treatment assessments, and then cover positive tracking, review of homework, a review of the week, a discussion of treatment gains, and specific recommendations for maintaining progress. It is especially important in this session that clients be encouraged to place a topic of their choice on the agenda, and to devote time to it. Frequently, couples experience considerable trepidation about stopping therapy. They typically bring into last sessions a combination of general worries that things will deteriorate without the weekly structure of therapy and specific questions about handling potential marital conflicts. The relapse-prevention focus of this session will directly address many of the couple's concerns about future functioning. In addition, it is useful simply to allow time for the partners to reflect on their experiences in this brief but intensive therapy, and to express any parting sentiments to the therapist.

Post-Treatment Assessment

Depending on the therapist's desire, clients can repeat the

set of measures from Session 1 (assessment) or a subset of these measures. At the very least, they should complete the Marital Adjustment Test, which provides a global satisfaction rating.

The couple should then complete another ten-minute problem discussion, ideally choosing the same topic as in Session 1. They should discuss the problem under the same conditions as in Session 1 (e.g., therapist present or not). Afterwards, the therapist can discuss this procedure with them, asking their impressions of changes in the tenor of the discussion from their initial experience with this exercise.

Positive Tracking

Positive tracking should occur as always. By now it should be ingrained for the partners to be mindful of each other's positive behaviors and to begin relationship-focused interactions with positive feedback.

Review of Homework

The therapist should review the homework on anger control by looking over each partner's Anger Worksheet with the couple. The therapist can ask clients what they learned from the exercise, and what outcome they achieved by attempting new coping strategies. As always, the therapist can take this time to clarify areas of misunderstanding, troubleshoot difficulties with the assignment, and praise the clients for their efforts.

Review of Treatment Gains

In promoting a discussion of treatment gains, the therapist can ask clients what improvements they see in their partners, what improvements they see in themselves, and what changes these improvements contribute to the functioning of the relationship. There may be a tendency to focus on the negatives here for fear of "speaking now or forever holding one's peace." While acknowledging areas still in need of attention, the therapist can offer general reassurance that the couple has now learned skills to handle problem areas and can continue to improve on their own. Couples must understand that just as their problems developed over a significant course of time, it may take a while to restore the relationship. That is why skills learned in treatment must be applied in the long run. So today's session will address strategies to foster ongoing attention to the relationship.

RELAPSE PREVENTION

What might be thought of as a "life support" notion of therapy, often held by couples, is that coming regularly to therapy and being connected to the therapist keeps their relationship alive. Couples with this perspective view therapy termination as "pulling the plug." Naturally, then, they will be terrified of treatment coming to an end.

By contrast, what might be labeled a "weaning model" of therapy, held by many therapists, regards therapy as a process in which the client (or couple) gradually comes to need less from the therapist as healthy autonomous functioning develops. Cognitive-behavioral therapists in particular view the weaning process as starting almost from the outset of therapy, as they actively teach skills to help clients sustain the marital relationship on their own. Therapy serves a largely didactic function, one that empowers a couple to become progressively less dependent on the therapy. From this point of view, the therapist gradually reduces his or her degree of directiveness and encourages the couple to become increasingly interactive and self-directive in session. This perspective conceptualizes couple independence from the therapist as a step-by-step process; termination of weekly contact comes as a natural step in this journey toward independence. This is where relapse prevention fits in.

Relapse-prevention methods supply the means to retain treatment gains and prevent a slide back to a clinical level of distress, and generally include strategies aimed toward maintenance and generalization of skills throughout treatment, as well as strategies to detect and cope with backsliding after treatment termination. Couples must understand that their relationship will need continued care and attention beyond therapy if they wish to avoid returning to old patterns. CBMT offers several methods of preventing relapse, including strategies used throughout therapy and strategies offered at the time of therapy termination.

Strategies Used throughout Therapy

Throughout CBMT, the therapist employs numerous strategies to generalize and maintain benefits of treatment. These include therapist modeling of new skills, in-session practice of skills with therapist coaching and feedback, and regular homework assignments with thorough reviews. In-session practice allows the therapist to assure proper application and acquisition of skills, while homework practice enhances generalization of skills to the home environment.

Another strategy the therapist employs throughout therapy involves the gradual encouragement of increased couple autonomy, both within each treatment module or set of skills taught and over the course of treatment. After the couple demonstrates some initial mastery of each new set of skills (e.g., communication, problem-solving), the therapist switches from a heavily didactic and modeling mode (to facilitate learning) to a coaching mode (to facilitate application). Within each topic area, the therapist increasingly fades the directiveness of prompts from providing specific instruction and feedback to having the partners perform the skills, critique their own performance, and get themselves back on track when needed. From the beginning of treatment the therapist urges the partners to communicate directly with each other and to face each other and maintain eye contact. This directive dissuades partners from talking to each other through the therapist, and helps them become accustomed to speaking face-to-face without the necessity of a third party playing a role in the interaction. Finally, by patterning treatment sessions after a basic structure (e.g., beginning with positive tracking), partners form lasting constructive communication habits (e.g., acknowledging the partner's positive behaviors as a routine part of problem discussions).

Strategies Offered at Treatment Termination

In addition to the therapeutic strategies used throughout treatment that help to ensure lasting effects, six relapse prevention strategies focused on post-therapy interaction include: (1) making time for home communication sessions, (2) anticipating future problems and planning solutions, (3) recognizing signs of backsliding, (4) reframing backslides as opportunities for learning, (5) reviewing the Relationship Deck (see p. 323), and (6) scheduling booster sessions.

Making Time for Home Communication Sessions

Some couples report that the therapy hour is the only time during the week when they sustain an exclusive, uninterrupted focus on their relationship. Embracing a life-support view of therapy, they fear that therapy termination signals a termination of this concentrated and regular attention to their relationship. However, this need not be the case. In fact, to ensure that the regular time couples have come to devote to their relationship does not decline, the therapist can suggest that the couple schedule regular home communication sessions. A couple's communication may be strengthened at the end of the initial training sessions, just as their physical strength may be improved by an exercise program with a personal trainer, but it will need regular "workouts" to maintain the gains and become even stronger. Explain to the clients that without care and attention to their interactions, their communication will likely deteriorate into earlier maladaptive patterns. Thus, the couple should plan to hold communication sessions weekly, setting aside at least thirty minutes to state gripes, address problems, and express positive feelings. Of course, during this time, the couple should remember to use constructive speaker and listener skills, and use the time to keep these skills fresh and to ensure continuity in the connection forged by therapy. Partners should be sure to pick a time when they are both able to focus (e.g., *not* before an important meeting at work) and a place where they are unlikely to be disturbed. They can even keep the general structure of the therapy sessions, beginning by setting an agenda and acknowledging positive partner behaviors from the previous week.

The therapist can ask the couple to agree to a time for these sessions right on the spot (the regular therapy hour is usually a good choice, and the couple can begin the following week), to increase the likelihood that they will follow through. By simply imparting the notion that they can continue the therapeutic work independently, couples may feel relief and may be more likely to recapture the feeling of the therapy sessions on their own.

Anticipating Future Problems and Planning Solutions

The time earlier in this session devoted to discussing treatment gains will provide a natural transition into discussing potential future problems and planning solutions. Couples will be aware of the areas they have mastered as well as potential trouble spots. The therapist can ask couples to state two or three areas of concern; these might include internal relationship conflicts (e.g., one partner may still tend to make overly negative attributions) or external relationship threats (e.g., an upcoming business trip when separation has posed difficulty in the past). The therapist can then prompt the couple to engage in brief, on-the-spot brainstorming on how to handle these problems. In addition, couples can build in prescheduled home communication sessions specifically to address these concerns. Even if couples have not yet mastered every skill, problems can be greatly mitigated by positive communication about the process of working on them, such as, "I'm still having a hard time with this but I want you to know I'm trying," or "I'm getting a little stuck trying to see this any differently but I still think we're doing great in other areas."

Although session time will not allow a lengthy discussion of potential future difficulties, the therapist might encourage the partners to continue this discussion on their own, or even have the discussion routinely as part of their home communication sessions. In other words, they can anticipate not only general areas of difficulty but specific problems they may be facing in the upcoming week. For instance, if in-laws pose problems and a visit with them is imminent, the couple might plan for anticipated troubles ahead of time; if partners know that they have clashing preferred styles of vacationing, they may decide to schedule a problem-solving session as a matter of course before leaving for each vacation together. In anticipating the types of conflicts they are likely to confront, couples can negotiate solutions *before* emotions get heated, expectations are dashed, and resentments set in.

Recognizing Signs of Backsliding

It is critical for couples to be able to perceive warning signs that their relationship may be heading back into the danger zone of discord. They may notice their pleasing behaviors trailing off, their thoughts and emotions becoming more negative, or patterns of criticism and defensiveness seeping back into their communication. In session, the therapist can ask each partner what signals might indicate difficulty for the relationship. By being alert to such signs, the couple can address them before they become (re)entrenched patterns. Perhaps an extra home-communication session will be needed, or maybe partners will wish to formally monitor their thoughts again for a specified period.

Reframing Backslides as Opportunities for Learning

Although couples will want to remain vigilant about relationship danger signals, they need not panic when they detect them. It will be helpful for couples to remain attuned to their cognitions about signs of relationship distress, and to challenge them when needed. For example, it is not uncommon for couples noticing problems to overgeneralize that "nothing has changed," or to reason emotionally, that "it's just not going to work out." It is important to send the message that even the best relationships encounter difficulty at times, and that sporadic slips are to be expected and do not reflect a loss of all treatment gains. It will be helpful for the couple to view backsliding as an opportunity for learning, rather than an indication of treatment failure. In the interest of learning from relationship danger signs, they might examine the troubling situation and ask questions such as, "Under what situations are we most likely to go through this?" or "What exactly led up to this?" or "Were there any signs that this was coming?" and, finally, "What are the various steps we learned in therapy to handle this type of issue?" Clients might be encouraged by remembering that they are far ahead of where they were when they entered treatment; they now have available a wide range of strategies for handling newly emerging problems.

Reviewing the Relationship Deck

Another technique for preventing relapse involves the therapist developing a personalized "Relationship Deck," which is a set of cards containing tips and strategies geared to a couple's particular areas of focus within therapy. Although CBMT employs a standard set of procedures, each couple brings in a unique constellation of problems and finds different aspects of the treatment particularly relevant or helpful. The Relationship Deck capitalizes on the couple's individuality, and serves as a sort of summary of the treatment while providing the partners helpful reminders of what was especially useful for them. This procedure is a variant of Weiss and Birchler's (1978) "cookie jar" strategy of filling a jar with slips of paper printed with various pleasing behaviors personalized for each spouse; routinely drawing slips from this jar serves as a reminder to engage in positive exchanges beyond the final therapy session.

Creating the Relationship Deck involves obtaining a set of index cards and writing on each card a general or specific communication strategy, caring gesture, cognition, or other item that emerged as particularly useful for the couple to address in therapy. Items can be written for each partner and for the couple as a pair. These may be formal elements of the treatment (e.g., reminding the couple to validate each other) or idiosyncratic findings that arose in working with the couple. For example, one couple might have discovered that keeping a sense of humor about problems helped diffuse the anger; a card in the relationship deck might remind the couple to maintain their use of humor. Another couple might have discovered that scanning the Internet together added new shared pleasure; a card might encourage weekly treks into cyberspace. Still another couple, plagued by negative automatic thoughts, may benefit from a general card reminding them to question their thoughts before jumping to conclusions, or a specific statement instructing: "Remember, when Andy withdraws it often means he's overwhelmed by work. Ask him what's going on first, rather than assuming he's upset with you." The therapist can capture what worked best for the couple by writing out a creative and individualized deck of cards; he or she can then present it to the couple tied with a ribbon. The therapist can urge the couple to periodically look through the deck, or draw cards from it during times of difficulty; this allows couples to continue to "draw from" the therapy long after its termination.

Scheduling "Booster Sessions"

Finally, booster sessions contribute to relapse prevention

and alter the concept of termination as we typically think of it. Rather than conducting a final session and saying goodbye to the clients forever, the therapist can suggest continued contact through periodic future sessions. Like dental checkups, booster sessions with the marital therapist allow for monitoring of "decay" or problematic "buildups." These visits can occur at a predetermined frequency (e.g., every six months), or can be arranged as the couple needs them. The idea is that the couple may need to come in for additional help if skills begin to fade or if new challenges arise. Since the therapist already knows the couple, a periodic single session can be effective in troubleshooting a problem and coaching the couple in handling it. Within this model, visits with the therapist become ongoing, but ultimately infrequent, as opposed to the model of therapy as intensive and finite. Alternatively, a therapist might choose to fade the frequency of sessions, gradually spacing visits further and further apart once the initial period of weekly treatment is complete (in the phase of acquiring new skills, we would not recommend spacing sessions; massed practice of skills will be most effective while mastering new ways of interacting).

Continuing to Practice

As an ending word to the couple, the therapist should stress that all of the new interaction strategies learned will require extensive continued practice to become automatic. That is, until the various techniques become habitual, the danger remains that partners will fall into their old habits when they are feeling emotional. The therapist therefore needs to emphasize that in addition to the relapse-prevention strategies mentioned above, couples should continually engage in all the various treatment components, such as critically evaluating their thoughts, managing their anger, communicating nondefensively, and working to maintain a high level of rewards in the relationship through positive sentiments, caring gestures, demonstrations of affection, and shared activities. Couples can continue to make use of the therapy tools as needed, such as the RTR, the Anger Worksheet, or the communication handouts. Because of the short-term nature of this treatment, the therapist can only introduce each strategy and offer limited opportunities for practice and coaching; he or she cannot see all of the new skills through until they are thoroughly learned by the couple. However, CBMT provides couples with the tools to work on their relationship independent of therapy; there is no reason, then, that with continued use of these tools the relationship cannot continue to improve after therapy.

This book presented an eight-session course of cognitive-behavioral marital therapy. Because of the structure the book followed, we were not able to address in detail some of the particular content issues that couples often bring to therapy. Thus, we have included Appendix II, which provides references for common marital problems, which are listed in alphabetical order by topic.

Appendices

I

Efficacy Studies

The following reference list consists of the collection of efficacy studies evaluating behavioral or cognitive-behavioral marital therapy interventions. A brief summary of the empirical status of CBMT appears in Appendix III.

Azrin, N. H., Besalel, V. A., Betchel, R., et al. (1980). Comparison of reciprocity and discussion-type counseling for marital problems. *American Journal of Family Therapy* 8:21–28.

Baucom, D. H. (1982). A comparison of behavioral contracting and problem solving/communications training in behavioral marital therapy. *Behavior Therapy* 13:162–174.

Baucom, D. H., and Lester, G. W. (1986). The usefulness of cognitive restructuring as an adjunct to behavioral marital therapy. *Behavior Therapy* 17:385–403.

Baucom, D. H., Sayers, S. L., and Sher, T. (1990). Supplementing behavioral marital therapy with cognitive restructuring and emotional expressiveness training: an outcome investigation. *Journal of Consulting and Clinical Psychology* 58:636–645.

Behrens, B. C., Sanders, M. R., and Halford, W. K. (1990). Behavioral marital therapy: an evaluation of treatment effects across high and low risk settings. *Behavior Therapy* 21(4):423–434.

Bennun, I. (1985). Behavioral marital therapy: an outcome evaluation of conjoint, group, and one spouse treatment. *Scandinavian Journal of Behavior Therapy* 14:157–168.

Boelens, W., Emmelkamp, P., MacGillavry, D., and Markvoort, M. (1980). A clinical analysis of marital treatment:

reciprocity counseling vs. system-theoretic counseling. *Behavior Analysis and Modification* 4:85–96.

Crowe, M. J. (1978). Conjoint marital therapy: a controlled outcome study. *Psychological Medicine* 8:623–636.

Ely, A. L., Guerney, B. G., and Stover, L. (1973). Efficacy of the training phase of conjugal therapy. *Psychotherapy: Theory, Research, and Practice* 10:201–207.

Emmelkamp, P. M. G., van der Helm, M., MacGillavry, D., and van Zanten, B. (1984). Marital therapy with clinically distressed couples: a comparative evaluation of system-theoretic, contingency contracting, and communication skills approaches. In *Marital Interaction: Analysis and Modification*, ed. K. Hahlweg and N. S. Jacobson, pp. 36–52. New York: Guilford.

Emmelkamp, P. M. G., van Linden van den Heuvell, C., Ruphan, M., et al. (1988). Cognitive and behavioral interventions: a comparative evaluation with clinically distressed couples. *Journal of Family Psychology* 1:365–377.

Epstein, N., and Jackson, E. (1978). An outcome study of short-term communication training with married couples. *Journal of Consulting and Clinical Psychology* 46:207–212.

Epstein, N., Pretzer, J. L., and Fleming, B. (1982). *Cognitive therapy and communication training: comparisons of effects with distressed couples.* Paper presented at the annual meeting of the Association for Advancement of Behavior Therapy, Los Angeles, November.

Ewart, C. K. (1978). *Behavior contracts in couple therapy: an experimental evaluation of quid pro quo and good faith models.* Paper presented at the annual meeting of the Association for Advancement of Behavior Therapy, Toronto, August.

Hahlweg, K., and Markman, H. J. (1988). Effectiveness of behavioral marital therapy: empirical status of behavioral techniques in preventing and alleviating marital distress. *Journal of Consulting and Clinical Psychology* 56:440–447.

Hahlweg, K., Revenstorf, D., and Schindler, L. (1984). Effects of behavioral marital therapy on couples' communication and problem-solving skills. *Journal of Consulting and Clinical Psychology* 52:553–566.

Hahlweg, K., Schindler, L., Revenstorf, D., and Brengelmann, J. C. (1984). The Munich marital therapy study. In *Marital Interaction: Analysis and Modification*, ed. K. Hahlweg and N. S. Jacobson, pp. 3–26. New York: Guilford.

Halford, W. K., Sanders, M. R., and Behrens, B. C. (1993). A comparison of the generalization of behavioral marital therapy and enhanced behavioral marital therapy. *Journal of Consulting and Clinical Psychology* 61:51–60.

Huber, C. H., and Milstein, B. (1985). Cognitive restructuring and a collaborative set in couples' work. *American Journal of Family Therapy* 13(2):17–27.

Jacobson, N. S. (1977). Problem-solving and contingency contracting in the treatment of marital discord. *Journal of Consulting and Clinical Psychology* 45:92–100.

——— (1978). Specific and nonspecific factors in the effectiveness of a behavioral approach to the treatment of marital discord. *Journal of Consulting and Clinical Psychology* 46:442–452.

——— (1984). A component analysis of behavioral marital therapy: the relative effectiveness of behavior exchange and communication/problem solving training. *Journal of Consulting and Clinical Psychology* 52:295–305.

Jacobson, N. S., Follette, W. C., Revenstorf, D., et al. (1984). Variability in outcome and clinical significance of behavioral marital therapy: a reanalysis of outcome data. *Journal of Consulting and Clinical Psychology* 52:497–504.

Jacobson, N. S., Schmaling, K. R., and Holtzworth-Munroe, A. (1987). Component analysis of behavioral marital therapy: 2-year follow-up and prediction of relapse. *Journal of Marital and Family Therapy* 13:187–195.

Jacobson, N. S., Schmaling, K. B., Holtzworth-Munroe, A., et al. (1989). Research structured versus clinically flexible versions of social learning based marital therapy. *Behavior Research and Therapy* 27:175–180.

Johnson, S. M., and Greenberg, L. S. (1985). Differential effects of experiential and problem-solving interventions in resolving marital conflict. *Journal of Consulting and Clinical Psychology* 53:175–184.

Liberman, R. P., Wheeler, E., and Sanders, N. (1976). Behavioral therapy for marital disharmony: an educational approach. *Journal of Marriage and Family Counseling* 2:383–395.

Margolin, G., and Weiss, R. L. (1978). Comparative evaluation of therapeutic components associated with behavioral marital treatments. *Journal of Consulting and Clinical Psychology* 46:1476–1486.

Mehlman, S. K., Baucom, D. H., and Anderson, D. (1983). Effectiveness of cotherapists versus single therapists and immediate versus delayed treatment in behavioral marital therapy. *Journal of Consulting and Clinical Psychology* 51:258–266.

Snyder, D. K., and Wills, R. M. (1989). Behavioral versus insight-oriented marital therapy: effects on individual and interspousal functioning. *Journal of Consulting and Clinical Psychology* 57:39–46.

Turkewitz, H., and O'Leary, K. D. (1981). A comparative outcome study of behavioral marital therapy and communication therapy. *Journal of Marital and Family Therapy* 7:159–169.

II

Supplemental Readings on Special Topics in Couples Therapy

Assessment

O'Leary, K. D. (1987). *Assessment of Marital Discord: An Integration for Research and Clinical Practice*. Hillside, NJ: Lawrence Erlbaum.

Children and Marital Distress

Cummings, E. M., and Davies, P. (1994). *Children and Marital Conflict*. New York: Guilford.

Co-Morbid Conditions:

Anxiety Disorders

Craske, M. G., and Zoellner, L. A. (1995). Anxiety disorders: the role of marital therapy. In *Clinical Handbook of Couple Therapy*, ed. N. S. Jacobson and A. S. Gurman, pp. 394–410. New York: Guilford.

Alcoholism

McCrady, B. S., and Epstein, E. E. (1995). Marital therapy in the treatment of alcohol problems. In *Clinical Handbook of Couple Therapy*, ed. N. S. Jacobson and A. S. Gurman, pp. 369–393. New York: Guilford.

Depression

Beach, S. R. H., Sandeen, E. E., and O'Leary, K. D. (1990). *Depression in Marriage*. New York: Guilford.

Cultural Issues

Falicov, C. J. (1995). Cross-cultural marriages. In *Clinical Handbook of Couple Therapy*, ed. N. S. Jacobson and A. S. Gurman, pp. 231–246. New York: Guilford.

Sue, D. W., and Sue, D. (1990). *Counseling the Culturally Different: Theory and Practice*, 2nd ed. New York: Wiley.

Divorce

Hodges, W. F. (1991). *Interventions for Children of Divorce*. New York: Wiley.

Walsh, F., Jacob, L., and Simons, V. (1995). Facilitating healthy divorce processes: therapy and mediation approaches. In *Clinical Handbook of Couple Therapy*, ed. N. S. Jacobson and A. S. Gurman, pp. 340–368. New York: Guilford.

Extramarital Affairs and Jealousy

Constantine, L. L. (1986). Jealousy and extramarital sexual relations. In *Clinical Handbook of Marital Therapy*, ed. N. S. Jacobson and A. S. Gurman, pp. 407–427. New York: Guilford.

Pittman, F. S, and Wagers, T. P. (1995). Crises of infidelity. In *Clinical Handbook of Couple Therapy*, ed. N. S. Jacobson and A. S. Gurman, pp. 295–316. New York: Guilford.

Spring, J. A. (1996). *After the Affair*. New York: Harper Collins.

Gay/Lesbian Relationships

Brown, L. S. (1995). Therapy with same-sex couples: an introduction. In *Clinical Handbook of Couple Therapy*, ed. N. S. Jacobson and A. S. Gurman, pp. 274–291. New York: Guilford.

Isensee, R. (1990). *Love between Men: Enhancing Intimacy and Keeping Your Relationship Alive*. New York: Prentice Hall.

Marital Violence

Ammerman, R. T., and Hersen, M. (1990). *Treatment of Family Violence: A Sourcebook*. New York: Wiley.

Caesar, P. L., and Hamberger, L. K. (1989). *Treating Men Who Batter*. New York: Springer.

Hamberger, L. K., and Renzetti, C. (1996). *Domestic Partner Abuse*. New York: Springer.

Holtzworth-Munroe, A., Beatty, S. B., and Anglin, K. (1995). The assessment and treatment of marital violence: an introduction for the marital therapist. In *Clinical Handbook of Couple Therapy*, ed. N. S. Jacobson and A. S. Gurman, pp. 317–339. New York: Guilford.

Remarriage

Sager, C. J. (1986). Therapy with remarried couples. In *Clinical Handbook of Marital Therapy*, ed. N. S. Jacobson and A. S. Gurman, pp. 321–344. New York: Guilford.

Schemas and Relationships

Dattilio, F. M., and Padesky, C. A. (1990). *Cognitive Therapy with Couples*. Sarasota, FL: Professional Resource Exchange.

Young, J. E., and Klosko, J. S. (1993). *Reinventing Your Life*. New York: Dutton.

Self-Help for the Couple

Fincham, F. D., Fernandes, L. O. L., and Humphreys, K. (1993). *Communicating in Relationships: A Guide for Couples and Professionals*. Champaign, IL: Research Press.

Gottman, J. M. (1994). *Why Marriages Succeed or Fail . . . and How You Can Make Yours Last*. New York: Simon & Schuster.

Gottman, J. M., Notarius, C., Gonso, J., and Markman, H.

(1976). *A Couple's Guide to Communication*. Champaign, IL: Research Press.

Markman, H., Stanley, S., and Blumberg, S. L. (1994). *Fighting for Your Marriage: Positive Steps for Preventing Divorce and Preserving a Lasting Love*. San Francisco: Jossey-Bass.

Sexual Dysfunction

Hawton, K. (1984). *Sex Therapy: A Practical Guide*. Oxford, England: Oxford University Press.

Heiman, J. R., Epps, P. H., and Ellis, B. (1995). Treating sexual desire disorders in couples. In *Clinical Handbook of Couple Therapy*, ed. N. S. Jacobson and A. S. Gurman, pp. 471–495. New York: Guilford.

III

Rationale for Brief Couples Treatment and Future Directions of Cognitive-Behavioral Couples Therapy

Changes in Health Care Delivery

The 1990s witnessed a dramatic restructuring of health care delivery, with managed care introducing third parties who intervene between doctor and patient by determining which services would be reimbursable. In both medicine and psychology, managed-care dictums increased demands for scientifically based treatment approaches and accountability of services provided through measurement of outcome. While the goal of eliminating payments for unnecessary or ineffective treatments remains laudable, many concerns have arisen regarding issues such as the appropriateness of business administrators making health-care decisions, the eradicating of artistry and individualized approaches in health-care treatment by the focus on data-driven manualized treatment protocols (which have been based mostly on large group outcome studies), and the over-reliance on short-term treatments to address complex problems.

Cognitive-Behavioral Therapy and Brief Treatment

Within psychology, cognitive-behavioral therapy (CBT) is no stranger to short-term, empirically based treatment. Throughout its evolution over the past four decades, CBT has aligned itself closely with the scientific method, routinely testing its approaches in randomized trials with a variety of new populations and new disorders. Given its active, directive, and problem-specific focus, CBT has fit naturally within a shorter-term model. In the field of behavioral marital therapy (BMT) in particular, a majority of treatment outcome studies have evaluated treatments ranging from eight to twenty sessions. The present volume, describing an eight-session, manualized treatment for relationship distress, might be viewed as undermining of other, longer-term approaches to couples treatment, or of ideographic case formulation. The following two sections address these issues.

Rationale for Brief Couples Treatment

Why propose a brief, eight-session treatment model? We do not wish to convey that marital distress can routinely be "cured" within eight sessions, or that this model is qualitatively preferable to a longer-term approach. In fact, research has demonstrated a dose–response relationship, such that increasing therapy time leads to significantly improved outcomes up to a point. Interestingly, however, evidence suggests that clients undergoing an eight-session treatment are more improved by the eighth session than are clients undergoing a longer course of treatment, regardless of therapy orientation; that is, change is accelerated in a shorter treatment (Barkham et al. 1996). In any case, this format was intended to offer a road map for situations in which available resources require a short-term treatment. Constraints such as limited insurance reimbursement (many health plans will initially cover only eight sessions of therapy, or refuse coverage of marital therapy altogether), short-term treatment settings (more hospital and agency-based clinics are moving in this direction), or the limits of couples' private payment budgets or time, necessitate more flexibility on the part of the clinician. That is, clinicians can benefit from knowledge of how to work effectively within a short-term model when needed. Thus, our treatment model aims to answer questions such as: How can the clinician maximize treatment gain when working within a brief treatment mandate? How can the clinician set feasible short-term treatment goals and apply interventions that directly serve these goals? What combination of practical strategies backed by research demonstrating their effectiveness can the clinician employ? In our experience, many clinicians feel anxious within the constraints of our current health-care system, feeling powerless to attain meaningful results when faced with a limited number of sessions. This book (and series) aims to help empower the therapist with concrete, data-supported intervention strategies that can be applied within a brief time frame.

Ideographic Case Formulation: Eradicated by Evidence-Based Psychotherapies?

Critics of manualized treatments also argue that following prescribed strategies prevents individualized approaches to cases. While it is true that manualized approaches may reduce strategic and structural variations across cases, they nevertheless allow for more individualization than is typically presumed. The various assessment components will present a unique profile of each couple. In turn, these profiles will result in markedly different targets for each couple. In other words, while a group of couples may uniformly engage in communication training, problem solving, and thought monitoring, no two will be alike in the issues they learn to validate, the problems they raise, the solutions they develop, or the cognitions they uncover. One couple may focus on issues of trust and dependency and another may focus on conflicts involving power and control, yet both can benefit from standardized treatment components such as identifying related thinking patterns that contribute to these conflicts, or learning communication and validation skills to express related feelings and needs.

In addition, behavior-therapy approaches incorporate functional analysis into assessment and treatment planning. By definition, functional analysis individualizes intervention by assigning greater importance to the underlying function of behaviors than to their topography. Thus, an anger outburst in Couple A may serve a different purpose in the relationship than a similar-looking anger outburst in Couple B; treating the anger involves examining the antecedents and consequences of anger in a particular relational context (see Chapter 9 on "Addressing Marital Anger"). Even so, some of the procedural aspects of the treatment will be the same for the two couples. For example, determining the advantages and disadvantages of anger with a client provides a routinized method of eliciting reinforcing and punishing consequences of anger *in the client's own relationship*.

Moreover, cases that require a different approach should by all means receive one; the brief treatment described in this volume will not meet the needs of every couple. Certain situations, based on either concrete assessment results or intuitive clinical judgment, will dictate a different course of treatment. Couples with little or no commitment to working on the relationship, a long history of severe marital distress, a recent crisis such as marital infidelity, a circumscribed problem such as sexual dysfunction, a significant psychological disorder in one or both partners (e.g., substance abuse, a psychotic disorder, or severe personality disorder), or spouse abuse will need longer or substantively different treatment. But even for such couples, many aspects of the treatment presented here will prove helpful in enhancing the relationship context in which these difficulties occur. In fact, several investigators have employed BMT components in combination with disorder-specific therapies in the treatment of mental health problems such as depression (Jacobson et al. 1991, O'Leary and Beach 1990), agoraphobia (Arnow et al. 1985), alcoholism (O'Farrell et al. 1993), and sexual dysfunction (Hurlbert 1993).

Empirical Status of Cognitive Behavioral Couples Therapy

This book was intended to provide the clinician with a "how-to" resource for conducting treatment backed by empirical demonstration of its effectiveness. Although the utility of other forms of marital therapy has been supported by empirical data, such as Greenberg and Johnson's (1988) emotion-focused couples therapy and Snyder and Wills's (1989) insight-oriented marital therapy, behavioral marital therapy (with and without cognitive marital therapy) has received by far the most research attention. A wealth of randomized studies, evaluating both whole treatment packages in various combinations (e.g., behavioral marital therapy plus cognitive restructuring versus wait-list conditions) and dismantled treatment components (e.g., communication and problem-solving versus behavior exchange conditions) have brought BMT the distinction of being the only couples therapy to meet criteria for classification as both efficacious and specific (Baucom et al. 1998).[1] *Efficacious* and *specific* here refer to demonstrating superiority over placebo or "nonspecific" treatment conditions, or over alternative treatments, in two or more investigations carried out by independent research groups (Chambless and Hollon 1998). Indeed, BMT has surpassed the minimal requirements for achieving this classification.

Treatments identified as efficacious have been classified as such based on findings of *statistical* significance. Recently, researchers have placed increasing importance on the additional evaluation of a treatment's *clinical* significance, which in marital therapy is typically assessed by looking for the proportion of clients falling into the nondistressed range on standard out-

---

1. Note that studies employing cognitive restructuring procedures yield improvements consistent with, but not superior to, behavioral marital therapy. Thus, at this time, cognitive therapy for couple distress is classified as a "possibly efficacious" treatment (cf. Baucom et al. 1998). However, several studies have demonstrated (1) the equivalent success of cognitive restructuring procedures to BMT (Emmelkamp et al. 1988), or (2) the superiority of cognitive restructuring procedures to wait-list conditions, either alone (Huber and Milstein 1985) or in combination with BMT (Baucom et al. 1990). Further, the couples therapy field has not yet established which components of couples therapy work best for which types of couples. Thus, we include procedures from cognitive therapy with couples to provide the clinician with a broad array of tools to employ with a range of couples who present for treatment.

come measures such as the Marital Adjustment Test (Locke and Wallace 1959) or the Dyadic Adjustment Scale (Spanier 1976). Using such criteria, the research indicates that approximately half of the couples receiving BMT evidence clinically significant improvement both at post-treatment and at follow-up periods of up to two years, with two-thirds of the couples benefiting at post-treatment and one-third of these couples relapsing over time (Baucom et al. 1998, Jacobson et al. 1987).

Future Directions in Cognitive Behavioral Couples Therapy

In recognition of the substantial number of couples who do not respond in terms of clinical significance to BMT or CBMT, or who respond but eventually relapse, some of the "founding fathers" of behavioral approaches to couples therapy have recently incorporated treatment elements from schools other than CBMT, such as emotion focused therapy, insight-oriented therapy, and additional, traditional psychodynamic therapies. Originally placing exclusive importance on observable problematic behaviors in couple interactions and the *changing* of such behaviors, many of the field's pioneers have come to emphasize the important roles of internal client experiences (i.e., cognition, affect, insight) and the *acceptance* of problematic relationship experiences.

Most recent and noteworthy in this trend is Jacobson and Christensen's integrative behavioral couples therapy (IBCT; Christensen et al. 1995, Jacobson and Christensen 1997), which balances acceptance strategies with traditional behavior-change strategies. Rapidly gaining recognition and reflecting a growing shift toward acceptance-based approaches in the field of behavior therapy as a whole (e.g., Gifford et al. 1997, Linehan 1993), this approach emphasizes acceptance of a partner's undesirable behaviors as well as acceptance of one's negative reactions to a partner's behaviors. Key thematic differences in the IBCT approach include a reduction of emphasis on behavioral specifics (or what the authors label "derivative" variables) and an increased emphasis on relationship themes (to reveal major, controlling variables in relationship distress), a focus on affect as indicator of crucial controlling variables, an emphasis on contingency-shaped versus rule-governed change strategies, and placement of increased importance on altering *reactions* to partner behavior compared with *changing* partner behavior. IBCT intervention tactics include facilitating couples' recognition of the positive as well as the negative side of their differences, focusing on couple interactions *as the source of their problems* rather than as means to *solve their problems*, basing the session focus on issues of particular salience to the couple in any given week, and minimizing use of formulaic communication skills while enhancing communication by working within clients' own styles. Acceptance is enhanced "by helping couples experience the problem in a different way, either as an understandable dilemma that causes both partners pain, or as a common, external enemy that they share . . . [or] by reducing the aversiveness of the partner's actions, either by increasing one's tolerance or self-care in the face of these actions" (Christensen et al. 1995, p. 54).

IBCT retains several aspects of traditional BMT techniques, including behavior-exchange strategies, constructive feeling expression and empathic listening skills, and problem-solving training when needed. Interestingly, although not explicitly labeled as such, acceptance is to a large degree the goal of cognitive interventions with couples, as described in this volume. For example, Chapters 7 and 8 highlight ways to enable clients to experience a problem differently through methods such as considering alternative attributions for a partner's behavior, or identifying underlying standards driving behavior and considering them in a nonjudgmental fashion. In any case, preliminary data suggest that IBCT surpasses BMT in outcome (Christensen and Jacobson 1996), and the authors contend that this new approach may be helpful to those clients who do not attain lasting benefits with the traditional methods of BMT. While additional research is needed to substantiate these findings, acceptance-based strategies will likely offer a promising enhancement to traditional behavioral approaches for couples seeking help for relationship distress.

References

Abrahms, J., and Spring, M. (1989). The flip-flop factor. *International Cognitive Therapy Newsletter* 5(1):1, 7–8.

Arnow, B. A., Taylor, C. B., Agras, W. S., and Telch, M. J. (1985). Enhancing agoraphobia treatment outcome by changing couple communication patterns. *Behavior Therapy* 16:452-467.

Bandura, A. (1977). *Social Learning Theory*. Englewood Cliffs, NJ: Prentice Hall.

Barkham, M., Rees, A., Stiles, W. B., et al. (1996). Dose–effect relations in time-limited psychotherapy for depression. *Journal of Consulting and Clinical Psychology* 64:927–935.

Baucom, D., and Epstein, N. (1990). *Cognitive Behavioral Marital Therapy*. New York: Brunner/Mazel.

Baucom, D. H., Epstein, N., Sayers, S., and Sher, T. (1989). The role of cognitions in marital relationships: definitional, methodological, and conceptual issues. *Journal of Consulting and Clinical Psychology* 57:31–38.

Baucom, D. H., and Lester, G. W. (1986). The usefulness of cognitive restructuring as an adjunct to behavioral marital therapy. *Behavior Therapy* 13:162–174.

Baucom, D. H., Sayers, S. L., and Sher, T. (1990). Supplementing behavioral marital therapy with cognitive restructuring and emotional expressiveness training: an outcome investigation. *Journal of Consulting and Clinical Psychology* 58:636–645.

Baucom, D. H., Shoham, V., Mueser, K. T., et al. (1998). Empirically supported couple and family interventions for marital distress and adult mental health problems. *Journal of Consulting and Clinical Psychology* 66:53–88.

Baucom, D. H., Wheeler, C. M., and Bell, G. (1984). *Assessing the role of attributions in marital distress.* Paper presented at the annual meeting of the Association for the Advancement of Behavior Therapy, Boston, November.

Beach, S. R. H., Sandeen, E. E., and O'Leary, K. D. (1990). *Depression in Marriage: A Model for Etiology and Treatment.* New York: Guilford.

Beck, A. T. (1988). *Love Is Never Enough.* New York: Harper and Row.

Beck, A. T., Rush, A. J., Shaw, B. F., and Emery, G. (1979). *Cognitive Therapy of Depression.* New York: Guilford.

Beck, J. (1995). *Cognitive Therapy: Basics and Beyond.* New York: Guilford.

Birchler, G. R., Weiss, R. L., and Vincent, J. P. (1975). A multimethod analysis of social reinforcement exchange between maritally distressed and nondistressed spouse and stranger dyads. *Journal of Personality and Social Psychology* 31:349–360.

Broderick, J. E., and O'Leary, K. D. (1986). Contributions of affect, attitude, and behavior to marital satisfaction. *Journal of Consulting and Clinical Psychology* 54:514–517.

Buehlman, K. T., Gottman, J. M., and Katz, L. F. (1992). How a couple views their past predicts their future: predicting divorce from an oral history interview. *Journal of Family Psychology* 5:295–318.

Chambless, D. L., and Hollon, S. D. (1998). Defining empirically supported therapies. *Journal of Consulting and Clinical Psychology* 66:7–18.

Christensen, A., and Jacobson, N. S. (1996). *Acceptance in marriage*. Paper presented at the meeting of the Association for the Advancement of Behavior Therapy, New York, November.

Christensen, A., Jacobson, N. S., and Babcock, J. C. (1995). Integrative behavioral couple therapy. In *Clinical Handbook of Couple Therapy*, ed. N. S. Jacobson and A. S. Gurman, pp. 31–63. New York: Guilford.

Dattilio, F. M., and Padesky, C. A. (1990). *Cognitive Therapy with Couples*. Sarasota, FL: Professional Resource Exchange.

Deschner, J. P. (1984). *The Hitting Habit: Anger Control for Battering Couples*. New York: Free Press.

Eidelson, R. J., and Epstein, N. (1982). Cognition and relationship maladjustment: development of a measure of dysfunctional relationship beliefs. *Journal of Consulting and Clinical Psychology* 50:715–720.

Ellis, A. (1962). *Reason and Emotion in Psychotherapy*. New York: Lyle Stuart.

Emmelkamp, P. M. G., van Linden van den Heuvell, C., Ruphan, M., et al. (1988). Cognitive and behavioral interventions: a comparative evaluation with clinically distressed couples. *Journal of Family Psychology* 1:365–377.

Epstein, N. (1982). Cognitive therapy with couples. *American Journal of Family Therapy* 10:5–16.

——— (1983). *Relationship standards sentence completion form*. Unpublished questionnaire. College Park, MD: University of Maryland.

Epstein, N., and Eidelson, R. J. (1981). Unrealistic beliefs of clinical couples: their relationship to expectations, goals and satisfaction. *American Journal of Family Therapy* 9:13–22.

Fincham, F. D., and Bradbury, T. N. (1990). *The Psychology of Marriage*. NY: Guilford.

Fincham, F. D., Fernandes, L. O. L., and Humphreys, K. (1993). *Communicating in Relationships: A Guide for Couples and Professionals*. Champaign, IL: Research Press.

Fincham, F. D., and O'Leary, K. D. (1983). Causal inferences for spouse behavior in maritally distressed and nondistressed couples. *Journal of Social and Clinical Psychology* 1:42–57.

Geiss, S. K., and O'Leary, K. D. (1981). Therapists' ratings of frequency and severity of marital problems: implications for research. *Journal of Marital and Family Therapy* 7:515–520.

Gifford, E. V., Hayes, S., Jacobson, N. S., and Marlatt, A. (1997). *Acceptance and change: reconsidering the goals of modern behavior therapy*. Panel discussion presented at the Annual Convention of the Association for the Advancement of Behavior Therapy, Miami Beach, FL, November.

Gondolf, E. W. (1985). *Men Who Batter*. Holmes Beach, FL: Learning Publications.

Gottman, J. M. (1993a). A theory of marital dissolution and stability. *Journal of Family Psychology* 7:57–75.

——— (1993b). The roles of conflict engagement, escalation, and avoidance in marital interaction: a longitudinal view of five types of couples. *Journal of Consulting and Clinical Psychology* 61:6–15.

——— (1994). *Why Marriages Succeed or Fail . . . and How You Can Make Yours Last*. New York: Simon & Schuster.

Gottman, J. M., and Krokoff, L. J. (1989). Marital interaction and satisfaction: a longitudinal view. *Journal of Consulting and Clinical Psychology* 57:47–52.

Gottman, J. M., and Levenson, R. W. (1986). Assessing the role of emotion in marriage. *Behavioral Assessment* 8:31–48.

———— (1988). The social psychophysiology of marriage. In *Perspectives on Marital Interaction*, ed. P. Noller and M. A. Fitzpatrick, pp. 182–200. Clevedon, England: Multilingual Matters.

———— (1992). Marital processes predictive of later dissolution: behavior, physiology, and health. *Journal of Personality and Social Psychology* 63:221–233.

Gottman, J. M., Markman, H., and Notarius, C. (1977). The topography of marital conflict: a sequential analysis of verbal and nonverbal behavior. *Journal of Marriage and the Family* 39:461–477.

Gottman, J. M., Notarius, C., Gonso, J., and Markman, H. (1976). *A Couples Guide to Communication*. Champaign, IL: Research Press.

Gottman, J. M., Notarius, C., Markman, H., et al. (1976). Behavior exchange theory and marital decision making. *Journal of Personality and Social Psychology* 34:14–23.

Greenberg, L. S., and Johnson, S. M. (1988). *Emotionally Focused Therapy for Couples*. New York: Guilford.

Greenberg, L. S., and Safran, J. D. (1987). *Emotion in Psychotherapy: Affect and Cognition in the Process of Change*. New York: Guilford.

Guerney, B. (1977). *Relationship Enhancement*. San Francisco: Jossey-Bass.

Hahlweg, K., Revenstorf, D., and Schindler, L. (1984). Effects of behavioral marital therapy on couples' communication and problem-solving skills. *Journal of Consulting and Clinical Psychology* 52:553–566.

Holtzworth-Munroe, A., and Jacobson, N. S. (1985). Causal attributions of married couples: When do they search for causes?

What do they conclude when they do? *Journal of Personality and Social Psychology* 48:1398–1412.

Huber, C. H., and Milstein, B. (1985). Cognitive restructuring and a collaborative set in couples' work. *American Journal of Family Therapy* 13(2):17–27.

Hurlbert, D. F. (1993). A comparative study using orgasm consistency training in the treatment of women reporting hypoactive sexual desire. *Journal of Sex and Marital Therapy* 19:41–55.

Jacobson, N. S. (1984). A component analysis of behavioral marital therapy: the relative effectiveness of behavior exchange and communication/problem solving training. *Journal of Consulting and Clinical Psychology* 52:295–305.

Jacobson, N. S., and Christensen, A. (1997). *Integrative Behavioral Couples Therapy*. New York: Guilford.

Jacobson, N. S., Dobson, K., Fruzetti, A. E., et al. (1991). Marital therapy as a treatment for depression. *Journal of Consulting and Clinical Psychology* 59:547–557.

Jacobson, N. S., Follette, W. C., and McDonald, D. W. (1982). Reactivity to positive and negative behavior in distressed and nondistressed married couples. *Journal of Consulting and Clinical Psychology* 50:706–714.

Jacobson, N. S., and Holtzworth-Munroe, A. (1986). Marital therapy: a social learning–cognitive perspective. In *Clinical Handbook of Marital Therapy*, ed. N. S. Jacobson and A. S. Gurman, pp. 29–70. New York: Guilford.

Jacobson, N. S., and Margolin, G. (1979). *Marital Therapy: Strategies Based on Social Learning and Behavior Exchange Principles*. New York: Brunner/Mazel.

Jacobson, N. S., McDonald, D. W., Follette, W. C., and Berley, R. A. (1985). Attributional processes in distressed and nondistressed married couples. *Cognitive Therapy and Research* 9:35–50.

Jacobson, N. S., Schmaling, K. R., and Hotlzworth-Munroe, A. (1987). Component analysis of behavioral marital therapy: 2-year follow-up and prediction of relapse. *Journal of Marital and Family Therapy* 13:187–195.

Johnson, P. L., and O'Leary, K. D. (1996). Behavioral components of marital satisfaction: an individualized assessment approach. *Journal of Consulting and Clinical Psychology* 64:417–423.

Johnson, S. M., and Greenberg, L. S. (1985). Differential effects of experiential and problem-solving interventions in resolving marital conflict. *Journal of Consulting and Clinical Psychology* 53:175–184.

Lederer, W. J., and Jackson, D. D. (1968). *Mirages of Marriage*. New York: Norton.

Linehan, M. (1993). *Cognitive Behavioral Therapy for Borderline Personality Disorder*. New York: Guilford.

Locke, H. J., and Wallace, K. M. (1959). Short marital adjustment and prediction tests: their reliability and validity. *Marriage and Family Living* 21:251–255.

Margolin, G., Christensen, A., and Weiss, R. L. (1975). Contracts, cognition, and change: a behavioral approach to marriage therapy. *Counseling Psychologist* 5:15–25.

Markman, H. J. (1979). Application of a behavioral model of marriage in predicting relationship satisfaction of couples planning marriage. *Journal of Consulting and Clinical Psychology* 47:743–749.

——— (1984). The longitudinal study of couples' interactions: implications for understanding and predicting the development of marital distress. In *Marital Interaction: Analysis and Modi-*

fication, ed. K. Hahlweg and N. S. Jacobson, pp. 253–281. New York: Guilford.

Marlatt, G. A., and Gordon, J. R. (1985). *Relapse Prevention: Maintenance Strategies in the Treatment of Addictive Behaviors.* New York: Guilford.

Meichenbaum, D. (1977). *Cognitive-Behavior Modification: An Integrative Approach.* New York: Plenum.

Navran, L. (1967). Communication and adjustment in marriage. *Family Process* 6:173–184.

Neidig, P. H., and Friedman, D. H. (1984). *Spouse Abuse: A Treatment Program for Couples.* Champaign, IL: Research Press.

Novaco, R. W. (1975). *Anger Control: The Development and Evaluation of an Experimental Treatment.* Lexington, MA: Lexington Books.

——— (1976). The functions and the regulation of the arousal of anger. *American Journal of Psychiatry* 133:1124–1128.

O'Farrell, T. J., Choquette, K. A., Cutter, H., et al. (1993). Behavioral marital therapy with and without additional couples relapse prevention sessions for alcoholics and their spouses. *Behavior Therapy* 27:7–24.

O'Leary, K. D. (1987). *Assessment of Marital Discord.* Hillsdale, NJ: Lawrence Erlbaum.

O'Leary, K. D., and Arias, I. (1987). Marital assessment in clinical practice. In *Assessment of Marital Discord*, ed. K. D. Leary, pp. 287–312. Hillsdale, NJ: Lawrence Erlbaum.

O'Leary, K. D., and Beach, S. R. H. (1990). Marital therapy: a viable treatment for depression and marital discord. *American Journal of Psychiatry* 147:183–186.

O'Leary, K. D., Fincham, F. D., and Turkewitz, H. (1983). Assessment of positive feelings toward spouse. *Journal of Consulting and Clinical Psychology* 51:949–951.

O'Leary, K. D., and Neidig, P. (1993). *Treatment of Spouse Abuse.* Paper presented at the 27th Annual Meeting of the Association for the Advancement of Behavior Therapy. Atlanta, GA, November.

O'Leary, K. D., and Turkewitz, H. (1978). The treatment of marital disorders from a behavioral perspective. In *Marriage and Marital Therapy: Psychoanalytic, Behavioral, and Systems Theory Perspectives*, ed. T. J. Paolino and B. S. McCrady, pp. 240–297. New York: Brunner/Mazel.

Patterson, G. R., and Hops, H. (1972). Coercion, a game for two: intervention techniques for marital conflict. In *The Experimental Analysis of Social Behavior*, ed. In R. E. Ulrich and P. Montjoy, pp. 424–440. New York: Appleton-Century-Crofts.

Patterson, G. R., and Reid, J. B. (1970). Reciprocity and coercion: two facets of social systems. In *Behavior Modification in Clinical Psychology*, ed. C. Neuringer and J. L. Michael. New York: Appleton-Century-Crofts.

Rappaport, A. F., and Harrell, J. A. (1972). A behavioral exchange model for marital counseling. *The Family Coordinator* 22:203–212.

Snyder, D. K., and Wills, R. M. (1989). Behavioral versus insight-oriented marital therapy: effects on individual and interspousal functioning. *Journal of Consulting and Clinical Psychology* 57:39–46.

Snyder, D. K., Wills, R. M., and Grady-Fletcher, A. (1991). Long-term effectiveness of behavioral versus insight-oriented marital therapy: a 4-year follow-up study. *Journal of Consulting and Clinical Psychology* 59:138–141.

Spanier, G. B. (1976). Measuring dyadic adjustment: new scales for assessing the quality of marriage and similar dyads. *Journal of Sex and Marital Therapy* 38:15–28.

Straus, M. A. (1979). Measuring intrafamily conflict and violence: the Conflict Tactics Scales. *Journal of Marriage and the Family* 41:75–86.

Straus, M. A., and Gelles, R. J. (1990). How violent are American Families? Estimates from the national family violence re-survey and other studies. In *Physical Violence in American Families: Risk Factors and Adaptations to Violence in 8,145 Families*, pp. 95–112. New Brunswick, NJ: Transaction.

Stuart, R. B. (1969). Operant-interpersonal treatment for marital discord. *Journal of Consulting and Clinical Psychology* 33:675–682.

———— (1980). *Helping Couples Change: A Social Learning Approach to Marital Therapy*. New York: Guilford.

Thibaut, J. W., and Kelley, H. H. (1959). *The Social Psychology of Groups*. New York: Wiley.

Weiss, R. L. (1978). The conceptualization of marital disorders from a behavioral perspective. In *Marriage and Marital Therapy: Psychoanalytic, Behavioral, and Systems Theory Perspectives*, ed. T. J. Paolino and B. S. McCrady, pp. 165–239. New York: Brunner/Mazel.

———— (1980). Strategic behavioral marital therapy: toward a model for assessment and intervention. In *Advances in Family Intervention, Assessment, and Theory*, vol. 1, ed. J. P. Vincent, pp. 229–271. Greenwich, CT: JAI Press.

———— (1984). Cognitive and strategic interventions in behavioral marital therapy. In *Marital Interaction: Analysis and Modification*, ed. K. Hahlweg and N. S. Jacobson, pp. 337–355. New York: Guilford.

Weiss, R. L., and Birchler, G. R. (1978). Adults with marital dysfunction. In *Behavior Therapy in the Psychiatric Setting*, ed. M.

Hersen and A. S. Bellack, pp. 331–364. Baltimore; MD: Williams and Wilkins.

Weiss, R. L., Birchler, G. R., and Vincent, J. P. (1974). Contractual models for negotiation training in marital dyads. *Journal of Marriage and the Family* 36:321–331.

Weiss, R. L., and Heyman, R. (1990). Observation of marital interaction. In *The Psychology of Marriage: Basic Issues and Applications*, ed. F. D. Fincham and T. N. Bradbury, pp. 87–117. New York: Guilford.

Weiss, R. L., Hops, H., and Patterson, G. R. (1973). A framework for conceptualizing marital conflict, technology for altering it, some data for evaluating it. In *Behavior Change: Methodology, Concepts, and Practice*, ed. L. A. Hamerlynck, L. C. Handy, and E. J. Mash, pp. 309–342. Champaign, IL: Research Press.

Index